Christians in Racial Crisis

A STUDY OF LITTLE ROCK'S MINISTRY

By Ernest Q. Campbell and Thomas F. Pettigrew
Laboratory of Social Relations, Harvard University

INCLUDING STATEMENTS ON DESEGREGATION AND
RACE RELATIONS BY THE LEADING RELIGIOUS
DENOMINATIONS OF THE UNITED STATES

Public Affairs Press, Washington, D. C.

Copyright, 1959, by Public Affairs Press
419 New Jersey Avenue, S. E., Washington 3, D.C.

Printed in the United States of America
Library of Congress Catalog Card No. 59-10228

FOREWORD

There is no greater urgency confronting American churches than effective leadership in contemporary race relations. All sections of the United States present challenges to both clergy and laity and to the churches as institutionalized bodies in interaction with their community environment. The distressing reality of Little Rock has invited a scientific analysis of factors bearing on the role of ministers and churches in questions of segregation, desegregation, and integration. Much can be learned from what happened in that city. Professors Campbell and Pettigrew have thoroughly analyzed a significant aspect of the problem and have developed a number of hypotheses which can be tested not only in Little Rock but in many other situations in the nation.

Students of the relationship of church and community have long noted the dilemma of the church in social action and along with it have noted the dilemma of ministerial leadership. The dilemma resides on the one hand in the given ideals and gospel of the church and on the other hand in the involvement of the church in material interests of society. On the one hand lies the ineffectiveness of utopian ideals and the irrelevance of noble but unimplemented ideas. On the other hand we have the betrayal of ideas through complete accommodation to the prejudices and interests of the world. The problem is to move men and society in the direction of the values to which the church by its very being is committed.

From a superficial point of view it would seem that the churches had failed Little Rock, but it is important to understand what actually happened and why it happened. The story as told in the following pages can be a source of great profit to all who are concerned for the effectiveness of the church in the interest of racial justice and integration. When the churches finally lapsed into silence they did not by this action freeze the status quo of that moment of Little Rock history. Their silence was followed by a steady deterioration of influence in terms of what they stood for as measured by the national pronouncements of their churches and their own earlier utterances.

v

The writers of this book present a persuasive challenge to the ministry because they believe that ministers are in a crucial position to influence decisively the course of race relations in the immediate future. In presenting this thesis they are thinking not only of the various types of parish clergy but also of the administrative leaders who can provide denominational and professional support or withhold it in times of crisis. This scientific analysis, therefore, has meaning for denominational strategy and for the implementation of the social pronouncements of the denominations. In this connection attention should be given to the complex and ambiguous role of class in American social structure and the various reference groups to which the minister is related.

There are some areas of the problem which this book does not undertake to analyze but which are illuminated in part by the hypotheses which are developed. Four of these can be briefly mentioned: (a) the structure of the congregational response analyzed into men, women, age groups, with special attention to youth; (b) the degree of preparation for social change undertaken within the congregation on the part of ministers and lay leaders; (c) the role of religious education with respect to social issues at all levels of the church school curriculum and the study groups of adults; and (d) the need to explore a complete theory of the art of handling controversial issues within the life of a local church as well as denominations taken as a whole. The writers of this book point to these areas in their recommendation that the churches need more adequately to institutionalize the social action role of the church and its ministry.

WALTER G. MUELDER

Dean, School of Theology
Boston University

PREFACE

This book is in effect a report on the predicament and behavior of the ministers of Little Rock, Arkansas. It is concerned primarily with what they did and why during the school desegregation crisis that engulfed their city in the period 1957-58. Our report is based on an intensive social science investigation that began in October 1957 and extended through December 1958. The basic data are derived from first-hand observations and repeated interviews with 42 ministers and rabbis in Little Rock. Included in this group are religious leaders who are segregationists as well as integrationists; some became deeply involved in the recent crisis, others remained detached.

It is well to recall the fateful events that initially aroused the nation's concern in the fall of 1957. Little Rock's school board had long been on record with its intent to comply with the Supreme Court decision of May 17, 1954, and a small number of Negro students expected to enroll in Central High School on Tuesday morning, September 3, 1957. But on Monday, September 2, the Arkansas National Guard surrounded the high school under orders from Governor Faubus, and on Wednesday, September 4, the Guard refused to permit nine Negro students to enter. On Friday, September 20, Federal Judge Davies directed Governor Faubus to stop interfering with integration at Central High. The Guard was withdrawn, and on Monday, September 23, the Negro students entered the school. But the threats of an angry mob outside led to the withdrawal of the Negro children under police escort before the end of the school day. The 101st Airborne Division of the U. S. Army arrived in Little Rock the following day under direct orders from President Dwight Eisenhower to enforce the decrees of the Federal Courts. The Negro students returned to Central High under soldier escort on Wednesday, September 25; eight of them completed the school year there. Military units remained on guard until the close of the school year in the late spring of 1958. The conflict was renewed the following fall when the city's high schools were closed to prevent continued racial integration.

Ministerial actions during this highly dramatic and troubled period have implications and significance far beyond the confines of Little Rock. For those concerned with the current racial desegregation process throughout the South, the behavior of the Protestant clergy is especially crucial because the clergy is the most important professional group in the South that still publicly defends integration. Likewise, Little Rock furnishes important data for those concerned with the social action potentialities and problems of modern Protestantism—especially since the church has become so deeply involved and committed in race relations. And, finally, the present study illuminates for social scientists some of the difficulties that men face when caught in the midst of a crisis-heightened conflict.

We are convinced that the Protestant ministry is potentially the most effective agent of social change in the South in the decade ahead. Chapter One documents the reasons for this conviction. Potentialities and realities do not, of course, always coincide. A reportorial review of clerical activity in Little Rock reveals that the ministry has not provided the united and forceful leadership many expected. Chapter Two details the activities on which this conclusion is based.

The reasons for the failure of religious leadership in Little Rock are several. One is the counter influence of the small sect, fundamentalistic pastors who stridently support the principle of segregation on moral grounds (Chapter Three). Another consideration is the fact that the clergymen most willing to defend their denomination's pronouncements favoring integration—young, recently arrived leaders of small, neighborhood churches—are not in a position to influence either their ministerial colleagues or the public (Chapter Four). A third factor concerns the conflicts faced by ministers who want to express their sincere beliefs to a hostile laity but who wish also to maintain a smoothly functioning parish (Chapter Five).

A continuing pattern of inactivity serves to substantiate our analysis (Chapter Six). Indeed, consistencies in behavior over a period of time enable us to present a number of testable hypotheses concerning ministerial actions in racial crisis (Chapter Six).

What has happened in Little Rock is highly relevant to the influence of modern Protestantism in America (Chapter Seven). We conclude that the forces underlying a basic "Protestant dilemma"—a dilemma between the organizational concerns of money and members and the effective expression of principle—must be balanced before the Protestant church can be expected to realize in actions its pronouncements on race questions. Several suggestions are offered as to how this balance might be achieved: unified ministerial action; early, pre-crisis indications of sentiment; and the full use of moral sanctions.

Depending on their own attitudes, some readers may interpret this report as a critical indictment, others as a bland apology. It is intended as neither. Those who read it as an indictment or an apology will miss the meaning we hope to convey. Our report is designed to contribute to the growing body of social science knowledge in the areas of race relations and religion. It is as fair and balanced an account as we can provide.

The reader is reminded, too, that both authors were born, reared, and educated in the South. And we have devoted most of our professional energies to the study of our region. If this volume can in the slightest way bring any understanding to the complex problems of racial desegregation and modern religion, it will serve its purpose.

ERNEST Q. CAMPBELL
THOMAS F. PETTIGREW

ACKNOWLEDGEMENTS

We wish to acknowledge our gratitude to Samuel A. Stouffer, whose suggestions and encouragement have been an invaluable part of this study since its inception.

We owe special debts, too, for the many helpful theoretical and editorial suggestions that we received from early readers of the manuscript: Gordon W. Allport, Sister Marie Augusta, the Reverend Mr. Colbert Cartwright, the Reverend Mr. Elbert Jean, Guy B. Johnson, the Reverend Mr. Charles M. Jones, Albert J. Reiss, Jr., George Reynolds, Howard Schuman, and Richardson White. A major contribution was rendered also by M. Richard Cramer, who served as an astute and insightful independent rater of the interview records. Charles Johnston, Barbara Long, and Lewis Long patiently briefed us on many aspects of Little Rock's dilemma; their full cooperation in this and other ways is gratefully acknowledged.

We owe much to our wives, Berdelle Campbell and Ann Pettigrew, for their understanding and help throughout.

And, finally, we wish to express our deep appreciation to the clergymen of Little Rock. Their patience, candor, and introspection made this study possible.

The entire investigation was financed by a research grant from the Laboratory of Social Relations of Harvard University. One of the authors, Ernest Q. Campbell, was a postdoctoral research training fellow of the Social Science Research Council during the time of this study.

The complete report is appearing for the first time in this volume, but three brief papers dealing with particular aspects of the study have been published previously: "Men of God in Racial Crisis," (*Christian Century*, 75, June 4, 1958, pp. 663-665), "Vignettes from Little Rock," (*Christianity and Crisis*, 18, September 29, 1958, pp. 128-136), and "Racial and Moral Crisis: the Role of Little Rock Ministers" (*American Journal of Sociology*, 64, March 1959, pp. 509-516).

E. Q. C. AND T. F. P.

CONTENTS

CHAPTER ONE

THE MINISTRY AND INTEGRATION:
"THE GREATEST THREAT TO SEGREGATION"

"In the South itself the 1954-57 period demonstrated that perhaps the greatest threat to the unity sought by organized segregationists came from the churches, themselves entangled in all but continuous debate."
—WELDON JAMES [1]

The white South today presents what appears to be a solid wall of resistance to racial desegregation. What sentiment there is to abide by the Supreme Court's rulings seems to be totally silenced—so silenced in fact that Hodding Carter, the editor of the *Delta Democrat-Times*, believes that "the First Amendment of our Constitution is probably in more danger in the South today than are our white and Negro children." [2]

Enforced silence necessarily implies that the South may not be as solid as it would like to appear. Indeed, many influential southerners do not fully approve of their region's position. [3] Neither martyrs nor moralists, they simply hold certain other values above the maintenance of segregation. The prominent businessman may not want integration, but he deeply fears the economic effects of community violence and disorder. The respected lawyer may have his doubts about the wisdom of the Supreme Court, but he firmly believes in the sanctity of the law. The dedicated educator may prefer separate schools, but he unhesitatingly chooses integration before the abolition of public instruction. And the popular newspaper editor may have reservations about the situation in his own locality, but he clearly sees the inevitability of desegregation in its national and international perspectives. Yet these ideas of the businessman, lawyer, educator, and newspaperman go largely unexpressed in the South at this time—in part because of the very involvements and commitments in the community that make these men influential.

One important group of southerners, however, has not been so easily silenced. Though by no means of one accord themselves, ministers provide "perhaps the greatest threat to the unity sought by organized segregationists." [4] They have become a threat simply by voicing anti-

1

segregationist sentiments at a time when no other respected leaders dared.

While the relatively fundamentalist sects typically have favored segregation, practically every major denomination in the South has publicly advocated compliance with the federal courts.[5]   Though these pronouncements vary somewhat in firmness, they are strikingly similar in intent and wording.   Thus the General Assembly of the U.S. Presbyterian Church (Southern) agreed in 1954: "The assembly commends the principle of the decision and . . .urges all our people to lend their assistance to those charged with the duty of implementing the decision."   The Southern Baptist Convention announced in the same year: "We recognize that this Supreme Court decision is in harmony . . .with the Christian principles of equal justice and love for all men. . .   We urge our people and all Christians to conduct themselves in this period of adjustment in the spirit of Christ."   The Episcopalians followed in 1955:   "The 58th General Convention of the Protestant Episcopal Church . . .now commends to all the clergy and people of this church that they accept and support this ruling of the Supreme Court. . . ."   In 1956 the Methodist General Conference made their statement: "The decisions of the Supreme Court . . .relative to segregation make necessary far-reaching and often difficult readjustments throughout the nation.   We call upon our people to effect these adjustments in all good faith, with brotherliness and patience. . . .Let these things, however, be done in love lest the cause of Christ suffer at our hands."

More recent pronouncements by these denominations have tended to be stronger and more detailed.   In 1957, for instance, southern Presbyterians reinforced previous statements with a widely publicized declaration of particulars that specifically condemned discrimination in education, employment, religion, and politics, admonished their communicants against Klan or Citizens' Council membership, and firmly supported the debated Koinonia interracial community in Georgia.[6]   Passed by an overwhelming majority, this declaration leaves little doubt as to the Presbyterian position.

But it is a giant step from the lofty ideals of national and regional conventions to the realities of a segregationist congregation back home. In regard to the integration resolution of the Southern Baptists one observer remarked to Robert Penn Warren: "They were just a little bit exalted.   When they got back with the home folks a lot of 'em wondered how they did it."[7]

Much of the minister's ardor is dampened when he returns to his flock though this is not to say that he bends completely to their will. It is not without significance that some fairly strong announcements have been made on the local level. Witness the 1954 statement of the New Orleans Council of Churches: "We believe that this decision is consistent with the spirit and teachings of Jesus Christ. . . .We call upon the members of our state legislature to find just ways of implementing in our state the decision of the U.S. Supreme Court." [8] Early in 1957 the Ministerial Association of Richmond, Virginia, issued a "Statement of Conviction" that indicted both the segregationist Governor and the General Assembly for their "exceedingly inept handling of the current racial situation." [9] And in the spring of 1958, 300 white clergymen, representing 13 Protestant denominations in Dallas, Texas, took a firm position on the school integration question facing their city when they announced flatly that "enforced segregation is morally and spiritually wrong." [10]

Keep in mind that such ministerial behavior has taken place in a milieu seething with dissent—a milieu in which outspoken pastors are censured by other members of the clergy and sometimes lose their positions. Yet, in spite of all of this, a few southern clergymen have ventured beyond the statement-issuing level into community action.

Roman Catholic authorities have integrated many of their educational facilities in the border and middle South. In 1947, seven years before the Supreme Court handed down its decision, Archbishop Ritter of St. Louis integrated all parochial elementary and secondary schools and sternly warned 700 parents that under Canon Law they would be "excommunicated if they presumed to interfere in the administrative office of their Bishop by having recourse to any authority outside the Church." Desegregation proceeded without incident. In a city that is 24 percent Catholic the Bishop's position was bound to have a marked effect on public school integration eight years later. It has been noted that a majority of the teachers in St. Louis attribute part of the success of their public school integration to the initial desegregation of the Catholic schools. [11]

At the present time Archbishop Rummel of New Orleans is attempting similar action. Believing segregation to be "morally wrong and sinful," he recently announced that his large parochial school system would be integrated. In view of lay protest, however, he set no date. [12]

The Protestant clergy is frequently involved when attempts at public school integration meet with violent opposition. For example, in 1956, when an organized segregationist protest in Henderson, Ken-

tucky, led to a widespread student boycott and a mob of 200 white
adults demonstrated before the school in question, the Henderson
Ministerial Association went into action. [13] Immediately, the Association issued newspaper and radio announcements urging the end
of the boycott; these continued until the resistance movement crum-
bled.

Sometimes activity of this sort has been physically dangerous for
clergymen. During the integration crisis in Mansfield, Texas, in September 1956, an Episcopal rector from Fort Worth had to be escorted
through a mob by a State Ranger after pointedly discussing "the
Christian merits of their demonstrations and of desegregation." [14]
Some months later the Baptist pastor of the largest church in Clinton,
Tennessee, led nine Negro children to an integrated school during
that community's disturbances. On his return from the school he was
attacked by segregationists who inflicted face cuts on him. [15] And
Ku Klux Klan cross burnings in small Alabama towns have been aimed
at intimidating white ministers. During the 1956 Christmas celebra-
tions in Opelika, a Baptist pastor invited a Negro high school delega-
tion to hear his church perform *The Messiah*. As a warning against
such "race mixing," a five-foot cross was burned in front of his home. [16]
Later, in Sylacauga, Alabama, threats against the families of two
outspoken ministers were made after a Klan demonstration and cross
burnings before their churches. [17]

The importance of courageous ministerial action for desegregation
is belittled by some observers of the southern scene who insist that
such gestures have been ineffectual. To be sure, single incidents do
not always reap immediate results. But when all of the ministerial
protests are considered together they become of crucial significance
for at least three fundamental reasons.

First, Protestant churches historically have profoundly affected the
culture of the "Bible Belt." Second, ministers are in a unique position
to attack one of the weakest links in segregationist armor—guilt over
past treatment of the Negro. And, finally, these actions are important
as publicized disruptions in what otherwise might appear to be
complete southern unanimity on integration. Let us consider these
three points in greater detail.

The pervasive authority of Protestantism has been felt throughout
southern history. The peculiarly rugged, forceful brand of religion in
the South stems in part from the frontier need for a strong God. [18]
W. J. Cash has convincingly shown how such frontier elements cling

tenaciously on in the South—far longer than in other regions of the country. [19] Since frontier days, too, church leaders have utilized their prestige in the secular realm, ranging from political office-holding to serving as generals in the Confederate Army. Early in this century, for instance, southern clergymen were active in re-establishing the Ku Klux Klan, in defending prohibition, in attacking evolution, and in supporting Herbert Hoover for president. [20] Most of these actions stemmed from a rigorously fundamentalist point of view; but, whatever their origin and subsequent direction, they maintained the tradition of a politically active clergy.

Events over the past three decades have wrought some vast changes. As the new South becomes more urban and industrial, its institutional forms become increasingly similar to the dominant American patterns. In religious terms this can only mean a decided trend toward secularism. Fundamentalism is slowly waning, and as it wanes the central role of religion in southern life is weakened. Today primitive forms of fundamentalism are confined to rural and urban working classes that lack regional prestige though fundamentalist overtones can still be noted in some of the larger denominations. And today the word of the Protestant churches in general lacks the complete authority that it once had throughout the South.

Over the past generation another religious trend has also been evident. Liberalism is gradually displacing the previous conservatism of the major denominations. F. S. Loescher reports that the 17 leading denominations adopted only six resolutions between 1908 and 1929 bearing upon the race problem. During the 1930's they adopted 60. But they adopted almost 100 in the first five years of the 1940's. [21] Moreover, the pronouncements became increasingly more specific (for example, against segregation of blood plasma) and more self-examining (almost one-third of the announcements during the early 1940's dealt with the church and its membership). The change is most striking when today's ministerial action against segregation is contrasted with the conspicuous silence in the 1920's on lynching. [22] Actually, for some time, most of the seminaries of the leading southern denominations have been producing young men with liberal racial views. Conservative congregations throughout the South are repeatedly replacing "extremist" clergymen with young men who are distinctly more liberal than their predecessors.

Though these changes are important they should not be exaggerated. Staunchly conservative elements continue to dominate the controlling bodies of the leading Protestant denominations. Fundamentalism still finds its strongest expression in the South. And the influence of Protestantism remains stronger in the South than in any other region of the United States.

The continuing importance of religion in southern life is amply evident. In one of the most extensive and thorough national public opinion polls ever conducted, Dr. Samuel Stouffer found Protestant church attendance to be considerably higher in the South than in the North.[23] Sixty-eight percent of his sample, chosen at random among southern Protestants, had attended church within the month as compared with only 55 percent of his northern Protestants. Other investigators have reported similar findings.[24]

This greater church attendance in the South is accompanied by corresponding differences in attitudes, values, and demography between the regions. For example, B. T. Prothro and J. A. Jensen have repeatedly noted that southern college samples are unusually favorable in their attitudes toward the church as an institution, frequently more favorable than even northern divinity students.[25] And investigators using the *Study of Values* scale have consistently found that southern college students score higher on the religious value than college students in other regions.[26] More religious activity is reflected, too, in 1950 census data indicating that the South employs more white ministers in proportion to its population than any other region in the nation. While three out of every 1,000 white males in the employed labor force in New York and California are ministers, for instance, the corresponding figure in Arkansas, South Carolina, and Mississippi is more than five.[27] Furthermore, the ministry as an occupation holds greater prestige in the South than in other regions. When a representative national sample was asked to evaluate 90 occupations, 61 percent in the South rated the minister as having an "excellent standing" as compared with only 53 percent of the Northeast, 47 percent of the West, and 46 percent of the Midwest.[28] Anthropologist John Gillin concludes from this accumulation of evidence that "Protestant morality is especially strong" in the South.[29] It is not the devoutly fundamentalist South of yesteryear, obviously, but, relatively speaking, the South remains America's "Bible Belt."

To point out that the Protestant churches are unusually strong in the South is not to imply that southern clergymen make community-wide policy decisions themselves. Like other institutional leaders, they are typically not found directly in the power structure; rather, they are important contributors to the milieu in which the decision-makers must realistically operate. Thus in his detailed research on a large southern city's power structure, Floyd Hunter notes: "We see both the institutions and the formal associations playing a vital role in the execution of determined policy, but the formulation of policy often takes place outside these formalized groupings. . . .It may be noted here that none of the ministers of churches in Regional City were chosen as top leaders by the persons interviewed in the study. The idea was expressed several times by interviewees that some minister *ought* to be on the listing. . . It is understood, however, that in order to get a project well under way it would be important to bring the churches in. . ." [30]

What may be uniquely southern about this description is that some of Hunter's respondents felt "that some minister *ought* to be on the listing." Though the churches are not directly represented in the power structure, they have such weight in the southern community that they must be taken carefully into account.

One more qualification must be made concerning the influence of the southern minister. Since fundamentalism and religion in general have slipped in importance in recent decades and since the minister is not directly a decision-maker, the significance of the clergy's actions can sometimes be denied. On a fairly superficial level, specific ministerial protests can be, and are, easily rationalized away by many religious and church-attending southerners. Thus the major denominational statements urging compliance with the Supreme Court are thought of "as pious declarations made for the national press and not intended for us down here." The civic ministerial associations who oppose the local segregationist politicians are "just full of Yankees." The Catholic archbishops who try to integrate their facilities "know better, but must take their orders from Rome." The rector who argued with the Mansfield mob "must have been a crackpot." The assaulted pastor of Clinton "had to expect the consequences of leaving his rightful place in his church." And the cross burnings in Alabama "were unfortunate, but those ministers stirred up the trouble themselves by raising the whole issue." One incident at a time, these rationalizations are frequently successful in allaying the individual conscience, but continuous religious protests against segregation in many different contexts and by all major denominations begin to have their effect. Finally the seed of doubt may be planted: "Perhaps they are right; maybe segregation *is* against the will of God."

Assuming that faithful Protestants desire to follow "the will of God," the task of the clergy in implementing their proclamations is to establish clearly that segregation is against "the will of God." That the efforts toward this end of at least some of the southern clergy have been partially successful is documented by the reactions of a variety of segregationist spokesmen. In a 1956 speech in Maryland John Kasper, the twice-convicted leader of resistance to integration, is reported by the press "to have attacked President Eisenhower, Vice President Nixon, Adlai Stevenson, Estes Kefauver, the Washington 'cesspool,' Quakers, Unitarians, Catholics, Congregationalists, some Southern Baptists, the Anti-Defamation League of B'nai B'rith and pro-integration activities of Parent-Teacher Associations." [31]

Note that five out of the eight groups Kasper assailed were religious organizations. Even segregationists who sharply disagree with him on many points seem to be impelled to counter the influence of the churches. One of these, Dr. W. C. George, professor emeritus of histology at the University of North Carolina, has declared: "There are people with good hearts, however, who for lack of information and understanding have espoused integration. The group most difficult to combat and the group most influential, perhaps, in bringing this evil upon us are the ministers. . . .You may remember that the Church used to assert that the earth was the center of our World and that the sun revolved around it. . . .Today ministers tell us that they know God's will on all sorts of worldly matters that they know little about, and they tell us what is the Christian thing to do, when a careful, critical consideration of the facts leads to the conclusion that the thing is evil, not good." [32]

Only when the clergy is actually influential can it draw such fire from segregationists.

To sum up: Ministers do not have as preeminent a position as they did 30 years ago; they do not directly make crucial decisions of public policy; and, taken one at a time, their anti-segregationist actions can be rationalized away. But the historically central role of religion in southern culture makes it certain that the repeated protests of the clergy are heard and are disquietingly effective in establishing moral doubt.

Establishing moral doubt may seem a minor achievement in the face of the considerable resources at the disposal of the organized segregationists. Yet it is precisely this weapon that makes the minister's role uniquely adapted to tapping the Achilles' heel of segregation—guilt. The importance of this factor—guilt—in southern race relations has been stressed by sociologists, psychoanalysts, and southern-born writers. Gunnar Myrdal makes the point forcefully in terms of the moral dilemma between the egalitarian tenets of democracy and the discrimination practiced against the Negro.[33] All Americans wrestle to some degree with the conflict, Myrdal points out, but white southerners are particularly susceptible for despite their more blatant restrictions on the Negro they believe as firmly and as deeply as their fellow citizens in other regions in the American creed as embodied in the Declaration of Independence, the preamble to the Constitution, the Bill of Rights, and state constitutions.[34] That the Protestant clergy is particularly qualified to deal with the guilt engendered by this dilemma is amply evident when we recall the origins of the equalitarian creed. "If," as Myrdal observes, "the European philosophy of Enlightenment was one of the ideological roots of the American Creed, another equally important one was Christianity, particularly as it took the form in the colonies of various lower class Protestant sects, split off from the Anglican Church. 'Democracy was envisaged in religious terms long before it assumed a political terminology.' "[35]

In short, the American creed—the dignity of the individual, the basic equality of all men and the right to freedom, justice, and opportunity—is derived directly from the value structure of the Protestant churches. Who, then, is better equipped to reinforce this guilt-producing creed than the Protestant ministry?

Psychoanalyst Helen McLean and Georgia novelist Lillian Smith emphasize guilt from another source.[36] The "sin, sex, and segregation" syndrome, they argue, accounts for the excessive emotional involvement of southerners in racial distinctions. The syndrome develops from the fact that many white southerners have warm, intimate personal relationships with Negroes and that these experiences lead unconsciously to the belief that the Negro has a greater capacity for expresssing genuine warmth. But both illicit sexual relations and intimate contact with Negroes are sinful, dangerous, and produce guilt. Segregation, in these terms, becomes a way of keeping those who represent the temptation in subservience. While this is in no sense a complete theory of racial conflict, abundant evidence supports these contentions. Consider the use of the derogatory term "nigger-lover" as applied to anyone who in the least way champions the rights of Negroes. Consider the exaggerated fear of rape, the sexual prowess stereotype of the Negro, and the immediate equating of school desegregation with miscegenation. Again, ministers who can provide guidance in all three realms—sin, sex, and segregation—are strategically positioned to deal with such guilt.

Southern guilt over the subjugation of the Negro from whatever source—democratic ideals, sex, or Christian teachings directly—demonstrates the region's potential for adjusting to the inevitable changes of the future. It reveals, in the language of Kentucky novelist Robert Penn Warren, the South's "fifth column of decency"—a fifth column the minister can expand and strengthen. [37]

The clergy's public support of values in conflict with segregation has the additional significance of disturbing the anti-integration unanimity of the South.

Recent social psychological evidence indicates that the crucial factor behind the anti-Negro attitudes of most white Southerners is conformity to the norms of southern culture. [38] And extensive laboratory experimentation of social psychologists shows that one of the most important variables underlying conforming behavior is the unanimity of the pressure placed on the individual. [39] Take, for example, the findings of Asch's classical work on conformity. A group of eight individuals, seven of them pre-instructed assistants of the experimenter and the eighth a genuine subject, were asked to estimate the lengths of 18 pairs of lines. On 12 of the line judgments, the seven stooges purposely reported aloud an obviously incorrect estimate. Thus the subject, seated eighth and believing that the other seven people were subjects like himself, faced unanimious pressure to conform by making a similar incorrect response. On approximately one-third of such judgments, he yielded to the group; like the others, he would estimate a five inch line as four inches. But when Asch disturbed the unanimity of the pressure by having one of his seven assistants give a correct response, a marked difference occurred. Only a tenth rather than a third of the subjects' responses yielded to the majority in this 6 to 1 situation. Once unanimity no longer existed, even when there was only one supporting colleague, the subject could better withstand the pressure of the majority to conform.

To carry through the analogy to today's crisis in the South, obvious five-inch lines are being widely described as four inches. When the minister is the only respected man in his community to announce aloud that the line is in fact five inches, the effects of such action in minimizing the conformity to the dominant pattern may be as striking as in Asch's controlled experiment.

There are, then, a number of reasons why clerical actions on the current integration scene are not to be regarded lightly. An aroused southern ministry that makes use of its historically central place in southern life by supporting and strengthening the American creed and the "fifth column of decency" and by destroying the "solid" South's unanimity on the issue could become the next decade's most important agent of social change.

This study examines the ministerial response to the most publicized of all desegregation crises—Little Rock, Arkansas. Two purposes prompted the study. The first comes from an interest in the desegregation process *per se* and a desire to predict the southern ministry's role in future integration efforts. Central to this forecast is the potential significance of the clergy in the process. The second purpose, closely related to the first, is a desire to learn more about the seldom examined ministerial role of social reformer. In time of crisis, clerical actions should stand out in bold relief, throwing sharp perspective on the reformer role when the community at large is opposed to the change.

Though social science has given little research attention to this ministerial area, C. Y. Glock and B. B. Ringer have thrown some light on the subject with their random sample, 1951-52 study of the members and clergy of the Protestant Episcopal Church.[40] They found the national governing body of the church "more receptive to social change than its parishioners" but nevertheless the church must tread softly on those issues on which parishioners have definite convictions and self-interests (such issues are war, labor, government control, and the political role of the church). The church must take its strong stands on ideological or moral issues on which lay opinion is more divided (intermarriage with Roman Catholics, treatment of conscientious objectors, and minority rights). In times of conflict between church policy and congregational opinion the position of the Episcopalian rector tends to adhere closely to the pronouncements of the church. Caught in between, rectors disagree most of all with congregational opinions concerning issues on which the church has taken a firm position. Furthermore, the rector can expect to receive his greatest opposition from precisely those communicants who are the most active. Thus Episcopalians who are most opposed to ministers taking an active role in politics belong to more church-related organizations and attend services more regularly than more liberal parishioners. The conservatives also tend to be less educated, older, of the female sex, and less politically informed than other members. The reformer role, these data suggest, may not be an easy one to play for many rectors. Though backed by his church, a clergyman who stresses the rights of minorities may well be faced with opposition from the older and active "pillars" whom he can least afford to offend.

Helpful as this extensive study is, many vital questions remain: How do ministers in the concrete situation pursue their reformer role? What are the differences in the manner in which the ministers of small sects and those of major denominations approach social issues? To what degree do ministers collaborate in community-wide efforts to influence social action? What are the pressures applied to ministers which make the reformer role difficult? And how does the minister resolve the conflicts that arise between what he expects of himself, what his denomination expects of him, and what his congregation expects of him?

The present study attempts to provide tentative answers to these questions. A number of considerations make Little Rock the ideal place for such a pilot study. Arkansas is in the middle South, not the deep South. Though the majority of white people in Little Rock, to judge from election results, believe in segregation, there has been more public opportunity for the clergy to express pro-integration views than in such states as Mississippi, Georgia, and South Carolina. In addition, liberal Little Rock ministers have been strengthened by having active world opinion marshalled behind them. Here in the Little Rock conflict, then, we might reasonably expect to find a particularly aroused clergy. And a survey of their behavior prior to the crisis further supports such an expectation. For example, the white and Negro ministerial alliances in Little Rock united into a single, interracial organization in 1956.

Another aspect of the Little Rock situation is ideal for our purposes. Following the September 1957 violence, 24 pastors of small, dissident Baptist sects sponsored a Friday night service in October to pray for the maintainance of segregation. The following morning, practically all of the Jewish rabbis, Roman Catholic priests, and major Protestant denominational ministers sponsored citywide prayers for a peaceful solution to the racial crisis. These two services provided the samples and the initial foci for the investigation.

Less than a week after the prayer services, the present study began. The method employed is simple and straightforward. First, background information was obtained by careful analysis of the ministerial action recorded in the local press. Then interviews were held with community leaders—newspapermen, businessmen, school officials, and church authorities—who could supply the further background and assistance needed to launch the ministerial interviews.

Forty-two detailed interviews with ministers were held: 13 participants in the segregation prayer service and 29 of the "peace prayer" group. Twenty-seven of the latter were Protestants and two were Jewish. Roman Catholic priests did not cooperate. The informants were not selected randomly. Rather, the so-called "snowball technique" was used in an effort to include the most influential sect and church leaders in the sample. Each interviewee was asked to name the "most influential" members of the Little Rock clergy, and then each man named was interviewed until all nominees were exhausted.

The first interviews were made with the announced leaders of the two prayer services. Since there was no overlap in membership of the two ministerial groups, this procedure amounted to drawing samples from two different populations. In addition to interviews with all of the ministers mentioned as influential, the sample included a number who had not been mentioned but who had taken strong positions during the crisis. Thus our sample is heavily weighted with pastors of the large, high-prestige churches and those from smaller churches who had assumed active roles in the racial conflict. We anticipated that these two types of ministers would have to contend with the greatest amount of role conflict.

The ministers were informed in the initial contact that the study concerned the clergy's role in time of community crisis, and that the interview would be conducted similar to a public opinion poll. No names would be mentioned in reporting the results. The investigators emphasized that they both had been born, raised, and educated in the South. One difference in approach was necessary, however, when dealing with the sect pastors. The peace-prayer leaders were told that the study emanated from Harvard University's Laboratory of Social Relations, but the sect leaders were not told of the interviewer's institutional affiliation.[a] This omission was made to gain better rapport with the segregationists. Save for Roman Catholic leaders, appointments were secured eventually with all of the ministers contacted.

The interviews lasted from 45 minutes to three hours each. Notes were taken, and a complete transcription was dictated soon afterwards. The basic data of the study consists of mimeographed reports of the dictated interviews.

Rapport was generally excellent with both sect and church ministers, judging from their relaxed candor. Both groups enjoyed the opportunity to tell of their part in the drama. Tension in Little Rock was still high, and no solution was in sight at the time of the interviews.

Thus the informants were discussing live issues that still plagued them and their community.

Open-ended questions sought information in three related areas. The first revolved around the minister and his church. When and where was he born and educated? Has he held office in any ministerial organizations? How long has he served his present church? Is his church largely a neighborhood or a community church?

How many members? What are the occupations of the members of the governing board (elders, deacons, stewards, or vestrymen)? Is there a fund-raising drive on now?

These "non-threatening" items helped to pave the way for a second battery of questions on the role of the minister and his church in the crisis. The transition was accomplished by two mild inquiries, one about the number of children in the Sunday school who attended Central High School. The other sought information on whether any of his congregation had approached him for advice concerning the conflict. Further queries of this type asked whether he had taken a public stand on the issue, whether his position reflected his congregation's views, what means his congregation used in letting him know their approval or disapproval of his position, and whether any members belonged to the White Citizens' Council.

The final section delved into his personal views. The transitional inquiry was whether he considered the racial matter as a religious issue.

Apart from your ministry, what do you privately think of this situation?

Do you think that the proposed visit of Billy Graham would help or hurt the present situation?

If you resided in an unsegregated state would your position be any different? (Only segregationists were asked this question.)

If you had an opportunity to advise Negroes on race relations in the South, what would you say?

How do you think this racial disturbance here in Little Rock is going to end?

After the completion of the ministerial interviews, spot checks were made of a number of selected congregations by interviewing 38 members of the eight churches in which we desired to obtain the congregation's view of the minister's activities. Four ministers from these churches encountered congregational opposition because they were vigorous champions of integration. The other four ministers were inactive during the crisis. The particular church affiliations of the members were known before the interviews began, but we requested them not to reveal the names of their churches. The purpose was to facilitate candor. After several warm-up openers, our questions touched on what the respondent perceived to be his minister's position in the crisis, then shifted to what he thought of this position, and finally ended with his interpretation of the congregation's attitude toward the minister's position. Most of these queries elicited fixed-alternative answers.

Data analysis was facilitated by our own independent ratings and those of a third person who had not been to Little Rock. Using the mimeographed ministerial interview material, each of the 42 respondents were rated low, medium, or high on such variables as personal commitment to, and internal conflict over, the desegregation issue. Subjective as such ratings must be, agreement between the judges was satisfactorily high. The final phase of the study was a continuous check on Little Rock ministerial behavior which extended through the fall of 1958. For this we utilized the local press and made several return trips to Little Rock.[42]

The results of the study are detailed in the following six chapters. The next chapter presents a reportorial review of the clergy's part in Little Rock's desegregation crisis during 1957. The small sect pastors who led the segregation prayer meeting are considered in detail in Chapter Three. We shall see that much of their behavior can be accounted for in terms of insularity from other points of view, hostility to other religious forms and ideas, and the feeling of support from almost everyone they considered of importance.

Chapters Four and Five focus on the ministers of Little Rock's leading churches. Within the framework of social movement theory, we shall see that three general types of ministers can be distinguished and that these three types differ considerably on a number of individual and social variables. Complementing this interpretation in Chapter Four, Chapter Five considers the individual actions of the ministerial leaders in terms of role conflict. We shall learn of the conflicting pressures placed on the minister during the crisis and how he attempted to resolve the resulting conflict between his conscience, his congregation, and his church superiors.

The sixth chapter tells of the clergy's actions during 1958 and presents a number of testable hypotheses. Chapter Seven interprets the study's results in terms of a more general "Protestant dilemma."

CHAPTER TWO

MINISTERS IN THE PUBLIC EYE:

"LET THE CHURCH BE THE CHURCH"

"Never have the Christian forces been given a greater opportunity to exert an influence for good than in this present crisis. This terrible disaster did not come because Christianity failed. Nevertheless the Christian church would not be worthy of itself if it did not speak out bravely and forcefully for the principles for which it stands. The real Christian must stand for obedience to law and orderly processes for settling differences within the framework of our government. He must express in his relationship to his fellow man love rather than hate . . .

"We are under the compulsion of God, if we are Christians, to 'lead the new life, following the commandments of God.' We cannot allow ourselves to drift into attitudes of ill will toward any man. Our responsibility is to discover the will of God and follow it . . .

"We recognize the differences of opinion shared by sincere men and women concerning the matter of integration in the schools. We are firmly convinced that the great majority of our citizens are law-abiding and are genuinely concerned that there be a right attitude demonstrated between all races . . .

"Now is the time for the Christian Church in the spirit of prayer to call upon all good people to encourage the forces that will unify rather than divide our people. Let us demonstrate to the world that peace and brotherhood are genuinely desired by an overwhelming majority of our citizens. In this crisis, let the Church be the Church."

—PAUL E. MARTIN, Methodist Bishop of Arkansas, 1957[1]

Like all other human events, the activities of the Little Rock ministerial community have a history. What individual ministers have done and said during the city's period of crisis is necessarily related to what was done and said on previous and less conspicuous occasions. Sermons on race relations, on love and brotherhood with explicit mention of the Negro, appearance before legislative committees, exchange visits between white and Negro congregations—these and other events form a part of the picture. Our purpose, however, is more limited. We intend to detail the ministerial actions that related directly to the 1957 racial crisis in Little Rock.

This chapter is based on a record of these actions as they were reported in the daily press, supplemented with relevant information

obtained in our interviews. The developments are presented chrono-
logically to give the reader a sense of the unfolding pattern of events.[2]

It is appropriate to begin this account with a sermon delivered
on July 7, 1957.[3] Speaking on the Sunday nearest the anniversary
of the Declaration of Independence, the highly respected "dean" of
Little Rock's Protestant ministers said: "I am not going to give aid
and comfort to segregationists and to the passions of violent men by
failing to speak out on a matter I know to be right." He felt reassured
because his stand was fully consonant with the position of his church
at higher levels.

The sermon itself was unequivocal. It defined the crucial test of
Christian citizenship: "Are we prepared to remove from our minds
the prejudices and from our statute books the legal hindrances that
stand in the way of full citizenship for our Negro citizens." To do
so "is so little for us to give and so much for them to receive." The
speaker pledged his support for the school board plan of desegregation
in Little Rock and invited all officers and members of the church to
join him in doing so. He gave three reasons why "the sooner [segrega-
tion] is eliminated from our minds and from our statute books the
better—

"Segregation by Law should be eliminated because it is a direct
contradiction to the Christian Doctrine of the Dignity of Man . . ."

"This legal disability . . . is in direct contradiction to the spirit
and purpose of American freedom . . ."

"A third reason . . . is the rising tide of resentment against it
throughout the world and the urgent necessity for continuing the
Missionary Enterprise."

The conclusion to this sermon is interesting because of its relation
to the analysis in Chapter Five. The speaker asked, "Why do I
preach on this subject when I run the risk of offending some of my
good members?" He said in answering his own question: "There are
some of our members who have already made up their minds and
who will disregard everything I have said here this morning. That
is their privilege. But there are also many loyal [church members]
who want light and guidance from their Church on this difficult and
complex question. They have a right as loyal [church members] to
know what position their Church has taken, and why. It is my responsibility and duty to tell them. It is for these that I have spoken
today."

He was almost unique among Little Rock ministers in his straightforward attack on segregation on moral and religious grounds. In

fact, during the city's crisis period that began in September 1957 only a small number of pastors delivered public utterances of comparable directness.

The response to the sermon was gratifying. Many members told their pastor they were proud both for what he had said and because he had made his position known so early. Members of other churches who heard of the sermon expressed the wish that their own ministers would take an equally forthright stand.

The city's pulpits touched only infrequently during July and August on the impending educational changes in the fall. Some ministers were on vacation during these months. Perhaps others were silent because the school superintendent had discouraged widespread discussion.

One might presume, however, that the first Sunday in September would be an auspicious date for sermons on Christianity and race relations. Yet so far as we can determine, only two ministers, pastors in leading citywide churches, devoted their sermons on the first September Sunday to the coming week's integration of Negro students into Central High School. The community was tense. Both sermons expressed sentiments favorable to integration. One of the ministers— who several days later heard a faithful member observe that he never thought he'd live to hear such a sermon preached from the pulpit of his church—called on his people to be kind, remain calm in the situation, and practice the Christian virtues. He reminded his listeners that the community had voted to accept the school board's plan, that the plan was carefully drawn, and that it deserved their full support. In similar vein, the second minister commended the school board for its wise procedure. He declared his support for the desegregation decision of the Supreme Court, and reviewed New Testament instances in which Jesus "openly cut across established social patterns." [4]

Both received predominantly favorable responses from their listeners. Even in the prominent church sometimes described by local ministers as "a hotbed of segregationists," many people in the congregation spoke to the minister in praise of his sermon.

Other ministers may have referred to the coming school year in less detail during the services of September 1. The *Arkansas Gazette* reported, for example, that a pastor in one of the city's leading churches "pointedly" instructed his congregation to "Be Christian this week and in the days ahead." In the meanwhile, the Greater Little Rock Ministerial Association released a letter urging the city's ministers to issue an appeal for orderly conduct.

The Arkansas National Guard, on orders from Governor Orval E. Faubus, surrounded Central High School on Monday, September 2. Schools opened the next day, September 3. On that evening 15 ministers in local churches issued a statement "to strongly protest the action of Governor Orval E. Faubus in calling out the armed forces . . . thereby preventing integration in compliance with the Supreme Court's decision of May, 1954 and the order of the Federal Court of August, 1957." The statement was a political rather than a religious document.[5] Those who signed it did not declare themselves as favoring integration nor as believing that Christian doctrine requires or even encourages its acceptance. Support for integration, educational or otherwise, as a legitimate or desirable social goal was left to inference.[6] It can be said that such support was widely inferred in the heat of the issue.

Those who signed this statement are ministers in six major Protestant denominations; 14 were interviewed in this study. Presbyterian, Baptist, Christian, Episcopal, Methodist and Lutheran pastors signed; Methodists were the largest single group represented. None of the several major church administrative officials in Little Rock signed. Ministers to the larger churches in Pulaski Heights, the high-status section of Little Rock, and to large community-wide churches around the downtown area dominated the list. Seven of the ten ministers of major Protestant community churches signed. In general, the list represented the city's ministerial elite.

Almost certainly, others of the city's ministry would have signed had it been possible to reach them. The statement originated with a small number of ministers late in the afternoon of September 3, and support was obtained by telephone before releasing the statement for a local television newscast later in the day. At least one minister refused to permit the use of his name; there may have been others.

It is difficult to know the extent to which this statement reflected the spontaneous reaction of the city's ministry to Governor Faubus's circumvention of school integration. Nor is it known whether the framework for the protest in "law and order" rather than in "integration" terms represented a tactical decision or a preferred principle. In the confusion of the time, it probably did not matter. The *Gazette* said editorially that the statement "condemned the governor's action in the strongest language permissible to men of God."

There was an immediate counter-response by another group of

ministers who came to the defense of Governor Faubus. Fifteen signed a statement on September 4, calling attention to the Arkansas state law that requires racial segregation in the public schools. They pointed out that it was the governor's duty to see that state law was enforced. Like its predecessor (and provocator), this statement was political rather than religious in tone.

The 14 churches served by those who signed this statement (two of the signers were a father-son combination in one church) are predominantly from two splinter-Baptist associations, not affiliated with the large Southern Baptist Convention.[7] The churches are small, with typical memberships of 200 to 250. At least half are located in autonomous suburban communities that retain strong rural ties; only one of the churches is in downtown Little Rock. It is doubtful that the combined memberships of the 14 churches would equal that of the city's largest church (Southern Baptist) whose pastor was among those who protested the use of the National Guard.

How many more signers of this pro-Faubus statement would have been produced by concerted effort is not known although it is obvious from later developments that the 15 believed themselves to represent a much larger body of like-minded ministers and laymen.[8] Seven of the 15 were in our interview sample, including all of those with churches in Little Rock proper.

Two other relevant events occurred on September 4th.

The president of the unaccredited Little Rock Missionary Baptist Seminary appeared at Central High School as a member of the threatening crowd gathered there. News sources reported that he tried to quiet the crowd by asking, "Let's cooperate with [the Guard]." On the same day, Governor Faubus was asked at a press conference to comment on the ministerial statement deploring his action in calling out the Guard. He replied that he had had "many or more" [sic] telegrams from white ministers, many of whom held churches in Little Rock, commending his action.

Also on September 4th, five Presbyterian ministers in the Clarksville, Arkansas, area released a letter to Governor Faubus.[9] Although this group is outside the geographic bounds of our study, it is interesting to contrast their statement with the critical one issued in Little Rock. These five endorsed the school board's plan of gradual integration "as a wise method of arriving at the situation of no racial discrimination in public education in Arkansas."

"We believe," declared the Presbyterian ministers, "in the dignity of all men as brothers under the fatherhood of God. We believe that freedom is a cardinal element of our national heritage and the product of the Christian tradition. We believe that the program of integration in the schools should continue and should not be thwarted by political pressure." Thus, they gave a clear moral declaration of support to integration in the schools which the Little Rock statement did not give. Indeed, no statement issued at any time by any group of white ministers in Little Rock was so unequivocal in its moral advocation of racial integration.

No public statement issued by Little Rock ministers attacked segregation on religious grounds with the strength of a statement adopted by a local Council of Church Women on September 9. Excerpts are indicative:

"It is our Christian conviction that enforced segregation of any group of persons because of race, creed or color is a violation of Christian principles. The national and state bodies of the denominations which we represent are all on record with statements saying that the Supreme Court rulings regarding segregation in the public schools are in keeping with Christian principles. We reaffirm these statements of our denominations. . . . We are shocked and dismayed that the governor of our state has placed military troops within our community to defy the order of the federal court instead of upholding the law of the land. . . .

"We deplore the un-Christian acts of some of our citizens expressing hatred of others, which have made the headlines around the world. . . .

"We call upon the Christian citizens of our communities and of our state to join us in . . . praying to God the Father of us all to forgive us for our failure to live as children of one Father. . . . We issue this call to prayer to all who will join us wherever they are at 12 noon Thursday, September 12, in a special time of prayer and meditation. . . ."

This statement is important for several reasons. The church women explicitly employed the stands taken by their various national denominations to support their own declaration, something the ministers did not do.[10] The statement also supports information received from other sources that many of the church women were "far ahead of" their ministers and the men of the churches, to the extent that some were pressuring ministers to explain their failure to take bold positions. Finally, the statement contained a call to community prayer and meditation at 12 noon, September 12—thereby antedating by exactly one month the public prayers sponsored by the city's ministers.

On September 12 the president of the Little Rock Ministerial Association called a meeting of Arkansas ministers to discuss the integration crisis. The number participating was reduced somewhat by walkouts when plans to have the group release a statement of principles were announced. Those who departed thought they had assembled only for prayer and discussion. Those who remained (35 ministers from 14 cities) issued a statement that "all are equal in God's sight" and declared that they had met to "witness to a unity given in Christ which transcends all racial, cultural, and denominational differences." Eight Little Rock ministers were among those who signed. No reference was made in the declaration to political aspects of the local situation.

Meeting on the same day, the board of managers of the United Church Women of Arkansas expressed "great concern" about the school situation and criticized the state's 1957 sovereignty laws as "embittering and delaying adjustments which eventually must and should be made." [11]

On Saturday, September 14, the president of the ministerial association made the most forthright statement by a local minister that had been carried in public print since the crisis began. Commenting on Governor Faubus' talk with President Eisenhower in Newport, Rhode Island, he said: "I am pleased that the President's statement means that gradual integration will proceed at once, and I am disappointed that the Governor did not say that the National Guard troops would be removed from Central High School. If the President does not mean that the integration will proceed at once in our high school, then I am disappointed with his statement also."

The events of the next week moved at a slower pace because of a hearing in the Federal District Court, at the conclusion of which the Governor was ordered to stop the use of national guardsmen to prevent desegregation at Central High. The order came on Friday, September 20. The Governor announced promptly that troops would be withdrawn. By Sunday, September 22, the *Arkansas Democrat* announced in its lead article that "both friends and foes of integration issued pleas for non-violence, including members of the Capital Citizens' Council and the Central High Mothers' League." The same article carried an excerpt from a statement by Little Rock's Mayor Woodrow Mann: "I respectfully request all ministers of all faiths to hold prayer during their Sunday services and ask that the love we hold for our neighbors and our respect for the dignity of God's children will lead us and direct us through the days ahead. Such

Christian charity will do more than anything else to keep peace and order in this community."

The *New York Times* mistakenly suggested a united clerical front in its report that "the clergymen here used their pulpits today [September 22] to pray for a peaceful acceptance of the integration program." The same issue reported that a sermon on fair play by the pastor of Little Rock's largest congregation made no direct reference to the integration issue; he told his congregation that it was not yet ready to hear what he had to say on this subject. [12] He did admonish them to stay away from any meetings called to encourage breaking the law, and in prayer he was reported to have asked for a blessing on the school authorities. On the same day, another prominent pastor chided his congregation regarding the lack of Christian brotherhood and fellowship shown a Negro girl who faced the jeers of a mob alone earlier in the month.

But the most dramatic event on September 22 occurred at a small, out-of-the-way denominational church in a working class neighborhood not far from the Little Rock Missionary Baptist Seminary. The minister was especially vulnerable because of the character of his congregation and because he had signed the Faubus condemnation. Several Negroes tried to attend services at the church, saying that they had received a telephone invitation from the minister's wife. The segregationists had chosen their target well; the Negroes were turned away. An out-of-state newspaper commented, "Perhaps these Negroes mistook this Church for the House of God." The city's staunchest segregationist ministers piously made public comments that they would not turn visitors away.

September 23 was Black Monday, the day of violence at Central High School. [13] The ministerial schism that had prematurely appeared in the alternate statements condemning and praising Governor Faubus broke into the open on September 24. That day, at the same meeting of the Citizens' Council at which a local pastor stated that "the Communist Supreme Court will keep after us and the South will continue fighting," a pastor from Malvern, Arkansas, offered a resolution calling on all "ministers who believe that children should have racially mixed schools forced upon them to immediately take steps to integrate their churches by publicly inviting the colored people to their services." The resolution was adopted. On the same day, a newspaper notice signed by 15 lay leaders in a local Presbyterian church asked citizens to peacefully accept or reject racial desegregation, and called on church and civic organizations to give urgent and prayerful consideration to the current threat to community peace.

During the following week the Episcopal Bishop of Arkansas called on all members of his Little Rock churches to "offer hourly prayers for God's guidance of our leaders in community, state and nation." His letter asked that all members "refrain from every word or deed which is not consistent with the teachings of Jesus Christ concerning the brotherhood of man." It cited a 1952 resolution of the Episcopal general convention which established the policy of "consistently opposing and combating discrimination based on color or race of every form, both within the Church and without, in this country and internationally." In addition, the letter declared that the physical violence at the high school "forces us to our knees in shame over our inability to exert an adequate Christian leadership in this hour." This letter was read from Episcopal pulpits on Sunday, September 29.

Two advertisements appeared in the *Arkansas Democrat* on September 27. The smaller of the two reproduced a 280-word telegram from a Missionary Baptist congregation in North Little Rock, signed by the pastor. Addressed to the President of the United States, it indicated that members of the church "lift [their] voices in strong protest against the unholy invasion of the customs, rights, and privileges of the citizens of Arkansas by Federal troops." The telegram expressed the "sincere conviction that if you had been spending as much time on your knees in prayer as . . . on the golf course you never would have sent troops into Arkansas." It declared "we are not extremists" and affirmed that "those of us here on the scene probably know a little more about the situation than those a thousand miles away, who are feeling called to go on the networks and speak their minds about it."

The second advertisement headlined that more than 1,000 people attending the Capital Citizens' Council meeting on September 24 unanimously adopted the following resolution:

"Whereas, consistency of action is the finest token of sincerity and

"Whereas, a number of Little Rock ministers have repeatedly spoken out in favor of mixing White and Negro children in our public schools, and

"Whereas, these ministers have not integrated their own congregations nor have made any move, or taken any steps in this direction, and

"Whereas, it would greatly clarify a confused situation, and help people to know what church to attend and support,

"Therefore, be it resolved, That we recommend and urge all ministers who believe that our children should have racially mixed schools forced upon them to immediately take steps to integrate their churches by publicly inviting the colored people to their services. Thus, with courage to match their convictions and a willingness to suffer for their principles, we feel this can be achieved as easily as the integration of our schools. Under this arrangement, the children would not be asked to accept a situation which the adults are unwilling to tolerate."

The text then listed the 15 ministers, together with their churches, who "on September 4 bitterly condemned Governor Faubus for his efforts to keep Central High School segregated." The notice concluded with a plea to "join the Council and help us fight for State Rights and Racial Integrity."

The *New York Times* of September 28 reported that the president of the ministerial association had defended Eisenhower's sending of Federal troops into the city; he was quoted as saying it was the only thing the President could have done. The same minister also defended the troops against Faubus' charge that they had been indiscreet in observing girls' legs in physical education classes at the high school.

Sunday, September 29 was in some ways especially significant as it offered ministers the first opportunity to refer in their services to Black Monday and the arrival of Federal troops. The *New York Times* dispatch was brief on this point: "Churches were thronged. Generally the Protestant clergy refrained from direct discussion of the crisis in their sermons. But several admonished their congregations to keep calm and say nothing to inflame emotion."

The local *Democrat* reported that the pastor of an independent Baptist church said that Arkansas' constitutional rights had been violated but that "though the provocations may be great, we as Christians must not yield" to violence. [14]

The *Gazette* reported that many ministers urged a peaceful compliance with the court-ordered school integration plan, deplored violence, and urged disregard for wild rumors. Moreover, the *Gazette* carried excerpts from the sermon preached by the president of the ministerial association. He encouraged those in his congregation who believed in gradual integration to express their views, and further declared: "There is something ironical about our putting this picture [of Jesus teaching little children of different races] up before our children throughout their early years in Sunday School and teaching them to sing the song, 'Jesus loves the little children—all the children of the world; red and yellow, black and white—all are precious in his sight,' if a little later they are to discover that all the children of the world's racial groups cannot come together to learn either the divine truth of Christ in our churches or the human wisdom presented in our schools."

On October 2, a group of business and civic leaders in the city issued a "Statement of Objectives and Rededication to Principles." One local newspaper said the 25 who signed condemned violence and urged citizens to be peaceful; the other said they urged peaceful compliance with court-ordered school integration. Their resolution called on citizens and organizations to uphold those who enforce laws, condemn violence and its encouragement, and "join unitedly in daily prayer for guidance and counsel for all who lead our people." On October 3, local church leaders issued a call for all Arkansas churches to join them in services at 11 o'clock on the morning of October 12 to pray for a solution to the city's crisis.

Plans for a citywide prayer service were formulated first in a meeting on Monday night, September 30, at the home of the Episcopal Bishop of Arkansas. The meeting, which had been preceded by a letter from Eisenhower in support of such a proposal, was attended by a small number of the city's religious leaders, and by United States Representative Brooks Hays, also president of the Southern Baptist Convention.

None of the pro-Faubus small sect ministers attended the meeting. Nor did any attend a meeting of about 45 ministers in the Episcopal Cathedral on Thursday, October 3, to lay final plans and secure a broad base of support for the prayer services.

A calculated and concerted effort was made to neutralize this prayer service relative to the segregation-integration, Eisenhower-Faubus disputes. Letters of support were secured from the President, the Governor, and the school board. The ministers expressed a desire to render "a ministry of reconciliation." Negro ministers were not invited to the planning sessions though expressions of their interest and support were conveyed to the group by an intermediary. When an unconvinced young minister remarked, "I don't want the action taken here in any way to be interpreted as sanctioning what has been done by the governor or any other element that has led to hoodlum rule in the city," leaders told him that ministers had already rendered their judgments of the situation, that now they were met "to find the cohesive factors in the situation." An insurgent's move to enter a clear moral and judgmental tone to the proclamation was unsuccessful. A statement by a church official at a news conference prior to the ministerial meeting clearly removed the services from what the speaker termed "the ministry of judgment." "There are Christian people who feel segregation is right and there are Christian people who feel that integration is right," he said. Individual church autonomy in conduct of the services was assured when plans were made to have each congregation conduct its own services in lieu of one or a small number of mass meetings. The *Democrat's* headline read: "Churchmen Talk Truce."

A vigorous effort was made to secure a unified religious support for the October 12 (Columbus Day) prayer services. A leading Catholic spokesman assured Catholic support and participation. At high mass on Sunday, October 6, the Catholic Bishop urged his listeners to attend the services. Sponsors sent out almost 250 letters requesting the participation of the churches.

Nonetheless, the vigorous segregationists, ministerial and otherwise, would have none of it. On October 4, the Citizens' Council re-ran its challenge to ministerial critics of Governor Faubus, urging them to open membership to Negroes as a token of their sincerity. On Sunday, October 6, the president of the local Missionary Baptist Seminary announced that his congregation would not participate in the special prayer service because he felt it was merely an attempt to promote integration under a veneer of prayer. On the next day, by means of a large advertisement in the *Democrat,* the League of Central High Mothers challenged the clergymen who were promoting the Columbus Day prayers. If the order of presentation in the advertisement is rearranged so as to see the arguments more clearly, a series of pointed and accusative questions emerges:[15]

Is the "peace" for which prayers are to be offered one with or without integration in the high school?

"In praying for peace to prevail, will it be peace—with the nine Negro children remaining in Central High School or peace—with the Negroes in [their own] Horace Mann School?"

Why not argue for integration rather than for law and order?

"You preachers who are planning this crusade are well-known. Your activities toward race-mixing are well-known. For years you have agitated the integration of our schools. Now that the issue is hot, you do not discuss the question on its merits but flee to the Law of the Land argument. Why not admit you are for race-mixing and fight the matter out on its merits? Do you feel integration cannot be defended? Do you lack courage? Why do you sidestep the real issue, do not deal with the cause, and say 'Brethren, Let Us Pray'?"

Who can escape the fruits of race mixing?

"Do we have a right to ask God to do for us what we can do for ourselves? You are asking God to heal our city. If the Negro children were in their own school our city would be peaceful again. How can you advocate race-mixing and pray to escape the fruits of race-mixing?"

Should advocates be conciliators?

"Is it proper for those who have for years advocated race-mixing to come forward as peace-makers? Are the ones whose philosophy created the problem the proper ones to prescribe the remedy?"

Can preservators be agitators?

"For over one hundred years the South has lived under the Plan of Separation of the races. It has been our code of life. Under it the colored people have made progress. The plan has made for excellent co-existence.

"The race-mixers are now telling us that all this must be changed. While the Segregationists want to continue on with our time honored plan. Now who are the agitators? Those who are fighting for upset and change? Or those who want things to continue as they are?"

Are the integrationist ministers morally consistent?

"Are the Churches to which you minister integrated churches or are they all-white churches?

"If integration of the races is so morally right that it should be forced upon our children at bayonet point, how can ministers serve churches that refuse to be integrated?"

Several things about this advertisement are striking. The all-too-apparent hostility toward the ministers sponsoring the prayer service extends even to some symbols regarded as sacred—for instance, the reference to "Brethren, Let Us Pray." It is apparent that this hostility had roots in the community extending back beyond 1957—reference is made to "those who have for years advocated race-mixing." The ministers are made to bear the responsibility for the crisis in the community—"How can you advocate race-mixing and pray to escape the fruits?" "Now who are the agitators?"

This League of Central High Mothers had been attacked by the pastor of the city's largest church on October 6, the day previous. The *New York Times* described his comments as "the strongest denunciation of segregationist agitators heard today." He praised the white high school students for resisting the effort by the "unscrupulous white Citizens' Council and the unethical Mothers' League" to organize a mass walk-out from the high school on the prior Thursday. "The attitude and response of our youth," he said, "is the one bright spot in all of this tragedy."

Formal organization of the hostility toward the Columbus Day prayer services and its sponsors was first announced in a front page story in the *Arkansas Democrat* of October 8. The story indicated that a prayer service open to all denominations would be held at an independent Baptist church on the night of October 11. "The purpose," explained the organizers, "will be to pray that a peaceful solution will be found for the present Central High School crisis in Little Rock. This, we feel, would be the transfer of the Negro students back to Horace Mann High School. The prayer meeting has no connection with the Saturday morning prayer service in several churches. We have nothing in common with those ministers, many of whom are modernists and liberals, while we are conservatives and fundamentalists."

In the meantime Governor Faubus seemed less than enthusiastic, even skeptical, about the prospect that practical good would come from the Columbus Day service—this in spite of his avowed support as indicated in his letter to the Episcopal Bishop. In a story about a press conference held by the Governor on October 9 the *Democrat* reported: "He was asked if he planned to attend any of the prayer services this weekend for peaceful solution to the situation. He said, 'Prayers without action are without avail' and quoted an old fable. It pertained to the man whose cart was stuck in mud and he prayed to the Lord to get it out. Nothing happened. Then he put his shoulder to the wheel and prayed for the Lord to help him get it out, and the cart came out. When he finished the fable the Governor looked around the big group of reporters and smiled. There were no more questions about the prayer service."

By contrast, the Negro interfaith ministerial group in greater Little Rock announced its unanimous support for the Columbus Day services and called on its members to participate. They would pray in their own churches.

"A Call to prayer at the Central Baptist Church" appeared in the *Democrat* of October 10. Services were to be held the next evening. The 24 pastors who signed the call stated their belief "in the constitutional rights of white citizens as well as colored" and affirmed that "the only way to have real and lasting peace in the Little Rock situation is for the nine negro [sic] children to return to Horace Mann High School where they legally and morally belong." They announced their intent to pray:

"For our National Leaders. That they be guided by Constitutional Law rather than politics.

"For our State Leaders. That they be given the wisdom and the courage to fulfill their responsibilities to the citizens of the State of Arkansas.

"For all citizens. That under these trying circumstances, no overt acts be performed for which we would later be sorry."

The invitation was extended to "Christians of all denominations." The signers represented 22 churches (an associate pastor and a "Moderator for Central Arkansas" were included). Virtually all were pastors of small, Missionary Baptist churches. Only one was a member of the large Southern Baptist Convention, and only 13 of the 22 churches were located in Little Rock; the remainder were in fringe communities. Ten of the 15 ministers who early in September praised the governor for calling out the National Guard were included among the signers.

The announcement suggested a broader base of ministerial support for the proposed Friday evening service than the number signing would indicate: "Time would not permit us to contact all of the pastors who believe as we do, of which there are many more. More than 100 Baptist pastors in the State have opposed the use of Federal troops as a solution."

Thus the effort of ministers in the city's major churches to serve as agents of reconciliation was frustrated at the community level not simply by failure to secure the cooperation of all religious elements in the community but by an explicit counter-effort by dissident religious leaders as well. [16] One religious leader, looking back weeks later on these events, felt the Lord had a good excuse for refusing to intercede: "I couldn't blame the Good Lord a bit if He got mighty confused by all that goings on."

Nevertheless, the plans went ahead, with considerable local and national publicity. [17] The rabbi who originated the idea of having the service on Columbus Day explained his choice of date as an "appropriate time to reiterate the principle of equality, justice and liberty on which the country was founded."

The Methodist and Episcopal Bishops of Arkansas, the rabbi of the state's largest synagogue, and the president of the Greater Little Rock Ministerial Association held a press conference on October 10 to discuss plans for the Columbus Day service. Eighty-five churches had given written notice of intent to cooperate; between 15 and 20 were said to be Negro churches. The Methodist Bishop emphasized that there had been no written refusals to the over 200 invitations, but one local newspaper thought it significant that well less than half of the invitations had been accepted. The Episcopal Bishop, commenting on Governor Faubus' ox-in-the-mud fable, said it may be valuable to drop to one's knees in prayer "to learn which side of the ox to push on." The ministers reiterated that they were not taking sides. "We are not pro-Eisenhower or pro-Faubus," the *New York Times* quoted one as saying.

Advertisements inviting public participation in the Saturday service appeared Friday evening and Saturday morning in the city newspapers. The invitation was issued by the 85 participating churches; the churches, but not their pastors, were listed. Less than half of the 85 are white congregations in the city of Little Rock. The best count available, although probably not exact, indicates that 53 churches in Little Rock announced their intent to participate, and that 15 of these are Negro churches. A numerical count is misleading, however. All Catholic and Episcopal churches, and most of the Methodist, participated.[18] Three of the four largest Baptist churches were among the 85; likewise, the four large Presbyterian churches cooperated. Virtually all churches in high-status Pulaski Heights took part. Also an indefinite (though probably small) number of churches not listed in the public announcement participated. After all, minimal participation required no more than unlocking the doors of the sanctuary on Saturday morning. In short, the larger and more prominent churches in the city presented an essentially solid front of participation.

The invitation indicated the objectives of the prayer services:

"Forgiveness for having left undone the things we ought to have done.

"The support and preservation of Law and Order.

"The leaders of our community, state, and nation.

"The youth in the schools of our community.

"The casting out of rancor and prejudice in favor of understanding and compassion.

"Resistance against unthinking agitators."

The objectives were offered as guides, nothing more. Each church or person was free to determine the content of his own prayers. No moral imperatives were stated, and no specific community goals were suggested. The objectives had to be sufficiently neutral to receive support from very divergent points of view.

Yet the statement was too strong for some ministers. One pastor of a small working-class church, for example, prepared an amended set of objectives in which participants were assured that "we are not asking God to keep the troops in Little Rock or to send them away, and not asking God to keep the Negroes in Central High or send them back to the all-colored school." Another pastor pointed out to his small assemblage that "contrary to what the segregationist [Missionary] Baptists are doing, we haven't gotten together to tell God our side and how He ought to look at it, nor to get God to come over to our side and work for us. We just want to know His Will."

Other ministers, to whom the statement was too mild, strengthened it with their own proclamations. In a special statement in their respective churches, three Presbyterian ministers, two of them pastors of large and affluent congregations, called for "an act of new dedication of heart, mind and will to the basic principles of American democracy, guaranteeing liberty and justice for all." Their statement also urged renewed dedication to these goals:

"The principle of obedience to the nation's laws.

"The maintenance of views and convictions by lawful and constitutional means, steadfastly refusing to take part in any mob action or violence of any kind.

"To refrain from boycotts or intimidation or slander or evil speaking against any who may differ in any matter of public interest.

"To refrain from joining any group whose purpose is to defy the nation's law.

"To commit themselves anew to the way of Christian love, and to resolve that they will carry no opinion to the point of disrupting the Christian fellowship."

Homer Bigart compared the two prayer services in his *New York Times* dispatch of October 11: "Citizens could take their choice whether to attend a Friday night prayer service sponsored by 24 Baptist pastors who are avowed segregationists, or wait for Saturday's meeting when the praying will be neutral."

In ironic affirmation of the neutrality of Saturday's prayers, James T. Karam—clothing store proprietor, friend and haberdasher to Governor Faubus, and active participant in the high school crowd on Black Monday—sat in a back pew at the First Methodist Church at 11 o'clock on the morning of October 12.

The spirit of conciliation also appeared in an interview the Methodist Bishop granted on October 10. The occasion was his return from a four months' tour of Methodist missions in Africa. The Bishop restrained any impulse he may have felt to make incisive remarks about the Little Rock affair. His only comment was that the situation hurt the nation: "The Communists play on it tremendously and there are so many people of color—yellow, brown, black—that anything about color disturbs them." [19]

The Prayer Services. The Central Baptist Church of Little Rock is a rectangular, concrete-block structure located on a principal artery some six or eight blocks from the heart of Little Rock's main business district. A neon sign shines brightly outside. On the night of October 11, the church was filled to capacity, and the crowd overflowed onto the lawn outside. Perhaps some 600 or 700 were inside the building. Newspaper reports indicated the presence of 35 to 40 ministers, 12 of whom appeared on the platform. The service lasted 25 minutes. Two hymns, "Amazing Grace" and "Stand Up for Jesus," were sung. The remaining time was devoted to introductory comments and to prayers led by an alternating group of ministers. Kleig lights were on so that motion pictures could be made. The host pastor explained the reason for the separate prayer service: "Jews do not believe in the deity of the Lord Jesus Christ . . . Catholics, while believing in the deity of the Lord Jesus Christ, pray through the Virgin Mary. Most of the Protestants involved in the call are of the modernistic persuasion. Modernists do not believe in the Virgin Birth or the deity of the Lord Jesus Christ. We feel, therefore, that since prayer must be made according to the Bible, in the Name of the Lord Jesus Christ, that a prayer meeting for those that are conservative in their beliefs about the deity of Christ should hold a separate prayer meeting."

Several interesting points were raised in the prayers offered at this service: [20]

The use of Federal troops is unconstitutional.

"Therefore we pray that our national leaders might follow constitutional law and remove the federal troops rather than follow political expediency. We should be a nation of law; and where federal and state laws are violated by our leaders in Washington, it means that it will not be long until we will be a nation under dictatorship as Russia and her satellites."

Governor Faubus is a preservator of peace.

"We pray that our Governor might be led to continue on the path that he knows to be right and to continue to fulfill his duties as chief executive of the state of Arkansas and to preserve the rights of all its citizens. Even though pressures may be strong, give him the courage of his convictions to stand fast for that which is right and just."

Negroes who are Christians are not causing the trouble.

"Those who are Christians among them [Negroes] are our brothers and sisters in the Lord, and they, too, are facing serious difficulties and are in need of Thy help. We know that this trouble is not of their making and we do pray that they might be led even as we need to be led by Thy Holy Spirit."

Political motives are paramount in Washington.

". . . we have the interest of the colored people at heart more than the politicians of this nation. We pray for the leaders of our nation . . . that they be as concerned about us here as what other nations might think of us.

"We pray for the President of the United States, who ordered troops down here and then went back to the golf course as if nothing had happened."

The turn-away crowd was gratifying to the hosts and their associates. By contrast, the turnout for the Saturday morning services was disappointing to many sponsors. Small numbers were typical, and females were dominant in most places. Of the estimated total of 6,000 who attended, 2,053 were Roman Catholic, according to a spokesman who said they represented one-third of the Roman Catholic population in the twin cities of Little Rock and North Little Rock. "The fact that 2,000 Catholics went to churches today to petition for guidance is powerful proof of their respect for authority," he said. The Protestant attendance was proportionately much lower. The Methodist Bishop said that the turnout was very fine considering that on Saturdays children are at home with their mothers and men cannot leave their work. These factors seem to have had much greater deterrent effect on Protestants than on Catholics.

The nature of the services themselves varied from church to church. At one extreme, the doors of the sanctuary were opened for the silent prayers of those who wished to enter. At the other, an hour-long service was held, complete with a statement of principles and readings from the letters of President Eisenhower, Governor Faubus, and the Little Rock school board in support of the services. The litany was recited and appropriate prayers read from the Book of Common Prayer in Episcopal churches. Responsive litany, rosary, and prayers were said in Catholic churches. In most churches the service was brief, lasting perhaps 15 minutes.

The Monday (October 14) papers did not mention any discussion of integration in the city's pulpits on the Sunday after the peace prayers.

A Personal Clash. The long-standing schism in the city's clergy, which played so prominent a part in the integration crisis, is neatly mirrored in a personal clash between two ministers. The dispute broke into the open when the Reverend Wesley Pruden placed a quarter-page ad in the *Arkansas Democrat* on Saturday, October 12, the day of the peace prayers. The advertisement was headed, "Can a Christian Be a Segregationist?" Its theme: that race-mixing is a Communist doctrine, segregation a Christian one. It quoted pastors of several large urban Baptist and Presbyterian churches in Tennessee, Arkansas, and Texas. Among those quoted was Dr. Robert G. Lee, three times president of the Southern Baptist Convention and pastor of the Bellevue Church of Memphis, the "largest Baptist church east of the Mississippi River." Dr. Lee was reported to have announced from his pulpit that "when the Negroes enter the front door of this church, R. G. Lee goes out the back door."

On Friday, October 18, the Reverend W. O. Vaught, critic of the Citizens' Council, pastor of Little Rock's largest church, brought a categorical denial from Dr. Lee to the offices of the city's newspapers. The *Gazette* carried the story in its next issue. "Not once in my life did I ever make any such statement or any statement that remotely resembled it or should in the least resemble or show kinship to it," he said. In a phone conservation with Reverend Pruden on October 15, Dr. Lee expressed his "deep resentment" and offered $1,000 to anyone who could find such a remark in taped recordings of his services. He described the false quotation as "almost libelous" and "wicked as the most wicked of words." He demanded a public retraction. Reverend Pruden offered his apology: "I am sorry Dr. Lee was quoted without his permission."

The affair did not end there. On Saturday, October 26, the *Gazette* carried an advertisement signed by Dr. Lee, and the *Democrat* carried an advertisement signed by Reverend Pruden. The latter, headed "Here Are the Facts," explained that Dr. Lee's alleged statement had been reported by "a member of his staff of professional publicity men." The matter, therefore, was a misunderstanding between Dr. Lee and a staff member: "Anyone knows it is not improper to quote a man's trusted press agent." His concluding judgment was this: "In my opinion, Dr. Lee was mistakenly identified with that glorious band of Christian patriots who are standing courageously by the South in her hour of crisis."

The same notice also questioned the good faith and proper motives of Dr. Vaught:

"On Friday, October 18, I learned that Dr. W. O. Vaught, Jr., pastor of Immanuel Baptist Church of this city, had taken it upon himself—for reasons still best known to him—to turn over Dr. Lee's denial to both Little Rock newspapers.

"Dr. Lee has sent his assurance that he did not ask or authorize Dr. Vaught or anyone else to give this to the newspapers. Interference of a third party into delicate personal matters of others never helps."

Dr. Lee's ad in the *Gazette* was in the form of a "To Whom It May Concern" letter. He demanded that Reverend Pruden strengthen his "evasive, puny, inadequate apology," and he included a letter sent to Reverend Pruden: "Your statement makes me mentally sick . . . I have made no comment about segregation or integration. I have not criticized segregationists or integrationists."

The affair came to its public end the Sunday after these notices appeared. Referring to Reverend Pruden as a man whose name was unworthy of mention in the sanctuary, Dr. Vaught devoted the closing portion of his morning service to a review of his part in the affair. He read Dr. Lee's telegram confirming that he had asked Reverend Vaught to give the newspapers his denial of Reverend Pruden's accusation.

This story would not be worth telling if it reflected only personal misunderstanding and animosity. The Reverend Pruden, member of the Southern Baptist Convention, is the only minister of a major denomination in Little Rock who has been active and vocal in support of extreme and organized segregation forces. Such others as have segregationist sympathies have been mild and quiet in their discussions of the issue. By all expectations the behavior of Reverend Pruden as a minister in a prominent denomination should have been more reserved and "respectable" than in fact it was. His critics accused him, among other things, of being uncouth. The animosity between the two men, then, revolving around the issue of whether someone in another state did or did not support segregation, may best be seen as symbolic of the deeper schism that divided the ministerial community and made truly concerted action impossible.

In the segregation dispute it is a mistake to minimize the dissident ministerial elements by saying that they are poorly educated, fanati-

cal pastors whose small flocks lack community influence. The fact
is that ministers like the Reverend Pruden more closely represented,
vis-à-vis the topic of segregation, the sentiments of almost any congregation in the city than did the city's moderate ministers, although
many congregations prefer more tact, restraint, and *savoir faire* than
the segregationists characteristically demonstrate. The Reverend
Pruden and his confederates encouraged partially latent but very
powerful sentiments present in every congregation in the city. Indeed,
they found themselves in the happy circumstance of expressing not
only the nearly unanimous views of their own congregations but also
feelings of a large part of the entire community. The ministers of
other congregations did not like this, which may explain their dislike
for Reverend Pruden. He made their job more difficult and their
status less secure.

After the Prayers. With the exception of the dissident segregationists, who if anything became more vocal than ever, religious participation in the integration dispute declined sharply after October 12.
The decline was so dramatic that it is tempting to impute a ritualistic
function to the Columbus Day services. It would appear that the
organized and highly publicized prayer services relieved the ministers'
compulsion to act and symbolized their desire to put the experience
behind them and "get on with the work of the church." This observation is considered in detail later.

On October 16, a committee in Shreveport, Louisiana, convened
to consider a proposal to dissolve the separate jurisdiction for Negroes
within the Methodist Church, heard the Bishop of Arkansas express
his support of the present segregated system; he said the Negro Central
Jurisdiction was working well. The *Arkansas Gazette* carried the
Associated Press dispatch under the heading, "Southern Methodist
Ministers oppose Integration. Later, a rabbi's suggestion to the
ministerial association that Christmas season would be a proper
time to rally the community's moral forces evoked little response.

There were some exceptions to this pattern of ministerial silence.
One minister announced plans on October 14 to appoint an interracial
committee to set criteria for selecting college scholarship recipients
among Central High School students who showed tolerance and good
citizenship under difficult circumstances. This sponsor announced
the committee members on October 18; significantly, he was himself
the only white Protestant minister in the city on the committee. In

November, a small number of ministers arranged an appointment with representatives of the school board to suggest remedies for the increasing harassment of Negro students within the high school. Generally, however, the ministerial voices had fallen silent, and this silence bespoke their actions.

Other instances of ministerial activity came from the side of the avowed segregationists. One local segregationist served as chaplain to the Capital Citizens' Council (CCC). The Reverend Wesley Pruden was elected its president. The Council, and especially its president, encouraged the segregationist Mothers' League of Central High School. [21] The CCC sponsored segregationist rallies, imported out-of-state speakers, and presented a slate of candidates for the city directors' election in November. One ministerial member of the CCC, who announced a rapid growth in the membership of his church, advertised sermons that would reveal the penetration of Communist doctrine into the nation's pulpits.

"Letters to the Editor" from various elders, reverends, churches, and church organizations among the Missionary Baptists and kindred fundamentalist sects throughout Arkansas supported segregation and Governor Faubus. Two examples of resolutions passed may suffice. One published on October 30 indicated that "the Pine Bluff Missionary Baptist Association, composed of 67 churches, had adopted the following resolution: 'Be it resolved that this body go on record as being opposed to integration, either gradual or otherwise. God, in His divine wisdom ordained that man should maintain a pure blood stream of their own race. Man sought integration at the Tower of Babel and God personally segregated the races. We believe that a line of demarcation must be drawn or else such a move will eat away at the foundations of civilization and greatly debase our moral and ethical code.' "

The second, titled "Resolution on Integration," appeared as a paid advertisement in the *Democrat* on November 22. It is reproduced in full:

"Whereas, various religious bodies and church groups have publicly set forth their attitudes and beliefs concerning the proposals and plans to integrate the black and white races in our schools and society;

"Whereas, both political and legal actions have been taken to bring about such change in our American way of life, and to force this change upon many of both races who do not want it, and this in the face of mounting tension between these races in all parts of our country, without counting the ultimate cost or the end result of weakening our nation by the mongrelization of our citizenry, a result clearly established by Biblical history, Nehemiah 13:23-25, as well as secular; and furthermore, without regard to the council of God's Word in this matter;

"Whereas, in His infinite wisdom, for His eternal glory and for the good of man, God formed the various races of men upon earth, separated them by geographical barriers, Acts 17:26, and encouraged their continued separation by differences in language, color, and other racial characteristics, Genesis 10:5, 32; 11: 1-9;

"Whereas, God has never set aside His decree concerning the three sons of Noah and their descendants, Genesis 9:24-27, but has taught in the Bible that segregation of the races was and is His desire and plan, Israel being a notable example, especially in that God forbid the intermarriage of the Israelites with the black races of Canaan, Genesis 24:3-4; 28:1; Deuteronomy 7:1-3, 6; Joshua 23:12-13; Ezra 9:1-2, 10-12; I Kings 8:53; and Exodus 33:16;

"Whereas, being law-abiding citizens, as Baptists ever have been, with a genuine love for all humanity and the souls of men, regardless of race or color, having proved our loyalty by giving the blood of our sons to defend the laws of our country, having never practiced violence to force the beliefs of Baptists upon others, and, consequently, being opposed to the use of physical force either to hinder or to promote the integration of free men anywhere;

"Be it therefore resolved that we, The Arkansas Missionary Baptist Association, herewith voice our opposition to any force within or without our country, whether communistic, socialistic or other, which seeks to destroy our democratic and American way of life; that we reaffirm our faith in the whole counsel of God's word; that we declare the integration of Negroes and whites in our schools and society to be a threat to the security of our nation and contrary to the teachings of God both in the Bible and in nature; and that we hereby describe the Supreme Court rulings which favor integration of blacks and whites, and the use of Federal troops to enforce those rulings, as being deplorable, unscriptural, and not in harmony with previous decisions of that body, nor with the beliefs and purposes of the God-fearing and democratic-minded men who at the first drafted the Constitution of the United States of America.

" (Paid advertisement from offering at annual session, November 19, 1957, of the Arkansas Missionary Baptist Association. Similar resolution passed at annual meeting of 485 churches of Baptist Missionary Association of Texas.) "

There were many other resolutions of similar tone from comparable bodies. But the time to expect counter-action from more liberal bodies had past.

Summary. Because we cannot cover all details, ours is necessarily not a complete story of public ministerial action in the fall of 1957 in Little Rock, but it is a fair and representative story. It is clear that the pastors of the large, high-status, and influential churches in the city favorably anticipated the first coming of Negro students to Central High School in September, and it seems apparent, moreover, that their enthusiasm, in many cases at least, expressed more than the "law and order" value on which they relied so heavily once the crisis broke. Whether they would have been as enthusiastic for a bolder, more forthright plan than the one adopted by the school board is uncertain.

This enthusiasm was transplanted into a spontaneous assertion against Governor Faubus when he took steps to prevent integration. Their force was soon spent, however. Later chapters may help the reader to understand why. Generally, the ministers tacitly consented to a public dissociation of moral criteria from the issue of segregation versus integration, to the extent that, contrary to the positions taken by the national and regional bodies of all major church groups, the loudest voices applying religious and moral criteria to this issue were those crying that integration violates the will of God. For most of the others, the religious and moral dimensions seemed simply not to be relevant. The Columbus Day prayer services were a dramatic symbol and fruition of this.

The spontaneous reaction in early September of 15 local pastors against Governor Faubus was countered within 24 hours by support for him from a like number. This schism, as we have shown, antedated the immediate issue and was based on other differences as well. The segregationists, however, far from subsiding, grew louder and stronger. They drew their support from a popular base in the community, a much broader base than any minister who wished to support the principle of integration could find. The punitive consequences generally befalling ministers who encouraged integration were threats of stronger sanctions if the encouragement continued. Ministers who were sympathetic to segregation faced no such sanctions. Under the circumstances, the growth of silence among the former and the increasingly strident voices of the latter may not be surprising.

CHAPTER THREE

SECTS AND SEGREGATION:

"THINGS PLEASING TO THE LORD"

"Just as sure as I know my own name, separate facilities for whites and Negroes—these are things pleasing to the Lord."
— A LITTLE ROCK PASTOR, 1957

This chapter deals with the small sect pastors who have been open and avowed opponents of racial integration. It is concerned with their values, their way of seeing things, their rationalizations, their sense of obligation and of certainty.

According to newspaper reports, between 35 and 40 such clergymen appeared at the Central Baptist Church meeting on October 11, 1957, to suggest to God, via prayer, that the return of Negro students to the all-Negro Horace Mann High School, "where they legally and morally belong," would be the desirable solution to the community's crisis. There is no available list of the names of these men. Presumably those who publicly sponsored the meeting constituted 24 of the number. We interviewed 13 of the 24.

The congregations of these 13 meet for services in small buildings of frame or cement block construction. With the exception of one adjoining a substantial new middle class residential area, they are located in the poorer sections of the city and outlying areas. Only three claim a total church membership as high as 400. None is a community-wide church in the sense the term is usually used.

Most of the pastors are either young or middle-aged. Nine were 45 or under at the time of interview, and the modal five-year age category was 40 to 45. One is affiliated with the Southern Baptist Convention. Eleven others are members of the two fundamentalist Missionary Baptist associations. Eight of the 13 are native Arkansans. Nine received or were receiving training at the Missionary Baptist Seminary in Little Rock. Most of these nine had not attended college before matriculation. This local seminary, which lacks accreditation, prefers but does not require that its students have high school diplomas.

The two religious associations are loose federations of member churches. No church sacrifices any of its autonomy through affiliation. Decisions made at the local level are final and binding; there is no control over the local church. Because of this, we were told uniformly, these churches have the most democratic, hence the best, form of church policy possible. Repeatedly we heard such statements as: "The Missionary Baptist is the most democratic of all churches. The local congregation has more freedom and more liberty than any organization in any other type of denomination." For illustration, we were told that no matter of importance is settled without putting the matter to the vote of the congregation. Yet it would seem that an important aspect of this local autonomy, as the minister views it, is the freedom he himself has to manage the affairs of the church. The development of lay leadership is discouraged, for example, and official church boards are small in number and weak in influence. Laymen are not allowed in the pulpit, and the number serving on church boards is often smaller than the number allotted. One church, for example, provides for seven deacons but in fact has only two.

Most of the pastors we interviewed were quite frank in discussing their opposition to a strong laity. Some stated that "running the church is my business and I don't want to encourage a leadership in my members." Several criticized the Southern Baptists for giving deacons too much power in the church. The tendency toward autocratic control was further strengthened in several instances by the fact that the minister organized the congregation and raised funds to construct the church building; he saw it as "my church" in a most literal sense. Interestingly, the minister's influence is not restricted to matters broadly sacred. One pastor, for example, gives a running commentary on the week's news from his pulpit each Sunday, since "My members work different shifts, travel, and what not, and they don't have time to keep up with the news. I regard it as a ministerial duty to report and explain headline news to them."

The congregations of the churches are working-class in origin and current status. Their limited education and sophistication encourage the minister's authoritarian dominance. Many members are recent arrivals from nearby rural areas. The occupations of members of the official church boards confirm the impression one forms about the class status of members from observing the condition of the church plant and the surrounding area. A few board members are in white-collar occupations, such as bookkeeper, shipping clerk, drug salesman, X-ray technician, and bank teller. A few more are private entrepreneuers—shoe-repair shop owner, builder's supply-house manager, wholesale grocery man, furniture-store owner. The large majority, however, are in such blue-collar occupations as barber, mechanic, carpenter, service-station attendant, hospital attendant, welder, dairy-man, letter carrier, fireman, baker, and policeman. Such occupations comprise approximately 70 percent of the total number of board members. Only one board member in the 13 churches is a professional person—a lawyer.

Insularity and Hostility. The most striking characteristics of the segregationist ministers are their general isolation from the community's higher prestige groups and their hostility toward those religious bodies and values in the community that are distinct from their own. Insularity and hostility are so related that it is to our advantage to consider them together; they appear to be the joint cause and effect of each other. Isolation might be expected on the basis of the ministers' mutual ties to the local seminary, their lower educational attainments when compared with those of other ministers, and their generally low prestige in the community. A significant part of their isolation, however, seems to be self-imposed, expressive of religious conviction and desire to be "a people set apart." [1]

Every person in our sample was asked to name a small number of ministers in the community who were especially influential and respected. They were also asked to name other ministers with whom they often worked and conferred.

Fifteen of the 30 "most influential" mentions by this group of segregationists were fellow Missionary Baptists. [2] Seen in the light of the general lack of prominence enjoyed by these ministers in the community—at least prior to the school crisis—this proportion is unusually high. When they named ministers outside their own circle, these were usually other Baptists. Ten of the 15 "outsiders" mentioned were pastors in the Southern Baptist Convention. Responses to the "co-worker" question mentioned previously give an even more vivid demonstration of the isolation of this group from other ministerial elements. Of the 35 times a co-worker was named, only one—the single avowed segregationist affiliated with the Southern Baptists—was outside the Missionary Baptist group. [3]

The small sect pastor named most frequently by his ministerial brethren as an "influential" responded to the influence question in a striking manner: "Well, from my reading it looks like Reverend X and Reverend Y (two prominent ministers in the regular ministerial association) are the most influential, but I really couldn't say. I don't know these two gentlemen, never met them, and what I say about them is strictly hearsay." A companion remark came from one of the city's leading "peace prayer" ministers as he reviewed the events leading up to Columbus Day: "Now, you know there was an out-and-out segregationist service here that was cooked up by that fellow, what's his name, Moseley, Moose, Mosler, Moore, something like that, you know who I mean, the preacher who has this barn-like, cinder-block church down the street here."

The Missionary Baptists maintain their insularity in part by refusing to take part in interdenominational cooperative endeavors. Even the popular evangelist Billy Graham incurred their disfavor by accepting sponsorship from ministerial groups of diverse sorts and by urging converts at his meetings to affiliate with the church of their choice. One pastor clinched his point that denominational differences are of paramount importance by asking rhetorically, "If there aren't any differences between churches in their power of salvation, what do we have them for?"

The isolation of the Missionary Baptists is expressed in the refusal of their ministers to join the Greater Little Rock Ministerial Association. Their disaffection with this body has a long history and their suspicions were confirmed in 1956 when the association combined with the Negro ministerial alliance. We were given a variety of reasons; some bear directly on the belief that association members are "a bunch of integrationists." A common expression, used to explain their refusal to join the association as well as their separate prayer service, was "We don't have anything in common with those fellows." As one said, "When the word came out about the Columbus Day services, the very first thing I thought [this was before plans for the segregation service developed], I just wondered whether I could pray with the people who were supporting this. The Jewish people have never recognized Christ as the Son of God, and about the Catholics, our Bible teaches us to pray through Christ. Now how could I get on my knees and pray with people like that? Baptists meet on common ground in prayer."

Another attempted to explain why he is not a member of the association: "Those fellows have nothing in common with us, and I have no idea of joining them. Those fellows don't even believe in the fundamentals of faith. They have people in there who don't believe in the Virgin Birth, they don't believe that the Bible is the Inspired

Word of God, they don't believe in the re-birth of man, and they don't believe in the Divinity of Christ in the Virgin Birth. I believe the Bible is inspired. They don't."

Most of our pastors explicitly accused leaders of the "uptown churches" of forcing the racial strife to become a religious issue and said that such ministers had used the Bible as a support for, of all things, desegregation. "This," said one, "is just plain blasphemy of the Bible."

Virtually all of these men had delivered defenses of segregation from their pulpits, discussed the racial issue in counseling sessions, sponsored advertisements in local newspapers, issued pamphlets, and in other public ways used their positions to defend segregation. At least five were prominent in the September crowds surrounding Central High School. One admits to having been almost arrested. Another told us that he counted 22 segregationist ministers there. Yet one of their most vigorous objections is to the "social gospel" preached, they say, by the city's more prominent ministers. To them the term represents departure from the practice of elaborating on the scriptures in sermons, an expansion of church activities into "social affairs," and the entry of the church into "politics." It also means religious support for liberal racial views and policies.

"I have strong convictions on this racial matter," explained one clergyman, "but it does not come up in my church as such because my church preaches the gospel and doesn't go running off on a lot of social problems. A minister simply cannot spend his time taking up social issues when he should be preaching the gospel." Some draw a distinction between their citizen and ministerial roles, maintaining that they do not "drag race into the pulpit."[4] Others interviewed dwelled at length on segregation's defense from the pulpit while protesting the "social gospel" of more liberal ministers. It is obvious that to the latter it is the content of the "social gospel," rather than its concern with social issues to which they objected.

Isolation from the remainder of the religious community is not merely a physical and personal matter; it also appears in matters of values, both sacred and secular. The conviction that most contemporary religious institutions are not true bearers of the faith was frequently expressed. One minister told us that he is opposed to "social affairs" in church activities on the following grounds: "The church's job is to attend to the scriptures and the ministry of the Lord; while sponsoring baseball teams, holding parties, doing this sort of thing, is not a proper part of the work of the church. There are a lot of churches that hold dinners and show movies, sponsor parties, this sort of thing, to attract their members to the church. Now if the members need this kind of ruse to get them into the church, then perhaps they are not saved, and they deserve my prayers, and I am giving them my prayers."

Comments such as these were couched in a framework of fundamentalism versus modernism. Modernism—which in their theology means denial of the Virgin Birth, the inspiration of the scriptures, and the deity of Christ, and which in secular terms means a broad social concern and program for the church—is a departure of the church and its ministry from the scriptures. One minister described the "modernist crowd" as follows:

"They are ministers who dabble in areas that are unscriptural. They substitute psychology and sociology for the gospel. The difference between my group, the fundamentalists, and the modernists in this community goes back a good deal farther than the integration crisis, and the integration crisis is just another instance of this split. As a matter of fact, it goes back before World War II; we have not seen eye to eye on a number of things that have come up. For example, before World War II some of these modernists got together and they brought this fellow, Kagawa, over from Japan. This fellow preaches the social gospel all the way down the line, and he sure took a pocketful of money back to Japan. We crossed swords over that because we couldn't see eye to eye. Another example is during the war, these modernists got together parties for the soldiers, things like the USO, and they wanted the parents to send their daughters down to help entertain these soldiers. One time there was a crowd of Oriental soldiers in the hotel and these modernists wanted the parents to send our young, tender American girls down to entertain these soldiers. A lot of bad things happened in situations like that.

"These modernists wanted parents to throw their young daughters at seasoned soldiers. Also, an Atlanta preacher named Louis B. Newton has close ties with some Baptist ministers and other modernists here in the city and he went to Russia with a group of eight or nine other ministers and came back and wrote a book that glorified the Soviet Union and the church freedom in that country, and made Russia sound like a paradise. The book was even put up in the Baptist bookstores here for sale, and there was a big crossing of swords over that."

Hostility is expressed in more general terms toward the large, more affluent churches in the residential areas. Such churches are accused of being cold, massive enterprises that fail to "get close" to the people. Typical of this sentiment is the pastor's remark that these churches number their members in the thousands, and then the caustic after thought: "I'll bet they can't find a third of their members."

This hostility and insularity has a strong secular dimension. There are significant and obvious social class differences between the sect congregations and the middle and upper class churches.[5] Members of the latter have more community influence, power, and prestige. Their ministers are better educated, more widely known, and more generally respected. The purely secular aspect emerges most clearly when we hear about Hall High School, on the western edge of Little Rock. Its school district encompasses the highest prestige residential area in the city—known to the people below as "the heights," the "silk stocking district," or simply as "up there." Some newer, substantial middle-class residential developments are also included. The school opened in the fall of 1957. It enrolled no Negro students, nor was it thought likely to enroll any in the foreseeable future.[6]

Many of the lower-class segregationists, whose most vocal spokesmen are the sect ministers, believe that a "deal" had been worked out by which middle-and upper-class groups would support the school board and the school superintendent in their program for token integration. In return the board would build a new high school in a restricted residential area and maintain it on a segregated basis. As the segregationist informants perceive the situation, this arrangement would permit the city's business and professional interests to "have their cake and eat it too." They believe that these leaders do not want their own children to attend integrated educational institutions, but nonetheless desire Little Rock to have a reputation as a progressive and enlightened city, thereby attracting northern industry. In the words of one pastor: "Those people up there didn't want integration any more than the rest of us did. But the board realized it had to have their support, so it promised them that they could have a separate high school. So Hall High School was built for them and the school superintendent himself traced off the school district lines so no Negroes would be in the district. Then the intelligentsia in the heights, who fall for this stuff about maintaining the community's reputation and being progressive, and what the rest of the nation will think, that sort of thing, those people went along with the board and heavily supported its plan for integrating Central High."[7] And another drew the following moral: "I'm against integration, but if we were going to have it, if it was going to come, it should have come all across the board. They certainly shouldn't have had a brand new school without Negroes in it, while the rank and file had to send their kids to an integrated school." Some of this hostility was applied to the several prominent ministers whose congregations were almost wholly composed of people in the Hall High School district. [8]

The Illusion of Unanimity. The amount of publicity and reinforcement given the sect segregationist during the months of crisis was a pleasant surprise to him. His conversations with us were liberally sprinkled with accounts of experiences which indicated to him that he had solid and massive support for his position. The cited evidence took many forms: praise from his members, increases in membership and in contributions, tales of troubles that integrationist ministers were in, telephoned calls of support, conversations with cautious Negroes, and letters published in local newspapers. The illusion of unanimity developing from these and comparable experiences suggested to him that his congregation, the white community, Negroes, Arkansas, and Americans in general agreed with him that segregation as a social system is preferable to integration and better for all concerned. Some of his evidence was highly selective. Other parts of it have a firm foundation in reality.

One sect leader volunteered the hearsay results of a public opinion poll. "Well, sir, one of those polls—an objective one made at the Pine Bluff Fair—showed that 87 percent of the people favored segregation, and most of the others were niggers." Another estimated, in response to our question, that "at least 95 percent of the people in Little Rock, generally, are opposed to desegregation." This support for their segregationist activities is thought to be so considerable, not only in Little Rock but throughtout the region, that revolutionary resistance could take place: "Here in Little Rock we didn't have any notice. We were the first, and a lot didn't dream troops would come in. In other places in the South that's not going to be the case. There's going to be bloodshed. They're going to resist the troops and there's going to be trouble, and this is why I think what could happen would be civil war."

The congregational responses to liberal ministers in other churches also assured the segregationist that his own position was a favored one. Although their accounts sometimes were garbled, most of our sect respondents had information about what had happened to the city's ministers who had assumed relatively liberal postures. They gave us a variety of leads to pursue, many of which we were able to verify. One estimated that "hundreds, maybe two hundred" members of other churches whose pastors had taken an "easier" stand on desegregation had come to him for guidance and to express unhappiness with their own pastor's position. Another had sent "spies" (members of his church) to various Columbus Day services to determine the number who attended the peace prayers. He gleefully reported that the attendance had been small: "One big integrationist had only 30 people out, and another didn't have but 70." He contended that probably more members of these churches had attended the segrega-tion prayers, and he reported that "many others" had telephoned to "wish me luck" and to assure him that the members didn't approve of the actions of their liberal ministers.

Frequently we heard the contention that even the great mass of Negroes were quite satisfied with a segregated society and that they were wary of an integrated one. As one sect pastor reported, "Why, for years we have held a Bible study class for Negro preachers around here who want to learn more about the Bible. One of those fellows was in here just the other day, and we had a very nice chat about segregation. He told me he doesn't want any of this integration busi-ness and he doesn't know any Negroes who do." Another estimated that if there should be a civil war, 80 percent of the Negroes would fight on the white man's side in the South. Still another told us, "You know, the Negroes themselves don't want this thing. There's an area over here, just a little ways from where we are now, and it's one of the biggest Negro areas all over Little Rock. All types of Negroes live there, from upper class to the trash, just like you find in any group. Now this colored man (the one who distributes the newspapers, he has eight boys working for him passing out news-papers) he assures me that 95 percent of the colored people over there don't want integration. They don't want any of this stuff."

The sense of massive popular approval for his segregationist position was also encouraged by "letters to the editor" columns in local news-papers, especially in the *Arkansas Democrat*. Almost daily during the fall of 1957 letters appeared from laymen in relatively liberal churches, and from various "elders," "reverends," and "conventions" of the segregationist sects. A wave of letters supported segregation and its defenders. It would be illuminating if we could review these letters in detail. In the main the letters were humorless and rigid protests against "forced" integration. A few, however, were humorous. One reader wrote that his white coon dog refused to hunt with his black coon dog and he wondered whether he could get an injunction to make them hunt together. Another proposed to Governor Faubus that Arkansas secede from the Union, declare war on the United States, surrender, and apply for foreign aid.

A final part of this general syndrome of unanimity is the conviction that the South and southerners are better for the Negro than the North and northerners. Variations on this theme are that Negroes are uncomfortable in integrated situations ("I was in an integrated area last summer and the colored kids weren't happy and they weren't getting equal treatment even when they were with the whites because they weren't given the same chances as the whites in the same situations") and that the southern white man has given the Negro much more than his tax payments provide ("Who trained their leaders? Who built their school houses? Who built their hospitals? Who gave them what they have? Not the foundations, but southerners. Not the North but the South. Not the National Association for the Agitation of Colored People, but whites right down here").

Another contention is that since the North lost its chance to help the Negro, it should leave him alone. Note the following soliloquy: "A Negro friend of mine said to me that the North liberated the Negro but didn't see to his needs, and left the poor white man and the Negro right up on the hill by themselves, alone as two jack-rabbits. Left 'em poor and stripped after having burned their farms and killed off their animals, even the ones they couldn't eat they just killed for the viciousness of it all. Now there they were, the white man and the Negro, on the hill like two jack-rabbits, and the white man turned to the Negro and said, 'Well, let's farm together, work together and I'll give you your share and we'll try to work it out as best we can.' At that time the Negroes were so uneducated they didn't know their right hand from their left, but his race made more progress here in the South than any other group in such a short time anywhere in the world."

God, Congregation, and Conscience. The small sect minister is armed with the firm conviction that God intends the races to be separate. He is prepared to quote the Bible chapter and verse to prove it. He has no hesitation or doubts on this matter. He can explain the minister who favors integration only by defining him as a poor student of the Bible: "I've never known an integrationist who was a good, sound Bible student," one of them told us. "What happens is that they go off to college and get loaded up with a lot of subjects; under these circumstances you simply cannot pursue the scriptures as you ought to. Even when they go on to seminary, they get a watered-down seminary version of the Bible."

We asked all ministers this question: "Some Christians say they believe in segregation while other Christians say integration is the right thing. Do you think the Bible gives clear guidance on the integration-segregation issue?" Quite in contrast to their integrationist counterparts, who speak of Bible "tone" and "theme" rather than of explicit source, 11 of the 13 segregationists gave an unequivocal and unhesitant "yes." Of the two answering "no," one said it is a hard question to answer but he believes segregation can be proved to be "religiously correct" by Biblical standards. The other responded that no law in the Bible says, "Thou shalt not integrate" just as none says, "Thou shalt not gamble." "But," he said, "gambling produces deterioration of character, as does integration, which breeds out the race, destroying the quality and vitality of all races. Just as God put safeguards around the Hebrew people by urging them not to associate with non-Hebrews, therewith to maintain their racial purity, so He favors segregation in the United States."

The Bible is a ready reference in these contentions. Chapter and verse are cited frequently. There follow excerpts from our notes on one interview. The reader's attention is called to the loose and folksy interpretation given to the Bible:

"Reverend R. says that segregation is scriptural. He first cited Genesis. He told me that God segregated Cain, marked him off, and the Canaanites became known as the sons of men, and the next son, Adam, took up the faith and his followers became known as the Sephites, the race of faith; hence, there is the race of men and the race of faith. He said that as long as these two bodies remained segregated, things would go pretty well, but when they integrated, this brought forth violence and wickedness. Then he carried me on down to the period after the Flood where there are three sons, one who became the founder of the Jewish peoples, one who became the founder of the Gentiles, and the Negroes are descended from the third. Descendants of the third are cursed with servitude. God scattered these people to different parts of the earth for the purpose of keeping them separate. Up until that time there had been no continents; there was only one body of land and one body of water and God caused the continents to be formed and water between to keep these bodies of people separate. The Negro was intended for Africa and that's where he should have stayed. Then, in a very confidential voice, he told me that the white man has brought this on himself by engaging in the slave trade and by bringing the Negro slaves over here, but, he hastened to add, it was the British who first did it. He went on to say that even the Israelites themselves were told not to take Canaanites for their wives and that there was to be no commingling with the Canaanites.

"I asked him about the brotherhood of man and the fatherhood of God theme in the New Testament. He said that we—meaning the fundamentalists in general and the Missionary Baptists specifically—reject the brotherhood of man and the fatherhood of God altogether as a doctrine. God is not the father of all people, he said. Some people are sons of the Devil."

Some gave terse reference to one or two Biblical references: the curse on Ham, the tower of Babel, and the separation of the continents were mentioned most frequently. Others gave elaborate detail, complementing their remarks with frequent Biblical references and numerous rhetorical questions. An excellent listing of the Biblical citations and arguments appears in the advertised resolution of the Arkansas Missionary Baptist Association that is reproduced on pages 38-39. These citations typically were given in a folksy manner of elaboration on the scriptures and in a spirit of absolute conviction. The most frequent rhetorical question was "If God had intended the races to integrate, what did He make them different for?" [9]

Several not only quoted scripture in support of segregation but found occasion to attack ministers who sought Biblical sanction for integration. They took particular delight in pointing out that ministers who quote *Acts* 17:26 ("And hath made of one blood all nations of men for to dwell on all the face of the earth,") usually stop at the comma, neglecting to quote the part that reads "and hath determined the times before appointed, and the bounds of their habitation." Uniformly, emphasis fell on the last phrase. "Now is that fair?" one asked.

The sophisticated reader may suspect that these men were struggling to legitimize a shaky position and lacked a sense of conviction. Our impression is strongly to the contrary. All evidence indicates that the arguments were given with assurance and conviction, in the spirit of those who have a sense of mission. Two points are of particular significance. In the first place, these arguments are not matters of facile rationalization or demogogic manipulation, but of basic certainty and assurance. Second, the sect ministers have a feeling

of unequivocal support from the Bible which the integrationist ministers fail to find for their position. This general sense of assurance
and certainty was expressed when a respondent said, "Just as sure
as I know my own name, I know that separate facilities for whites
and Negroes—these are things pleasing to the Lord."

Just as they feel assured of God's support, they are also confident
that their congregations agree with their views on racial matters. If
one of these men was correct when he said, "There is not a single
congregation in town which will support an integrationist minister"
(and our data tend to support this judgment), how much more is
this true of the small sect congregations!

We asked a battery of questions designed to determine whether
the minister had experienced any criticism from his congregation
because of his stand on the racial crisis. We inquired about attendance, contributions, personal comments, membership transfers, congregational opinions, and so forth. Several noted a significant increase
in attendance during the fall: they inferred that they were attracting
the alienated members from other, more moderate churches. Some
made object lessons of their support from the congregation in contrast
to unrest in other churches over the city. [10]

In striking contrast to other ministers, each of the segregationists
reported that all or almost all members of his congregation support his
views on the racial issue. A number of them had asked their congregations to vote on whether they preferred segregation or integration.
The reported vote of "187 to 0 in favor of segregation" was not
atypical of the results. [11] Whereas some integrationist ministers
perceive that as few as 5 percent or 10 percent of their congregations
fully support their views, the segregationist reported possibly "five
or six families who I suppose are fence sitters, since they haven't come
to me to express their appreciation of what I am doing." The significant fact here is that the best he could produce by way of opposition,
in answer to questions, was a "hunch" that a limited number might
be neutral. The closest evidence of actual opposition came from a
woman who had written the church that because she differed with
the minister, she wished to transfer to another church. The minister
said he did not know what the differences were, but he assumed they
were on the segregation issue. It seems apparent that most of these
men have strengthened their hand and increased their influence in
the church by following the segregation line, and that none of them
has done damage to himself in this respect.

As with God and congregation, so with conscience; the conviction among these men that they are doing what is right is easily observed. Indeed, most of them have a sense of mission, of doing what they must. Not one expressed misgivings about segregation or any of its consequences; none indicated concern for the international implications of the Little Rock crisis.

We thought that the problem of advising parents whose children were enrolled in Central High School might cause these men some trouble. After all, on the question of whether children should remain in school there was a possible conflict in values between segregation and education. [12] And on the question of how white students who remained in school should treat the Negro newcomers, there was a possibility that the expression of segregationist sentiments in action would violate other values sufficiently to make even the staunchest segregationist uncomfortable. Accordingly, we inquired whether the sect pastors had been asked for advice on these matters, and if so, the nature of their advice.

Virtually all had been approached by concerned parents and students. In addition, four were personally involved in the sense that their own children were of high school age. There was, however, considerable variance in the advice they gave on what to do with students enrolled in Central High.

Several explicitly advised parents to remove their children. This advice was based on both principle and practicality. In terms of the former, they argued that attending school with Negroes is wrong; they wanted their people to do the right thing. Practically, they reasoned that the students did not want to go to school with Negroes and that the general situation was not conducive to good education. Uniformly, ministers who advised the withdrawal of students actively assisted in making suitable arrangements for transfers to other, segregated schools.

None tried to dissuade parents from transferring their children to another school. They did encounter situations, however, in which to remove the child to another school was not a practical solution. Hence, each faced the problem of giving advice on the proper conduct of students who remained at Central High. Here again, advice patterns varied. Several suggested attending "under protest," which meant, in the words of one central figure, "telling the school authorities that they were there against their wishes, seeking an education but not wanting to go to school with 'nigras,' and that they have not in any wise changed their opinions about the value or necessity of segregation." One advised his own ward, and several children of parishioners, that they could best register their protests by returning to school under a program of passive resistance: "I told them to stay away from the 'nigras' and that they can help make them withdraw from Central in other ways than direct violence; for instance, by walking away when they approach and by not speaking to them." Still others, however, explicitly advised against violence or intimidation as conduct unbecoming a Christian. As one expressed it, "I told them that although I am opposed to integration as much as the next man, violence doesn't settle any problems. I have told them to go on to school and to treat the Negro children in a Christian way. This means being kind to them."

In summary, then, some sect leaders so strongly viewed segregation as a Christian virtue that they advised parishioners to withdraw their children from an integrated school. The need to express disapproval of integration was so strong for others that they either were unconcerned or unaware of what this involved in inhumane treatment of Negro students. Only a minority were aware of this as a possible conflict in conscience values. This small group advised their constituents to be friendly to Negroes while sustaining the conviction that integration as a system is wrong.

We also tried to explore the dimension of conscience, and possible conscience conflict, by asking about a publicly advanced proposal that evangelist Billy Graham help allay racial tensions in Little Rock. Graham is widely admired, especially among fundamentalist religious bodies, for his evangelical work and his expositions of the Bible. Yet he has also taken quite visible, albeit tentative, steps in support of racial desegregation. We wanted to find out what the sect segregationists felt about the proposal to bring him to Little Rock.

The answer was not hard to get. All 13 ministers were opposed to his visit. Nine explicitly mentioned his views on race as the basic reason for their opposition. [13] To some, the reason appeared to be that Graham's comments on race would destroy his influence as an evangelist: "He would slant his sermons toward integration and that would destroy his religious effectiveness to the people. Besides, most people in this town are Baptists and they just couldn't possibly go to services that were unsegregated, so all in all I just think it would stir things up and worsen things." Others were more thorough in their rejection, denouncing him as "a straight-out integrationist who would just pour fat on the fire."

The point is that, faced with a conflict between their support of a renowned evangelist and his views on segregation, these men handled the conflict by withdrawing their respect for a religious hero. In doing this, they opposed a visit by a man whose religious philosophy and work in many ways would complement and aid their own. [14]

The American Creed and Segregationists. One of the interesting characteristics of the segregationist ministers, as we have shown, is their effective isolation from the power and prestige elements of the community. In a real sense, too, they are ignorant of the main currents of American political, social, and religious thought. Their insularity is not sufficiently complete, however, to protect them from the need to incorporate into their ideologies a series of arguments counter to those advanced from more liberal sources. Were there complete insularity, there would have been no need to develop answers to the claims of the opposition.

When insularity is not complete, leaders must maintain group morale and solidarity by supplying rejoinders to the negative influences to which their followers may be exposed. These counters appear in the interview data we obtained.

For example, those who favor racial reform often complain that the Russians make use of American patterns of segregation in propaganda campaigns in Africa and Asia. There is a simple "answer" to this, given us by several respondents: "The United States must do what is right, rather than letting Russia determine our policies."

To the assertion that segregation is unconstitutional in its defiance of the law of the land, there is a standard rebuttal: "Who says its the law? Congress hasn't passed any law, and laws of the state of Arkansas require segregation in the public schools. Furthermore, if segregation is wrong, why did the Supreme Court discover this just a few years ago?"

To the contention that segregation is inhumane and that it is cruel to deny Negroes the privileges of first-class citizenship, the sect segregationist declares that the Negro is much happier and better understood in the South than in the North, and that the Negro masses were quite content with established systems until a few hotheaded agitators began to stir them up. He further asserts that the southern white man is the friend of the Negro, understands his needs, and has given him much more that his tax-dollar would ordinarily buy.

To those who believe in freedom, equality, and brotherhood, and who think that segregation is a violation of these conditions, the segregationist replies that there are the rich and the poor, the saved and the unsaved, the policeman and the criminal, the powerful and the powerless, and (with particular relish since in this next instance he is speaking about the President of the United States) plush clubs for army officers and less plush clubs for enlisted men. We have already seen how easily he manages the argument that segregation is violative of the will of God simply by asserting the opposite proposition.

Gunnar Myrdal, who has written persuasively of the dilemma the segregationist faces in trying to reconcile his racial values with what is called the American creed, contends that the essential qualities of the American race problem lie in the consciences of white Americans.[15] It is difficult, he says, to reconcile the beliefs in individual dignity, fundamental equality, and inalienable rights— central components of the creed—with the practices of racial discrimination and segregation. The segregationist recognizes this discrepancy because he too accepts and values the American heritage; hence, the oft-called "Negro problem" in fact is the "white man's problem." It is "a problem in the heart of the American." In Myrdal's judgment the solution seemingly lies in the expectation that between the tenets of the creed and the tenets of racial discrimination the former ultimately will prevail.

The crux of Myrdal's argument, insofar as it concerns the Little Rock situation, would seem to rest on the directness with which the American creed translates into injunctions prohibiting the practice of racial segregation. Or, stated in other terms, the appropriate question would be: "Do the tenets of the American creed lead so inevitably to the negation of segregation that the creed generates guilt and other discomfort in those who have internalized both the creed and the values of segregation?" We may state this central issue in the form of three specific questions:

How thoroughly is the American creed (as described by Myrdal) internalized?

How much guilt is generated by holding simultaneously the values of the creed and the values of segregation?

What degree of difficulty does the affected person encounter in "handling" whatever amount of guilt develops?

There seems little doubt that the American creed is as much a part of southern life as it is of life in the rest of the nation. Competent observers have long noted that the white South "wraps itself in the Constitution" when defending customs and interests in relations between the races. Even in pre-Civil War debates a century ago,

southerners contended staunchly that the North, not the South, was
departing from the Constitution. Our data give many examples
of the contemporary operation of creed values. For example, these
pastors consistently affirmed belief in equal rights and opportunity,
cornerstones of the American value-system. And these affirmations
frequently represented for them new and more liberal thinking. "If
I can vote, then Negroes should be allowed to do the same ," said
one. "I'm no integrationist," said another, "and I''ll fight it to the
last. But I am for equal facilities and equal rights because Negroes
are human beings also." Often these assertions were accompanied
by admissions that historically the South had been negligent in these
respects.

But the sect segregationist also affirms that the procedures used
to "force" changes in established social patterns have been themselves
violative of the American heritage: "It's those integrationists, not
us, who are un-American." [16] Remarks granting the Negro's right
to equal facilities were followed typically by arguments that the
desegregation order of the Supreme Court and the President's decision to send troops into Little Rock were deeply offensive to this
heritage. One pastor told of watching the 101st Airborne Division
rush into the city: "I saw it and many of my people saw it and it
was a frightful sight. It made you realize you no longer lived in a
free America." Another ventured the prediction that we will have a
dictatorship "within five years" as a result of the use of federal troops
to "coerce people against their will."

An especially interesting explanation lies in the following lecture on
civics:

"Now, the Supreme Court has devoured the very body that created
it, has devoured the Constitution, in other words. The way the
Federal government operates, there are three bodies: the legislative,
the executive, and the judicial. The legislative comes first, then the
judicial comes second, and the executive comes third. Have you ever
been to Washington and noticed how the Supreme Court building
stands just a little higher than the others? That's because the Court
is supposed to adjudicate, not legislate. The judicial branch has been
created by the legislative branch, and now for the court to turn
around and devour the will of the legislature, is like a son devouring
his mother. A man told me the other day that he thought we ought
to go ahead and obey this law outlawing segregation and I said to
him, 'What law? There is no such law.' It reminds me of a joke I
heard. Two Negro men were talking. One said to the other, 'You go-

ing to vote?' The other said, 'What are we voting for?' 'Oh, we're voting for a president,' said the first. 'But we've already got a president,' said the second. 'I know we have,' the first one said, 'but the white folks are electing them one now.' The Executive is definitely supposed to come last."

It is tempting to speculate that the sect segregationist is fundamentally uneasy in his defense of segregation; that the elaborate supports he has erected in its defense are actually reaction-formations that testify to a threatening awareness that what he defends is not worth defending. His quick readiness to affirm the virtues of his stand exposes the guilt he tries to suppress; the American dilemma is really working.

It is, however, difficult to know whether in fact this is the case. The American creed is, after all, a set of abstract values that require translation before application into the everyday affairs of everyday men. The manner in which it is presented to the segregationist minister would seem of crucial significance to this issue. There are alternative possibilities. One such possibility is that the creed was presented to him intact, that is, in pure form, and that he accepted it. This is not likely in lower-class southern culture. Another possibility is that it came to him intact but that because of his own personality dynamics he modified it while acquiring it. Yet a third possibility is that the net thrown around him by the southern subculture protects him from exposure to the creed except in quite distorted form.

In a practical sense, these various alternatives are not mutually exclusive, for all of them have been partially true for most southern segregationists. Some elements of the creed get through and are accepted in relatively pure form. Others come only with qualifications appended. The limited range and nature of the segregationist's contacts so effectively protect him from other elements that they can hardly be said to be familiar to him. The specific forms of exposure and internalization no doubt vary among seemingly similar individuals.

Relatively speaking, the sect segregationist is insulated by his social and cultural milieu from the prevaling interpretations of the American creed. He is quite well protected by his social contacts from situations in which he might comprehend the rationale that supports these views. In our interview materials there are definite traces that the creed is operating among the sect segregationists. But there is also an elaborate and extensive creed of segregation which bisects, contradicts, and interprets the American creed in ways both devious and intricate. This creed of segregation contains the following features:

• Americans should establish their own racial policies based on God's Will. It should not be determined by the African, Russian, or Asiatic peoples nor by their reactions to it.

• Forced, as contrasted to voluntary, racial desegregation is un-Constitutional since it violates traditional American freedoms of self-determination and local autonomy.

• Racial integration cannot be American since segregation is pleasing to the Lord and America is a Christian nation.

• Segregation is mutually desirable to both races since under such a system the progress of the Negro has been more substantial than that of any comparable body for any comparable period in the history of man.

• Accordingly, the southern Negro appreciates the dual system as fully as the white southerner, at least when left alone by outside agitators.

• Equality is in some ways desirable, but it is unattainable. If equality does not exist within racial groups, by what justice is it foisted between racial groups?

• Were segregation un-Christian, then all of the major Christian bodies would not have established segregated churches.

• Were segregation un-Constitutional, then the Supreme Court, under any reasonable assumption of competency, could not have delayed the discovery until 1954.

To determine the precise ways and manner in which this creed of segregation supplements, conjoins, contradicts, or supplants the values Myrdal calls the American creed, requires more intensive data than are available. Of this much we are sure: Whatever its dynamics or its origins, it is a staunch bulwark. It will not quickly dissipate.

Summary. The sect segregationists are important to an understanding of the unfolding pattern of race relations in the South.[18]

We may say that their basic function is to give religious legitimization in current efforts to maintain racial segregation. The status quo need not be defended or explained because it is customary, economically feasible, psychologically functional, nor because of hatred and prejudice; it *must* be defended by those who claim to obey God's will. A Christian cannot do otherwise. He need not support segregation from the basest of motives; he supports it for the highest of motives. God who made the races separate intends them to remain that way. Those who wish His favor must follow His dictates.

The 13 men we interviewed were lower-class pastors, without direct access to the middle or upper classes. Yet on the single theme of segregation they spoke a message keenly attuned to popular sentiment in the South, not limited by class barriers. At all class levels in the South, the majority is for segregation. The minister to the congregations representing the middle and upper classes, generally speaking, does not legitimize this sentiment. Instead, in Little Rock, as we shall see, the higher class minister typically wishes to legitimize integrationist sentiments.

Hence, although of limited prestige and influence, on the one subject of race the sect segregationist expresses a value common to many white southerners in all walks of life. By the single act of defending segregation, he secured publicity and prestige for himself, legitimized the preferences of the public majority, and effectively neutralized the denominational minister's efforts to aid the cause of integration by appealing to the Christian conscience.

The further significance of the sect segregationist lies in the fact that he has contact with those who resort to violence. Ministers of major established denominations, however vocal their protests or brave their acts, lack this contact; without it, they lack an influence with the violent-prone. To assay the prospects for violence, one is better advised to seek out the pastor of the small sect than the minister to the prominent downtown church. Indeed, the small sect pastor almost certainly has better lines of communication with extreme racist elements in Little Rock than has any other professional group.

This is not to say that the sect segregationist intends to encourage violence. None of the ministers interviewed suggested that violence is a proper means although some admitted that good Christians can easily be caught in the spirit of a violent crowd. It is apparent, however, that the segregationist pastor helps create a climate of opinion in which violence becomes increasingly probable. As an apologist and legitimizer for segregation, he has considerable influence, and we should not be misled by his lack of sophistication and his lapses into logical inconsistency. His role is especially significant because lower-class groups, contrary to classes above them, have limited access to alternatives other than violence by which to secure their preferences.

Because of Little Rock's sect segregationists, ministers in major denominations were less effective in their efforts toward moderation. Similarly, their voices carried less weight with their own congregations, and their difficulties caused them to lapse into silence. Not all of the troubles of the liberal minister were caused by the sect pastors, however; indeed, most were not. In the chapters that follow our account of the activities and limitations of ministers in the major denominations will be accompanied by an analysis of why they behaved as they did.

CHAPTER FOUR

THE PROTEST THAT FAILED:

"PEACE, PEACE—WHEN THERE IS NO PEACE"

*"I objected to the peace prayers being described as a ministry of reconciliation. My Bible teaches me that you can't have reconciliation without repentance, and there has been no repentance for what these people have done in this city during the last two months. Why cry 'Peace, Peace—when there is no peace'?"—*A LITTLE ROCK MINISTER, 1957

Although the sect ministers who banded together to sponsor the segregation prayer meeting held different views on religious and other matters, they were of one accord during the racial crisis. By contrast, the denominational ministers supporting the prayers for peace were defiinitely not of one accord and did not offer united support for integration—even though they were formally organized into a single biracial association. The positions of these ministers' churches, congregations, and consciences did not coincide so neatly as they did for the sect leaders. Hence a variety of individual reactions resulted. Some were in deep conflict over the issue, some moved with extreme caution during the crisis, some compromised when segregationist pressures were applied to them; some, however, displayed considerable courage in following the dictates of their conscience.

With such a diversity of responses, it is not surprising to find that very few clergymen—approximately eight—were responsible for most of the religious support publicly given integration in the city during the fall of 1957. What factors encouraged these eight men to prod the city's clergy into forceful action? Why did their efforts fail? Who are these men and how are they different from other Little Rock ministers? Such questions are the chief concern of the present chapter.

History of the Protest Movement. The eight active integrationists can be best described and understood as innovators of a ministerial protest movement. [1] They attempted to persuade ministers of greater influence (the influentials) and ministers of modest influence who were less active (the inactives) into taking strong public stands favoring school integration. [2] The history of this effort can be traced briefly by emphasizing the role of the innovators in the events detailed in Chapter Two.

Before the fall of 1957 few clergymen suspected that a racial explosion was imminent. True, pro-segregation laws had been enacted in the spring by the state legislature and the Capital Citizens' Council had been active during the summer, but it was difficult to imagine what lay ahead for Little Rock. Together with most of the community, ministers—innovators, influentials, and inactives alike—tended to accept the school superintendent's strong assurance that school integration would be successful.

But even in this period of optimism a number of the clergy, the innovators particularly, were active in race relations. One innovator became the president of the Arkansas Council on Human Relations, a small, liberal group with a full-time staff centered in Little Rock.[3] This post gave him a vantage point from which to promote integration. Other innovators, joined by a number of influentials, appeared before an Arkansas legislative committee to protest vigorously against pending segregationist bills. And each innovator dealt directly with the integration question on repeated occasions in sermons to his congregation (save for a few notable instances, other pro-integration ministers explicitly avoided the topic, preferring to dwell on the less specific themes of love and brotherhood).

All three types of ministers combined in the ministerial association on several important issues before the crisis. First, there was general approval in 1956 of the integration of the Negro and white ministerial groups. General agreement, too, led to an association offer to the school board to help sell the board's gradual integration plan to the city.[4] The group also elected an innovator as its president for 1957-58.[5]

When September arrived the innovators and influentials joined hands again. The president of the ministerial association issued to all members an official letter urging them to appeal for orderly conduct in the coming weeks. But Governor Faubus intervened and within hours the ministerial protest movement took shape. Innovators countered immediately with the idea of a ministerial condemnation of the governor's interference.[6] The support of fifteen ministers, including both innovators and influentials and even a few inactives, was secured for the pronouncement. The following morning two innovators and several out-of-town ministers escorted seven Negro children on their first attempt to enter troop-guarded Central High School.[7]

The anti-Faubus announcement marked the pinnacle of the protest movement. From this point on the most influential ministers increasingly withdrew from the public scene. Without their support the protest movement of the eight active integrationists was doomed to failure. We can only speculate as to precisely what reasons were behind the shift of the influentials. The influential minister who was most interested in race relations before the crisis became so ill he had to remain relatively quiet.[8] Other powerful clergymen became silent, even in their own churches, without any explanation. Probably the crucial factor was the generally unfavorable reaction within their congregations to any condemnation of Faubus. As opinion polarized rapidly in the community, leaders who did not openly espouse segregation were suspected of being integrationists. So in spite of the clergymen's extreme care to avoid outright advocacy of integration, their Faubus statement and their overall "law and order" posture were now widely interpreted as favoring school desegregation. The influentials immediately detected serious congregational rumblings: casual remarks at a social event, discussions among the deacons concerning whether to seat Negroes who might visit the church, threats not to contribute to the vital building fund, and even an abortive petition for dismissal.

The consequences of the innovators' activities frequently were more severe and direct: reduction in church giving (not just threats), requests for membership transfer, lowered Sunday morning attendance, and rumors of dismissal sentiment. After one innovator professed in a moment of anger that he would rather have his daughter marry "a Negro Christian than a white heathen," many members of his congregation stopped speaking to him. Reports of such consequences, many of them exaggerated, were circulated among the city's ministry and served to keep the other ministers more inactive than they might have been otherwise.

But the innovators continued their protests. On the Sunday before the riot they gave stern warnings to their churches against contributing to the lawlessness generally expected in the community. One went further in his remarks to his congregation: "I will regard it as a personal favor if any member who feels he must participate in the Central High School demonstrations this week will first drop by the church and withdraw his membership." On the day of the rioting several ministers representing the association personally urged the mayor and the police chief to prevent trouble. The innovators also attempted a broader and bolder move. They brought together selected ministerial leaders from all over Arkansas to draft a declaration of Christian principles with regard to racial desegregation. Some refused to sign, but the announcement had the advantage of being a statewide interracial and interdenominational ministerial proclamation made in the midst of crisis.

And in the face of their parishioners' opposition, all eight innovators persisted in delivering sermons that dealt directly and forthrightly with the issues facing the city. Disturbed by segregation within their own churches, several extended their racial concern to the point where they advocated to their congregations—with little success—the admission of Negroes to their churches as members. One innovator dwelled on the evils of segregation in five consecutive sermons. When he chose another topic on the sixth Sunday, one of the leading laymen in his church confessed bluntly: "Reverend, I'm sure glad you talked about something today besides all this racial mess. I almost didn't come this morning, and I do believe that I and others never would have returned if you had repeated all that stuff again."

As conflict continued, pressures mounted for the influentials to aid their faltering colleagues. Since no solution evolved, their desire to do something besides watch from the sidelines grew stronger. National church organizations began to inquire about their ministers' activities, and national mass media questioned why Little Rock's ministry was not taking a more active role. In this context plans for the peace prayers were formulated by the three most influential ministers in our sample together with several of the innovators. The leader of this group, it is important to note, was an influential minister, not an innovator.

As described in Chapter Two, compromise and neutrality were the main themes of the peace prayer plans. The prayers did not really signify an effective reunion of the influentials and innovators. More accurately, they represented the end and failure of the protest movement. [9] The prayer services relieved the influential ministers' compulsions to act, answered national pressures on them to act, and symbolized their desire to put the whole experience behind them and get on with the uncontroversial aspects of church work.

In view of these factors it was obviously more important to assure that the peace prayers be conducted than to quibble over the form they should take. Hence, compromise and reconciliation were stressed above other principles. [10] The services were never described as organized prayers for integration, but rather as prayers for "law and order" and for divine guidance. No moral commitments beyond this purpose were implied or suggested. To further strengthen this neutrality, endorsements were secured for the prayers from three sides of the controversy: from President Eisenhower, from Governor Faubus, and from the school board. Arrangements were not made through the ministerial association for fear that the presence of Negroes at the early planning stages would make the cooperation of segregationists impossible. Later Negro churches were invited to participate and many did. Even the date—Columbus Day, October 12—was selected with care. It not only lent a national note to the prayers, but it also served as a gesture to the co-sponsoring Roman Catholics. As a final touch, the organizers added autonomy to their arrangements by holding separate services in the cooperating churches.

One of the influential sponsors expressed precisely the underlying assumptions of the services: "Good Christians can honestly disagree on the question of segregation or integration. But we can all join together in prayers for guidance, that peace may return to our city." Such compromises resulted in a widely supported and publicized movement with a broad base of support: Jewish, Roman Catholic, and all major Protestant denominations. Most of the inactive ministers participated.

The effects of the prayer services later became subject to question. [11] One of the influential ministers who had been active in arranging for the prayers had some distinct doubts: "I guess about one-third of us prayed to a segregation God, another third to an integration God, and the last third was so humble as to pray for guidance."

Many of the innovators sensed that the prayer service would serve as a ritualistic ending of ministerial activity in the crisis. [12] At one of the prayer service organizational meetings, the protest movement made its final effort when several innovators strenuously objected to the conciliatory tone of the arrangements. One insisted that the ministers were unrealistic in trying to go it alone in such a weak fashion; he urged that they solicit more general support throughout the community, particularly among leading businessmen. Another protestor pointedly remarked that the compromising nature of the proposed service completely neglected the ministers' moral responsibility. This was the time for a great moral message to the world from Little Rock. He cited the Old Testament story of Esther and told how she had been destined to be queen to save the Jews from annihilation at the hands of Haman. "Who knoweth whether thou art come to the kingdom for such a time as this?" [13] His implication was clear: They were dedicated to the ministry and destined to play a courageously moral role in the Little Rock conflict. But these pleas were ineffective.[14] The compromising tone of the prayers for peace remained. Somewhat reluctantly, the innovators went along with the services; three of them, however, read special pro-integration prayers in their own churches.

The neutral tone of the peace prayers did not succeed in attracting segregationist ministers outside the association. Upon being invited to participate in the prayer services they declined quite unequivocally.[15] Most interpreted the prayer movement as a thinly veiled pro-integration operation. However, they organized their own pro-segregation prayer service so "that people reading the newspapers wouldn't think all of us Little Rock ministers favored race mixing."

Though the press emphasized the neutral nature of the prayer services, many Americans made the same mistake as the sect segregationists, identifying the services as prayers for integration. The error was easy to make since the services were publicized in juxtaposition with the segregationists' gathering. But the misinterpretations actually helped to fulfill the vital functions of the services. Without arousing congregational opposition (members responded favorably to the compromising tone of the prayers), the ministers were at last able to do something about the situation—something that the world outside Little Rock regarded as positive and courageous support for integration. It met their own needs to act. It complied with the national demand for ministerial action. And it terminated the whole unpleasant business.

With this ritual, the influential and inactive members of the association symbolically washed their hands of the conflict. As we have noted, the absence of their public participation in the integration dispute afterward was conspicuous. Even on the Sunday after the prayers none even mentioned segregation in their pulpits. Later in the fall, two efforts at further clerical proclamations failed completely.[16] A few parishes did organize discussion cells on integration[17] and the Arkansas State Council of Churches did authorize distribution of two pro-integration pamphlets at its annual meeting in December 1957, but the protest movement had failed.[18]

A month after the services an irate minister (an innovator) confided: "Those services needed a Trumanistic, not a compromising approach. You can't compromise with a Hitler or a Stalin or a Faubus. An extremist simply doesn't compromise. The prayers' reconciliation theme was doomed from the beginning because the ethical and moral issues involved were simply ignored."

Another minister (also an innovator) expressed pointed views:

"I objected to the peace prayers being described as a ministry of reconciliation. My Bible teaches me that you can't have reconciliation without repentance, and there has been no repentance for what these people have done in this city during the last two months. Why cry 'peace, peace—when there is no peace'?" [19]

Individually, the innovators continued their efforts though they made no further attempt to influence the entire Little Rock clergy. Several helped to start a small group of Negro and white leaders which met weekly. One became the local chairman of the Goodwill Scholarship Fund, a trust set up "to reward youth of Little Rock Central High showing a belief in fair play." Two other innovators continued their attempts to influence their own immediate superior into taking a firmly pro-desegregation position. Still another wrote nationally-circulated articles analyzing the Little Rock conflict and carried on his work as the president of the Arkansas Council on Human Relations. None, be it noted, allowed his congregation to forget the religious implications of their city's turmoil.

The Three Ministerial Groups. Who were the innovators and how do they differ from their more powerful and their more inactive colleagues? The tables that follow provide twelve comparisons between these three types of ministers.

Individual Characteristics. A glance at Table 1 reveals that innovators, influentials, and inactives differ in age, in length of service at their present post, and in where they were educated, but not as to birth in Arkansas. The eight active integrationists among the 29 ministers are in their thirties. They have been at their present churches only a few years. Nearly all were educated outside Arkansas, Louisiana, and Texas.

Since it requires time and stability to become prominent, it is not surprising to find that the seven influential ministers are in their late forties and fifties and have generally been in their present position for more than a decade. A majority were educated in Arkansas, Louisiana, and Texas. The inactive ministers include the oldest group of all. Like the innovators, they have been in their Little Rock pulpits only a few years.

Two exceptions to these trends contribute only minor qualifications to the preceding generalizations. One influential minister had been in Little Rock only a few years, but his power derives largely from his important position as bishop of his denomination in Arkansas.

One innovator, a rabbi, is in his sixties; he has been in his post for more than 30 years. His special role as liberal spokesman of the Jewish community partly accounts for his integrationist behavior. [20]

Each of the three types of ministers is predominantly southern; only three of the 29 interviewees were born elsewhere than in the South. [21] Although the three types do not differ in their percentage of Arkansas-born members, they do differ in where their members were educated. Since most of the Protestant ministers in Arkansas were educated and trained in Arkansas, Louisiana, or Texas schools, it thus is a fair index of local ties to ascertain the percentage of each group educated in these states. The rank order of this index is the same as the length of service at present post index: influentials constitute the highest percentage, inactives the next, and innovators the least. The agreement between the two indices lends confidence to the inference that this rank order (influentials, inactives, and innovators) reflects degree of involvement in the Little Rock community.

TABLE 1.

INDIVIDUAL CHARACTERISTICS OF THREE GROUPS OF MINISTERS*

Group	Number	Median Age (years)	Median length of service at present post (years)	Percentage born in Arkansas	Percentage educated in Arkansas, Louisiana, and Texas
Innovators	8	36	4	38	25
Influentials	7	50	12	29	57
Inactives	14	55	4½	36	43

*Those participating in the October 12, 1957, peace prayer movement.

TABLE 2.

CHURCH CHARACTERISTICS OF THREE GROUPS OF MINISTERS*

Group	Number†	Median church membership	Percentage of churches with community-wide membership	Percentage of churches of congregationally structured denominations
Innovators	8	400	25	63
Influentials	5	2,800	80	40
Inactives	13	1,200	46	54

†Two influentials and one inactive were denominational
officials and had no church in their charge.

*Those participating in the October 12, 1957, peace prayer movement.

Church Characteristics. Even sharper differences between the three ministerial types can be seen in Table 2. Innovators lead small, neighborhood churches, inactives lead medium-sized churches, and influentials lead the large, community-wide churches. In fact, the largest church headed by an innovator is smaller than the smallest church led by an influential. Furthermore, the five churches of the influentials are among the eight largest churches in Little Rock.[22]

The next comparison reveals an unexpected finding. It could be reasoned that a clergyman who heads a congregationally structured church (for example, Presbyterian, Baptist, Christian) would be less likely to take a strong public stand on the desegregation issue than a clergyman who headed an episcopally structured church (for example, Episcopalian and Methodist). The conservative congregation should be able to put more effective and direct pressure on the minister in the former situation while the hierarchy can protect, bolster, even reward the pastor who takes a church-supported but congregationally opposed position in the latter situation.[23] But this was not the case for our limited sample. Though differences were small, innovators were more frequently from congregationally-structured churches and influentials were more frequently from episcopally-structured churches. In any event, it seems clear that the size of the church was a more important variable than the structure of the church. In addition, it should be noted that the three types of ministers cross-cut denominational lines. Innovators represented three different denominations and the Jewish faith; influentials represented four denominations; and inactives represented six denominations.

Rated Characteristics. From the protocols, five variables rated independently by three judges are compared with the three ministerial types in Tables 3 through 7.[24] The variables compared are attitude toward racial integration, personal commitment to the integration issue, "accumulated capital" of the minister, internal conflict, and conflict with members.

For our purposes, an integrationist is a minister who believes that a society free of all artificial racial barriers would be a morally superior one to the present segregated society. With this definition, Table 3 shows that the clergymen who participated in the peace prayers are predominantly integrationists. Only five segregationists are in this sample; four are inactive ministers. The three types vary considerably, however, in their personal involvement in the issue: innovators

were highly involved, influentials tended to be only moderately
involved (Table 4). Whether these differences partly account for the
differential public actions of these groups or whether the differences
are largely after-the-fact postures the ministers assumed in support
of their action or inaction cannot be determined in the present data. [25]

TABLE 3.

INTEGRATIONIST VIEWS OF PEACE PRAYER MINISTERS

Group	Pro-integration	Pro-segregation
Innovators	8	0
Influentials	6	1
Inactives	10	4

TABLE 4.

PERSONAL COMMITMENT IN RACE ISSUE OF PEACE PRAYER MINISTERS

Group	High commitment	Medium commitment	Low commitment
Innovators	8	0	0
Influentials	1	5	1
Inactives	3	2	9

TABLE 5.

ACCUMULATED CAPITAL* OF PEACE PRAYER MINISTERS

Group	High accumulation	Medium accumulation	Low accumulation
Innovators	4	2	2
Influentials	6	1	0
Inactives	4	8	2

*"Accumulated capital" refers to the reservoir of support from and rapport with
his congregation that a minister collects during service in a particular post.

TABLE 6.

INTERNAL CONFLICT OF PEACE PRAYER MINISTERS

Group	Considerable internal conflict	Little or no internal conflict
Innovators	0	8
Influentials	1	6
Inactives	4	10

TABLE 7.

CONGREGATIONAL OPPOSITION TO PEACE PRAYER MINISTERS*

Group	Serious opposition	Moderate opposition	No opposition
Innovators	3	3	2
Influentials	1	2	2
Inactives	1	4	8

*Again, two influentials and one inactive are not included in this table because they are denominational officials and do not have a church in their charge.

"Accumulated capital" refers to the reservoir of support from and rapport with his congregation that a minister collects during his service in a particular post. One could reasonably argue, as one could do for ministers of episcopally structured churches, that ministers with a great deal of "accumulated capital" will venture forth more daringly on public issues because they may expect to face less congregational opposition. But, as with the church structure variable, this was not the case in our sample. Table 5 shows that the influentials have the greatest amount of "accumulated capital" while the inactives and the innovators vary considerably in their amounts of "capital." Note, also, that two of the four ministers among our 29 who were rated as having very little "accumulated capital" still took aggressively pro-integration positions.

The ratings of conflict within the minister and between the minister and his congregation over racial integration are provided in Tables 6 and 7. Only five of these men were in internal conflict, and four were passive ministers. Fourteen, however, had some degree of conflict with their members; the innovators received the most severe opposition, as might be expected. One influential ran into strong resistance because of a national television appearance in which he made his strongest statement of the crisis against the Citizens' Council, a Little Rock organization that claims as members a number of the parishioners of this minister's predominantly lower-middle class congregation. Just how most of the clergy so skillfully avoided serious trouble and parried the congregational conflict they faced is detailed in the next chapter.

Attitude Characteristics. Four of the standard questions asked tended to elicit different responses from the three types of clergymen.

Is the racial matter a religious issue? Percentage answering yes:

Innovators	100%	(8 gave codable answers)
Influentials	57%	(7)
Inactives	38%	(13)

Should a minister take a public stand on an issue such as the racial issue? Percentage answering yes:

Innovators	100%	(8 gave codable answers)
Influentials	86%	(7)
Inactives	46%	(13)

More than other ministers, innovators feel that the racial crisis is a religious matter and that they should take a firm public stand. Their uniformly negative response to an additional query, "Do you think the achievements of the church in the area of race relations have been satifactory," rounded out their thinking. [25] Race problems are of deep concern to these eight men. And since they view these problems as being intimately related to religious concerns, they feel that the church should make a significant contribution toward their solution, but they are dissatisfied with its role in race relations. Furthermore, they feel compelled to act publicly themselves on these issues. That these attitudes are not simply the products of the crisis can be inferred from their actions before September 1957.

Most of the influentials and nearly half of the inactives agree that ministers should take a public stand on integration. But the contexts in which they couched their responses make it apparent that their view of a public stand is a much more timid, if public at all, gesture than the innovators have in mind.

Does your position reflect the wishes of your congregation? Percentage answering yes:

Innovators	0%	(8 gave codable answers)
Influentials	57%	(7)
Inactives	56%	(9)

The active integrationists are aware that their views do not reflect their congregations' wishes, but a slight majority of the other two types of clergymen feel that their positions reflect their congregations' wishes.

Does the Bible give clear guidance on the segregation-integration issue? Percentage answering yes:

Innovators	50%	(6 gave codable answers)
Influentials	25%	(4)
Inactives	22%	(9)

We have noted that the segregationist ministers much more often

than the peace prayer leaders believe that the Bible gives clear guidance in the segregation problem. But only the innovators among the
latter seem to feel that the Bible lends direct guidance; though, of
course, their interpretation of "guidance" is diametrically opposed
to that of the sect segregationists.

Profile of the "Innovator" Minister. Collating these findings, we
begin to see a reasonably clear profile of the innovator. Usually he
is a young man, not long out of seminary. Though southern-born, he
is typically not rooted in the Little Rock community. That is, he
was usually not educated in the schools attended by most ministers in
Arkansas, and he has been at his present post only a few years. He
heads a small, neighborhood church, usually a congregationally-control-
led church though not necessarily of any particular denomination.

The young innovator feels strongly about race relations. He is
an integrationist, deeply involved and without internal conflict over
the issue. He sees the race question as of definite religious concern.
More often than his colleagues, he thinks that the Bible straightfor-
wardly supports his position. Disappointed over what he considers
to be the church's failure in the race issue, he thinks it his duty as a
minister to take a firm public stand for integration. He realizes that
such a stand does not reflect the conservative wishes of his congregation, but this does not deter him. And frequently he meets with anticipated opposition from his parishioners.

Profile of the "Influential" Minister. The influential member of
our sample either heads a large, community-wide church or is a church
official. Again, he may be from any one of a variety of denominations.
A man in his late forties or fifties and sometimes early sixties, the
influential type of minister is deeply involved in the local community.
Typically, he has been in his present position for more than a decade,
was educated in one of the popular schools for Arkansas ministers, and
has accumulated a great deal of church "capital."

Generally an integrationist, the influential minister is not in personal
conflict over and is only moderately involved in race problems. He
may or may not feel that they are directly of religious significance
though he does feel that a minister must take a public stand on race
issues. He considers the Bible to be vague and ambiguous in its position on integration and therefore not a source of clear guidance for him
on the issue. He may or may not express racial views counter to his
parishioners'; and he is in fact likely to receive only moderate parishioner opposition to his mild stand.

Profile of the "Inactive" Minister. Leader of a medium-sized

church of any one of a number of denominations, the inactive minister is in his fifties or sixties. [27]   Like the innovator, he is not firmly
established in Little Rock. He was called to his present church only
a few years ago and has had an opportunity to accumulate at best
only a modest amount of congregational "capital."   While the innovator usually has just begun his career and the influential minister
is at the successful height of his career, the inactive minister is frequently a man who has already served a large number of churches in
other communities and is now nearing the close of his career. (Why
should he stick his neck out at this late stage in the game?)

Though generally rather conservative, the inactive minister is
at heart an integrationist. However, he has had little involvement in
the race issue, does not feel that it is a religious matter, and does not
think that the Bible gives clear guidance. He may or may not feel
that a minister should take a public stand on race, and he has typically not encountered congregational opposition to the gentle gestures
that he may have made.

The passive minister is a particularly important type, for he un-
doubtedly typifies in many respects many of the ministerial association members. The "snowball" manner with which the 29 men were
selected would, of course, greatly under-represent in our sample this
relatively uninfluential and quiet variety of minister.

Community Protest Pattern. Now we can ask if these findings are
consistent with the generalizations that social science has been able
to establish in past studies of social protest movements.

Community-level protest movements—and many broader movements as well—tend to follow a general pattern. At first, there is
initial ambiguity and unrest in the situation. Then an incident trig-
gers off the unrest, and the movement begins as a direct response to
the incident and attempts to reduce the ambiguity by defining the
situation in both thought and action terms. At this particular stage,
the movement tends to have a narrow focus and consequently specific
objectives and actions. But, as the movement progresses, both the
focus and the actions are liable to become broader and more general,
encompassing more and more related goals. And community opinion
begins to polarize sharply for or against the movement. In addition,
there is a concurrent evolution of leadership. The originating zealots
who were never deeply rooted in the locality become dysfunctional.
To broaden the focus and to appeal successfully to the general public,

more "routine," influential leaders are needed. If the movement shows signs of winning popular favor, influential members of the community come forward willingly; but if the movement fails to catch public imagination, the influentials do not join and the movement ends. The culminating stage of a successful movement's history is usually reached when it attains institutional form within the framework of the general society.

To assess the closeness of fit between this typical pattern and the ministerial protest movement, we must consider seven aspects in detail: initial ambiguity and unrest, the trigger incident, broadening focus, broadening action, polarization of opinion, leadership evolution, and final institutionalization. For comparative purposes, we will discuss at the same time another community protest movement arising from a desegregation crisis, the much-publicized bus boycott in Montgomery, Alabama. [28]

Initial Ambiguity and Unrest. Protest movements, from revolutions to community protests, emerge from charged atmospheres. Before fires arise, there must be tinder. Thus R. D. Hooper finds that "mass excitement and unrest" is the preliminary stage in the natural history of revolutions. [29] Similarly with charismatic movements, Max Weber says that "any situation where an established institutional order has to a considerable extent become disorganized, where established routines, expectations, and symbols are broken up or are under attack is a favorable situation for such a movement." [30] The desegregation now occurring in the South is just such an end to an established order, upsetting "routines, expectations, and symbols." We need not be surprised, therefore, at the rise in the South of numerous protest movements on both sides of the question.

Racial tension has marked Montgomery, Little Rock, and other southern cities in recent years. In Montgomery, resentment against the inferior status assigned them has been growing for many decades among Negroes. The 1954 Supreme Court ruling against public school segregation serves to heighten unrest. In Little Rock many white ministers have long wrestled with the dilemma of Christian values and segregation. And as September 1957, the announced date of Central High desegregation, approached, community uneasiness mounted. But how could anyone specify precisely the source of these tensions? And what could an individual do about them? The answers awaited the incident which would trigger off the formation of protest movements.

The Trigger Incident. Finally, the incident occurs which ignites the unrest. It may be trivial in nature, it may be devastatingly crucial, but in any event it succeeds in bringing the conflict into the open. Protest movements now arise, offering interpretations of the crisis and suggesting specific channels for action.

In Montgomery the trigger incident was a relatively minor occurrence. A widely respected member of the Negro community became involved in an argument with a city bus driver over seating arrangements and was arrested.[31] This particular event was only another in a long series of similar bus altercations, yet it proved to be the necessary spark. Immediately following it, the Montgomery bus protest movement was initiated.

In Little Rock the igniting incident drew international attention. In an effort to maintain school segregation in something resembling the Mansfield, Texas, manner,[32] Governor Faubus suddenly stationed National Guard troops around Central High. His action triggered the ministerial innovators in the city. Within hours after Faubus had called out his troops the ministerial protest movement began (with the initiation of the announcement condemning the governor's move).

Broadening Focus. Social movements typically begin with a specific focus. Usually the trigger incident provides the dimensions of the initial goal. Thus the Montgomery bus protest began with a limited focus on particular aspects of the public transit system, and the Little Rock ministerial protest began with a limited focus on the governor's attempt to prevent integration at Central High School, no mention of the moral implications of integration being made.

But once the movement gets rolling, the goals tend to become more ambitious and expansive. The basic issues are stressed rather than the immediate problem posed by the trigger incident. For example, as the Montgomery boycott met with some success, the bus movement began to range widely over the entire spectrum of civil rights and race issues that underlay the original dispute. Likewise, the Little Rock ministerial protest broadened its focus from the immediate high school desegregation problem to race relations in general, even to the point of questioning openly the segregation practices of the all - white churches.[3] Beyond the immediate focus of National Guard troops maintaining school segregation, the ministers we have called innovators began to challenge the whole inactive role of the ministry in the entire realm of race relations.

Broadening Actions. Beginning with narrowly prescribed efforts, a protest movement tends to gather force as its focus broadens. In

Montgomery, for instance, the original boycott was aimed merely at rectifying a number of specific injustices in the city's bus system. But as the objectives increased in scope, the boycott demands became more sweeping and other protest forms became necessary: support of bus boycotts in other areas, speeches by the movement's leaders in other parts of the country, careful attention to international publicity, and so forth.[34]

The widening focus of the Little Rock movement was accompanied by varied techniques. The first move was an announcement opposing the behavior of the governor. Somewhat restricted were the repeated sermons by the innovators in their own churches. The next actions—escorting the Negro children through a mob and interviews with the mayor and the police chief—were more direct but still somewhat limited in scope. A more expansive effort came with the statewide, interdenominational declaration of Christian principle on the issue. The innovators made their most general effort when they tried but failed to convert the neutral peace prayers into an uncompromising, pro-integration prayer service.

Polarization of Opinion. As a movement grows and the issues are hotly debated, attitudes begin to polarize toward two extremes—either for or against; the middle ground becomes almost impossible to maintain. This phenomenon is characteristic of a special case of Pitirim Sorokin's "law of polarization" pertaining to dual effects of crises.[35] On the individual level, Gordon W. Allport, J. S. Bruner, and E. M. Jandorf observed in studies of the personality effects of living through the Nazi revolution: "In Germany, as in Austria, when battle lines were drawn, political opinions departed from a normal distribution wherein the Great Undecided sits comfortably on the fence, to a state of bimodality in which one had either to be for or against 'The Revolution.' Here we have evidence of a general law of public opinion: in times of grave crisis, the central tendency in attitude-distribution disappears; its place is taken, as opinion is forced to the extremes, by a U-shaped curve." [36]

The polarization tendency operates in community conflicts as well as in sweeping revolutions. J. S. Coleman has observed it in fluoridation disputes in American communities. [37] Once the issue becomes important and movements arise on both sides of the question local residents find it difficult to have a middle-of-the-road opinion about fluoridation of public water systems.

In Montgomery attitudes about the bus boycott sharpened quickly. The split was largely, though not entirely, along racial lines: the

Negroes were for the boycott, the whites were against it. Negroes
and whites alike soon found that it was difficult to remain neutral.

In Little Rock's white community any position that was not bla-
tantly pro-segregation was regarded as dangerously pro-integration.
This circumstance caused the reconciliatory peace prayers to be viewed
as favoring integration by many segregationists in the community.
Just how emotionally charged and polarized attitudes became is
indicated by one clergyman: "Longtime friends have learned that
their opinions are being supported with too much heat. Business
partners have found in many instances that it is a case of being silent
or dissolving the partnership. Families are as divided on the subject
as they were in 1860. A son takes one position publicly, his mother
another. A wife becomes active with one group, her husband with
another." [38]

Within the Little Rock ministry, attitudes toward the protest
movement also polarized. Some persons looked on the innovators
as "publicity seekers" or as "young men who have let their enthusi-
asms run away with their sense of reality." Others admired their
courage and were tempted to help, at least indirectly.

Leadership Evolution. The zealous individuals who start community protest movements are typically young, mobile, educated, and
not deeply rooted in the community. These characteristics point to
some of the social dynamics behind their protest. They are not now
influential in the locality themselves, and so from a purely power
point of view they have everything to gain by upsetting the status
quo. And they (the innovators) do have new ideas. Their youth,
education, and wider experience in other regions almost assure this.
Their ideas are often, though not always, somewhat liberal—social
science data consistently show that the young, educated, and more
urban elements in our population tend to be the most liberal. [39] Moreover, the innovators' lack of local roots mean that they are not particularly committed to the community's traditions nor are they en-
meshed in the established and antagonistic interest groups. With
new ideas to espouse, no special influence to risk, and little involvement in the old order from which to break, the young innovators are
in an ideal position to initiate protest movements.

But before a local protest movement can attain success a "routini-
zation of charisma" must generally take place. [40] More "routine" and
influential leaders must replace the original zealots in order to assure
the popular acceptance of the movement. Older and thoroughly
established in the community, these new leaders have real power. A

movement's success or failure, then, is reflected in whether or not evolution of leadership can be effected. Actually, the shift appears to have a catalytic effect, hastening whatever trend has already begun. Thus, when the movement is gaining popularity, the influentials assume its leadership eagerly—sometimes so eagerly that it is easy to lose sight of the innovators. But if the movement meets with stern resistance in the community, influentials will typically not come forward, and the protest may soon flicker out.

F. V. Cantwell provides an interesting example of this wait-and-see attitude by influentials on the national legislative level.[41] In 1937, President Roosevelt proposed a sweeping expansion of the federal judicial system; his opponents referred to it as an attempt "to pack the Supreme Court." At first, national polls showed that public opinion was evenly divided on the issue, and the Senate Judiciary Committee began a series of slow, time-consuming maneuvers. Months later, events such as the resignation of one of the anti-Roosevelt Associate Justices on the court shifted public opinion against the measure, and the committee soon announced its opposition. "As long as any doubt remained about public sentiment toward the bill, the committee remained in session, and only when it was perfectly plain that public support for the proposal would not be forthcoming did it make its unfavorable report."

Based on his research in community conflict, Samuel A. Stouffer has cogently summarized this evolution of leadership phenomenon:

"The existence of different types of leadership must be recognized, and the reactions of each type to given situations demands further analysis. One fundamental distinction in regard to the leaders can be advanced, and that is the distinction between the 'zealots' or 'innovators' and the 'influentials.' The former are more mobile, less rooted or established in their communities. They will initiate changes, and will often be sacrificed to the resistance of the community. The influentials, on the other hand, seldom initiate change. They tend to remain on the sidelines until an issue has developed and its ultimate outcome seems fairly assured. Nevertheless, the final decision of these influentials will often decide the success or failure of any social movement, since these individuals do carry the community with them. Small group research has demonstrated that the most effective combination for the successful accomplishment of given tasks is the cooperation of the 'innovator' and the 'moderator,' who, when working together, can easily sway and dominate the remainder of the group."[42]

The leadership pattern of the Montgomery bus protest fits this general scheme within the context of today's rapidly changing Negro community in southern cities. Many of the older Negro leaders achieved their positions largely because of their ability to deal effectively with whites within the constraints of racial segregation. But now that working within the segregated system is becoming unacceptable to southern Negroes, new, militant leaders who will attack segregation are needed. Consequently, the time is ripe for young innovators to replace older influentials as leaders of urban Negro communities in the South. This situation is illustrated in Montgomery.

The Reverend Martin Luther King, Jr., acknowledged head of the Montgomery boycott, is an ideal leader in many ways. Young, militant, and vigorous, he meets the need for a new type of Negro leader. Not previously influential and not long a resident of Montgomery, he fits the innovator role perfectly, involved neither in past policies nor past politics. Southern-born and a persuasive pastor, he is not so radically different from former leaders as to be unacceptable to the more conservative Negroes.

The Montgomery protest gained rapid and thorough support; the vast majority of the city's Negroes joined in wholeheartedly, many of them representing previously hostile factions. One notable influential—the state leader of the Brotherhood of Pullman Porters and former president of the State Conference of the National Association for the Advancement of Colored People—had been active in the movement from the start. Other influentials, however, tended not to cooperate until the protest had clearly gained wide acceptance. Though their endorsement clinched the success of the movement, an older influential did not replace the Reverend King as leader, as would typically be the case. Three reasons for this exception to the general outline are suggested. First, on both social and personality criteria, King is too ideal a leader to be replaced easily. Second, the real power of these influentials has waned rapidly with the changing racial scene. And, finally, the influentials came into the movement too late; King had already built up such a devoted following that he had become essentially an influential himself. In a sense, then, the evolution of leadership from innovator to influential took place within the same remarkable man in Montgomery.

The leadership and history of the Little Rock protest movement agrees closely with the typical pattern we have described. We noted earlier that the eight men most actively engaged in the protest are young men who are not themselves particularly influential nor firmly established in Little Rock. Usually in their thirties, not long in their present posts, frequently educated in other parts of the country, and ministering to small, neighborhood parishes, they are obviously well suited to their role as innovators. Likewise, the powerful ministers fit the typical influential picture of older men who have deep attachments to the locality: men in their late forties and fifties, called to their present positions a decade ago, educated in nearby institutions, and leading large, community-wide parishes.

Some of the influentials cooperated with the early efforts of the innovators (in issuing the anti-Faubus announcement, for example) but they deserted the movement when their congregations' opposition became increasingly more apparent. Some of the techniques that church members used to make their opposition clear we have discussed. And we have seen how in rapid succession the protest actions soon included only the innovators: escorting the Negro children through a mob, forthright sermons dealing directly with segregation, and the statewide announcement of Christian principle. Without influential support, the innovators failed when they attempted to transform the reconciliatory peace prayers into a defiantly pro-integration ceremony. The prayers spelled the end of the protest movement by remaining so neutral as not to achieve the purposes of the movement while at the same time ritualistically draining off any motivation on the part of more conservative ministers for joining it.

Thus Little Rock's ministerial protest fits neatly into the general pattern of unsuccessful movements. The innovators attained a certain measure of initial success and some influential support. Then, because the movement encountered stern resistance, the influentials pulled out entirely. And, finally, with neither popular nor influential backing, the movement ended in failure. The unique feature of this particular case lies in the symbolic death of the movement in the form of the peace prayers. Such an end strongly suggests a latent willingness on the part of many of Little Rock's clergymen to do something about the crisis; they simply could not see the protest fail without a token, community-wide effort. Yet restraining factors that we will consider in detail in the next chapter prevented them from making this activity forceful and effective.

The present data throw light on an additional aspect of the ministerial protest: the inactive ministers—men who are neither active nor powerful. The majority of these men are in their fifties and sixties and have been leading their medium-sized churches for only a few years. In age they resemble the influentials; and in depth of roots in the community they resemble the innovators. From their point of view, they had little reason to join the protest movement. Most of them are reaching the end of their careers in the ministry; they are without firm footing in Little Rock and too old to consider transferring to another area. In general they are conservative. Many, however, would have given at least fringe support to the movement if the influentials had backed it. For instance, several of the inactive ministers placed their names on the announcement condemning Faubus when it was clear that many of the powerful ministers were also signing.

Final Institutionalization. Successful protest movements frequently attain institutional form within the framework of the broader society. Sometimes, institutionalization may signify that the movement has undergone such a vast degree of "conservatization" that it has lost much of its protest vigor, and its values and aims have become almost indistinguishable from those of the larger society.[48] But institutionalization usually signifies success in achieving many of a movement's objectives and an acceptance of the movement by the larger society as an agent for further change in the same direction. The Montgomery boycott is an example of successful institutionalization. Today the movement has taken the form of the Montgomery Improvement Association, an organization with permanent headquarters, a full-time staff, an active, dues-paying membership, and a continuing program of social action.

In Little Rock no permanently organized, pro-integration group of clergymen was formed. The protest movement met with defeat so early that it never achieved any semblance of institutionalization.

Summary. Eight men account for most of the public ministerial support for school desegregation in Little Rock. These men differ from their colleagues on a number of meaningful variables. Findings in this connection coincide closely with previous social science generalizations about community-level protest movements. On the basis of these results and general social movement theory a number of specific hypotheses concerning the ministerial response to racial crisis as a group phenomenon can be formulated. These predictions will be presented in the sixth chapter.

In this chapter we have looked at the actions of clergymen in the ministerial association exclusively from the social movement point of view. But this type of analysis leaves unanswered many important questions about individual ministers and their role conflicts. It is to these questions we now address ourselves.

CHAPTER FIVE

THE MINISTERIAL ROLE:

"RUNNING WHILE STANDING STILL" [1]

"You'd think we had our heads filled with sawdust, an empty cranium, suh, the way we parked our minds on the sidelines here weeks ago. We've been running on nothing but feeling lately. The trouble is, none of us liberals have been able to do anything effective. Matter of fact, suh, all these good moderates, ministers included, have been running while standing still." — A Little Rock Minister, 1957

The behavior and motives of the missionary pastors who defend segregation have not been too difficult to understand. In their view, the Bible, God, conscience, congregation, and personal and professional associates all mutually reinforce their segregationist sentiments. Should one of them decide to support racial integration, he would be a sociological and psychological freak worthy of intensive scientific analysis.

But about the remaining ministers in our study much more can be said. We have reviewed the numerous reasons for expecting the leading denominational ministers in the South to support racial integration. And we have noted that only a few men of God in Little Rock are active defenders of school desegregation, and that their efforts to enlist general clerical backing has failed. The vast majority of the city's denominational pastors were passive in 1957's crisis.

Of course, it might be said that they failed to give ringing support to integration because they do not believe in integration as a principle. It may be argued that they are products of southern culture, with attitudes and values fixed by that culture. But southerners though they are, the emphasis of their occupational role increasingly alienates them from traditional secular race views. As we have seen in Table 3, most of the Little Rock ministers with whom we talked are integrationists.

There must, then, be other reasons. Let us discuss the conflicting pressures on the minister; the explanation for his passivity lies therein. Let us consider first the contrary expectations to which he has been exposed, and then his personal decision-making efforts within

the context of these pressures, for he must manage somehow to reconcile his public behavior with his private values. We shall then be in
a position to state some generalizations and hypotheses that emerge
from this analysis.

For both scientific and practical reasons, ministers who believe in
integration but who were passive during the 1957 crisis are the most
interesting segment of our study. They were numerically dominant—
more than half (16) of the 29 non-sect ministers. (This number
includes the six pro-integration influentials and the ten pro-integration
inactives noted in Table 3.)   Further, their actions were inconsistent
with their racial attitudes. Those who stoutly defended segregation
on Scriptural grounds, those who were silent because they did not
believe race is a religious issue, and those whose activity in behalf of
integration expressed moral and religious convictions— these groups
shared a common compatibility in attitude and behavior. It is a
different matter with the silent integrationist. Why did he, believing in racial integration, shy away from expressing this belief
and implementing this goal?

As things turned out in 1957 the Little Rock minister who believed in
integration was confronted by an impossible pressure between personal
integrity and social pressure. Somehow he had to extricate himself.
The demand for personal integrity would lead him to stoutly defend
integration and condemn as un-Christian those who supported segregation. He would feel he had to do this to be true to his convictions.
He would feel proud and courageous if he did, cowardly and ashamed
if he did not. However, his ministerial responsibilities carry explicit
obligations such that he felt required to consider the preferences of
his congregation. The drama of ministerial endeavor as it unfolded
in Little Rock in the fall of 1957 must be interpreted as an effort
to reconcile these mutually incompatible role requirements.

One thing all 29 of our ministers have in common is a congregation
whose major view favored segregation. Without exception, our
respondents believe that the majority of their members are strong
opponents of racial integration in the schools as elsewhere. The
highest estimate given by any integrationist of the percentage of his
members who share his views was 40 percent. The median estimate
of the percentage of segregation sympathizers among their congregations was 75 percent. [2] There was almost as much agreement in their
perceptions of the degree of support members would give them for
defending integration. Only three of the men interviewed thought

that a majority of their members would "accept" a strong public defense of integration by their minister.

It is important not to miss this point. Significant pressures to give vigorous defense to integration did not arise from any congregation in the city.[3] Since most church members in Little Rock, even in the established denominational churches, preferred school segregation to integration, the integrationist minister had to reckon with conflicting pressures, a crossfire of expectations. He experienced, in other words, role conflict.

For discussion of role conflict, we may distinguish three role reference systems as relevant to behavior. These we may term the self reference system (SRS), the professional reference system (PRS), and the membership reference system (MRS).[4] The self reference system consists of the demands, expectations, and images the actor carries regarding himself. Analytically, it may be thought of as what he would do in the absence of any possible sanctions from external sources. Typically for our sample the SRS would produce action supportive of racial integration goals. By definition, this would be true of those who are integrationists.[5]

The professional reference system consists of several sources mutually related to his occupational role as minister yet independent of his congregation. It includes national and regional church bodies, the local ecclesiastical hierarchy (if any), the local ministerial association, personal contacts and friendships with fellow ministers, and an image of "my church" in an abstract sense.

The membership reference system consists simply of the minister's congregation.

The net effect of these reference systems would seem from certain points of view to favor the cause of integration. Were each of these three forces equal in strength, and were there no contrary forces internal to any of these systems, this conclusion is obvious. So viewed, we would expect that the minister would feel a commitment to support the official national policy of his denomination regarding integration, that his knowledge that fellow ministers were similarly committed would reinforce him in this inclination, and that the local hierarchy would encourage him to make this decision and reassure him of its support should he encounter congregational disaffection. These external influences would reinforce his own values, resulting in forthright action in stating and urging the Christian imperatives as he and his church perceive them.

Realistically, however, internal inconsistencies in the nature of both the professional reference system and the self reference system restrain what on first examination appears to be an effective influence toward the defense of integration. We will discuss these inconsistencies in turn.

PROFESSIONAL REFERENCE SYSTEM. There are two overriding characteristics of the PRS that minimized its liberal influence in the Little Rock case. First, most of its component parts could not or did not impose explicit sanctions for nonconformity to their expectations on racial policy. Second, those parts of the PRS that could impose sanctions also impose certain other demands on the minister that are inconsistent with the expectation that he defend racial integration to a membership that in large part believes in racial separation and whose beliefs are rooted in deep emotions. The effect of these conditions internal to the PRS was to minimize the external pressure on ministers to advocate national church racial norms.

Inability to Impose Explicit Sanctions. It seems certain that some abstraction such as that suggested by the term "my church" enters into the minister's role definitions. The image may be closely tied to a particular set of actors in a church hierarchy, or it may transcend any formal body in the sense of the "church universal." In one form or another, the minister internalizes it, letting it influence his sense of duty and responsibility. On the other hand, the image by virtue of its abstractness cannot itself impose explicit sanctions. Similarly, the national and regional associations that serve as the official "voice of the church" are not organized to confer effective rewards or punishments on individual Little Rock ministers. [6] Especially is this true in the case of negative sanctions, that is, in the case of failure to espouse national racial policy or to act decisively in a period of racial tension. The same is even more true of the local ministerial association. As an organized body, it does not presume to censure or praise its members in any formal or explicit sense. Conversely, the local church hierarchy is a realistic and immediate source of both positive and negative sanctions, having as it does the responsibility of assigning parishes and of assisting in the development of the local church.

The probability and nature of sanctions from fellow ministers with whom one has personal contacts and friendships is somewhat more difficult to specify. Since the expectations of one's primary contacts are known to be major determinants of his behavior, it seems obvious that a minister's statements and other actions on racial matters are affected by the expectations of his closest ministerial associates. However, it does not appear that the Little Rock minister is subject to negative sanctions if he does not conform to these expectations. Indeed, it seems quite unlikely that their expectations could be so rigid and his behavior so deviant as to induce them to impose negative sanctions in this instance. Had he given endorsement and active support to segregationist and violent elements, it would have been another matter. If he was silent or guarded, however, this caution was not likely to subject him to sanction. The silent integrationists in Little Rock described the innovators as courageous men; nevertheless they expressed doubt as to the ministers' timing and effectiveness. The innovators were disappointed at the inaction of their associates even though they suggested that possibly there were mitigating circumstances. No evidence indicates that personal or professional ties have been damaged or threatened.

Among the various components of the PRS, then, only the local Little Rock ecclesiastica, which did not exist for some, and, to a lesser extent, fellow ministers, were likely to impose significant sanctions in reference to the integration minister's decision to be silent, restrained, or forthright. To demonstrate further that these sources did not in fact negatively sanction inaction or extreme caution, and why they did not do so it is necessary to consider at this point a second inconsistency.

Conflicting Expectations and Mitigated Pressures. For purposes of elaborating the distinctly role variables that concern us, we assume that the local church administrative officials and close ministerial associates are sympathetic to integration. Our central contention is that the role of the minister as community reformer or issue-advocate is not as institutionalized (it does not have as significant a built-in system of rewards and punishments) as certain other roles associated with the ministry.

The minister is the administrative head of an organization. He is responsible for the overall conduct of the affairs of the church. He is judged successful or unsuccessful according to how these affairs prosper. He is expected to oversee and coordinate the varied activities and projects of the congregation. He must encourage cooperative endeavor, reconcile differences, bring people together. Where he succeeds, the vigor and high morale of the congregation are reflected in increased financial support and a growing membership. Both his fellow ministers and his church superiors are keenly sensitive to these twin criteria of effectiveness. An important though elusive goal is full and maximum support from all members of an ever-growing congregation. The effects of discord and dissension, or of ministerial alienation from the members, are too obvious to need elaboration.

The church hierarchy keeps records. It hears reports and rumors. It does not like to see congregations divided, ministers alienated, membership reduced, or contributions decreased. Responsible as it is for the destiny of the denomination in a given territory, it compares the changing fortunes of the denomination with those of rival churches. Responsible as it is for recommending or assigning ministers to specific parishes, it looks for performance clues on the basis of which it rewards some ministers with prominent assignments and punishes others with assignments carrying low prestige or promise. However exalted the moral virtue the minister expounds, the hierarchy does not wish him to damn his listeners to Hell unless somehow he gets them back in time to attend service each Sunday. His promotions are determined far less by the number of times he defends unpopular causes, however virtuous their merit, than by the state of the physical plant and the size of the coffer.

This is not to say that defense of unpopular causes and statement of moral imperatives are without merit. It is especially commendable if the minister can defend the cause and state the imperative with such tact that cleavages are not opened and loyalties are not alienated. If, however, moral imperative and church cohesion are mutually incompatible, there is little doubt that the administrative officials favor the latter. One Little Rock church administrator told two of his ministers, "It's OK to be liberal, boys, just don't stick your neck out." Indeed, the advice relationship between ecclesiastical officials and (especially) younger ministers was systematically used in Little Rock to dampen a minister's enthusiasm for purposive action by urging him to "go slow" and by reminding him of the prospects of permanent damage to the work of the church through what could appear to be rash action. [7]

It is obvious that under such circumstances the pressure from above (the national church and its administrative representation) to take an advanced position on racial matters loses much of its force. The minister is rewarded for his efforts in this area only if he does not endanger the fellowship of the church—"Don't lose your congregation." Similarly, the prospect of an unfavorable response from his congregation gives the minister an effective immunity from negative sanctions that conceivably might be imposed by a liberal church hierarchy. He has only to say that, with feelings running high among his members, he dare not discuss racial issues. He can point to Pastor X, who didn't heed his congregation. The higher officials, themselves keenly aware of local values and customs, will surely understand.

Conditions of a similar nature reduce the prospect that pressures toward advanced positions from fellow ministers will have much force. They are, after all, in the same boat, faced with heavy sentiment against racial liberalism. They offer sympathy, not censure, when he says "My hands are tied." An informal rationale assures the pastor he cannot have done wrong by refusing to take severe risks— "These things take time; you cannot change people overnight; you cannot talk to people when they will not listen." There is strong sympathy when a forthright pastor is in real trouble, but there is also a strong object lesson. Thus the ministers tend to reinforce and reassure each other in their inaction despite their common antipathy to segregation. These conditions largely dissipate external pressure to advocate national church norms on matters of race.

Two central points emerge from this analysis of the professional reference system: The local sanctions are stronger than the national sanctions, and the weight of the professional sanctions points toward passive conduct on the local level.

THE SELF REFERENCE SYSTEM. We still must reckon with the demands the minister imposes on himself. It is obvious that the actor has the power of self-sanction through the mechanism of guilt. There is no need to argue the significance of this sanction nor to suggest that it is especially potent among the religiously oriented. A threatened sense of unworthiness, of inadequacy in God's sight, cannot be taken lightly. Similarly, to grant oneself the Biblical commendation "well done" is a significant reward. We have said that in Little Rock the self reference system is an influence favoring action in support of desegregation. Is the silent integrationist, then, able to control his guilt? If so, how does he do it?

We cannot affirm in any conclusive sense that he avoids a sense of guilt while refusing to defend a pertinent moral conviction in a crisis. Our data are not entirely appropriate to the question. Nevertheless, four factors, readily generalizable beyond the Little Rock case, at least partially support such a contention. These include major characteristics of the ministerial role, several ministerial values and "working propositions," certain techniques for communicating without explicit commitment, and the gratifying reactions of extreme opposition forces.

The Role Structure.   The institutional structure of the church, within which ministerial role obligations are determined, specifies a set of evaluative criteria to which the minister as actor may compare his performance as manager of a religious enterprise.   It does not so specify comparable criteria by which to evaluate himself as an agent of community reform and change on controversial issues. [8] The effect of this is to encourage, even compel, the minister to base his self-image, hence his sense of worth or unworth, on his success in managing a corporate enterprise.   Thus, when social action is seen as interfering with institutional goals because church members do not share the minister's goals, three major sets of institutionalized responsibilities restrain reform activity:

1.   Coordination.   The minister is required to be a cohesive force, to "maintain a fellowship in peace, harmony, and Christian love," rather than to encourage action that divides the members.   During the Columbus Day services some ministers prayed that members "carry no opinion to the point of disrupting the Christian fellowship." Significantly, several Little Rock ministers, even those who were inactive in the controversy, scheduled conferences with lay leaders and other membership groups in late 1957 and early 1958 to assess the effects of community race tensions on the individual church.

2.   Evangelism.   The minister is expected to show a progressive increase in the membership of his church, thereby providing a tangible measure of both the personal goal of salvation and the institutional goal of growth.   Lacking mass support, pro-integration activity is likely to secure converts for other churches from the church whose minister so engages himself. Thus, a small sect minister prominent in Citizens' Council work claimed that his membership was growing fast because disaffected members from congregations with liberal ("law and order") ministers transferred to his church.

3.   Administration.   The minister's task is to encourage maximum annual giving and to plan for the improvement and expansion of the physical plant.   It is hardly surprising that several inactive integrationist ministers who were engaged in vital fund-raising campaigns shrank from action that might endanger the success of these campaigns. [9]

Working Propositions.   Certain assumptions in the minister's work pattern reduce the probability of guilt when he does not defend the moral convictions that his members reject. In contrast to his counter-part of an earlier period, who was more likely to believe in the efficacy of sudden change through conversion, he is, first, a devotee of the process of education, by which he means gradual growth and devel-opment of spiritual assets. Consequently, he is vulnerable to the argument that change in the racial structure is a long, slow process, and that the South cannot tolerate rapid change. He also believes that communication with the sinner must be preserved at all costs—"You can't teach those you can't reach." It is important to maintain relations that allow the possibility of effecting gradual change in attitude and behavior over a longer time period. Especially, then, in a crisis period, when feelings run high, the time is not ripe for decisive action that risks alienation of those one wishes to change. Take Pastor X, whose actions, though decisive, damaged the church fellowship and threatened his pastorate—"Look at him; he can't do any good now." Such working values—the efficacy of the educative process, the necessity to maintain communication, the intrinsic worth of a preserved fellowship, the mistake of Pastor X—provide a rationale by which the minister in Little Rock might control the flow of guilt for inaction.

Communication Techniques. The minister can, of course, use certain techniques in discussing topics on which he does not wish to commit himself. (Some of these are discussed in a later section.) As with the 'line' in flirtation, the speaker uses the language of diplomacy to provide an escape from an untenable position. Hence the minister may talk in vague generalities which he hopes his listeners may apply to the racial situation. He seems to supply, as it were, a do-it-your-self moral kit. He may hint darkly that he would say many things if his audience were able to receive his (unstated) message. He deals in innuendo and ambiguity, even innocuity. Whatever the impact, if any, on his listeners, he has the satisfaction of telling himself that the connections are there to be made; after all, he cannot force his listeners to apply what he says.

It would appear that the desire to express his convictions, though doing so may damage the work of the church, leads the minister to give much thought to choosing even ambivalent remarks. He writes and rewrites, discards and reorganizes, erases and starts again. When the remarks have been made, he may believe that he has said more than in fact he has since he has considered saying so much. Thus these techniques are psychologically valuable to him. It is not impossible under these circumstances for an ambiguous, cautious statement favoring "law and order" to become in the speaker's memory a forceful, impassioned condemnation of all things segregationist.

Reaction of the Opposition. The ministerial body in Little Rock, except for pastors of dissident fundamentalist sects, was viewed with suspicion by active segregationists. In fact, the segregationists, including sect pastors, described the denominational ministers as "a bunch of race mixers and nigger lovers." So defined, the leading clergy of the city became the object of public and often vitriolic attacks. The charge was made that the "peace prayers" were intended to "further integration under a hypocritical veneer of prayer," and the small sect pastors sponsored their prayers for segregation "to show that not all of the city's ministers believe in mixing the races." Indeed, ministers of major denominations were charged with having "race on the mind" so much that they were straying from, and even rejecting, the Biblical standard to further their un-Christian goals.

The effect of this stern and critical opposition by segregation extremists was to convince silent integrationists that indeed they had been courageous and forthright in expressing the moral imperative. An interesting process took place here. The minister did not hesitate to accept the segregationists' contention that he was an active exponent of desegregation. But whereas to the segregationist this was cause for censure, the clergyman accepted this judgment as proof that he had performed as he should have. Accepting the opposition's evaluation of his behavior, he reversed its affective tone. This disapproval by a negative reference group gave him reassurance that his personal convictions had been adequately and forcefully expressed.

Returning now to consideration of the three role reference systems, we may see why any analysis that suggests stronger pressures for defense of integration than for silence or support of segregation is misleading. Were the force of the membership reference system not what it is, the professional reference system and the self reference system would have produced effective support of integration, not limited to "law and order" appeals and denunciation of violence. However, since "don't lose your congregation" is itself a strong PRS pressure, the force of the PRS is neutralized.[10] The pastor's demands on himself, consisting as they do of loyalties and obligations to the membership as well as of the desire to defend moral imperatives, tend to become confused and conflicting. Inaction is a typical response to conflicting pressures within both internal and external systems.

Seen in this manner, it is not surprising that most Little Rock ministers have been far less active and vocal in the racial crisis than a knowledge of the policies of their national church bodies, their sense of identification with these bodies, and their own value systems would lead one to expect. Rather, what is surprising is that a small number of them continued throughout the crisis to express vigorously the moral imperative as they saw it, in the face of congregational disaffection, threatened reprisal, and the lukewarm support or quiet discouragement of their superiors and peers.

THE MINISTER AND HIS DECISIONS. It is within the context of related but opposed sets of expectations and pressures that the minister's decision-making takes place. We will discuss this—by way of a series of progressive questions—in the specific terms of the Little Rock incidents during late 1957. It is obvious, however, that some of the minister's decisions were made before that fall and that others are predictable outgrowths from his more general ways of relating himself to the church and community.

1. The basic decision the Southern minister must make is whether he favors racial integration or racial segregation as a social pattern. Stated simply, the question is: "Do I basically prefer to participate in a society that continues its present patterns of race contact or do I prefer a society in which artificial, legal barriers to race contact are removed?" In its pure form, this is a question of principle only and not of implementation.

The question of principle, however, becomes immediately a question of policy. Not only must the minister decide whether he favors integration or segregation, but he must also determine in what areas he favors it. And if he supports integration, with what speed is its attainment desirable? There are integrationists who propose a gradual transition from a segregated society as there are integrationists who want immediate all-out efforts. And how complete should the process be? Is the presence of nine Negro students in one high school more or less preferable to the presence of more Negroes in all public schools in the city?

2. Having decided his goal-preference, the minister faces the question: "Is this a matter on which I should express myself in my ministerial role?" The question is not simple, and its answer is not likely to be categorical. Some ministers believe that, though they may have their personal preferences, racial matters are not religious issues.

Others attempt to draw a line between religious aspects and legal and political aspects. Still others feel that it is one of the primary ministerial responsibilities to apply religious evaluative criteria to the matter of race relations. The integrationist ministers we interviewed ranged from belief in intensive discussion and action to belief in silent detachment from the issues.

3. Up to this point, the minister may assume any value position— integration, segregation, neutrality, indifference—and yet be publicly silent. If, however, he decides he should express his convictions on the matter, then he must define a target group for his remarks. Should he address himself to his congregation or to the community? Or to both? If he limits himself to his congregation, the role position from which he speaks is clear: "I come to you as your pastor." [11] If on the other hand he aims the expression of his convictions at some extra-congregational target, he faces the additional question of defining the position from which he speaks. Does he speak as a private citizen, as a Christian minister, or as the pastor of First Metropolis Church?

These questions are not insignificant—especially if the minister speaks in favor of integration. Church members will complain that no matter how he prefers to be regarded he nevertheless is the pastor of their church and spokesman for the members. Such complaints have been voiced in many of the churches in Little Rock. One example may suffice. A minister was called by telephone to sign a statement condemning Governor Faubus. This happened while he was meeting with his official board. He sympathized with the statement and authorized his signature, thinking of it as an act of individual preference. He did not consider it important enough to mention to his board when he returned to the meeting. But he was later criticized by his board and other members on the grounds that he was not authorized to appear to represent his church in this manner.

4. If the minister favors segregation, his decision-making is an easy task. He is under little local pressure to restrain his behavior or to adopt a different attitude. He is aware that the defense of segregation will alienate only small numbers, and in many churches it will offend virtually none. Finally, he is likely to have full conscience-support on the matter. Believing that God and right are on his side, he often has a sense of mission. We encountered one possible exception to this last point, and this was the case of northern-born ministers turned segregationists. Their over-adaptation to local values may have left residues of guilt. Nevertheless, the general picture of full support from God, conscience, and congregation is clear.

If, however, the minister favors integration and believes it to be a religious issue, the matter is much more complex. Although he has the support of his conscience, generally he does not translate the Bible to his purposes with the same chapter-and-verse conviction observed among segregationists. More crucially, the integrationist minister is in a position in which his values digress from those of large segments of his congregation, and in which the congregation's beliefs are overlaid with heavy emotional conviction. He faces the decision: "What shall I say or do, and how shall I say or do it?" The answers to these questions are affected by the social characteristics of his congregation and by aspects of his prior relations with them.

Generally speaking, the higher the socioeconomic and educational level of the congregation, the greater the freedom of the minister to defend and support integration values. The racial attitudes of those in higher social class and educational levels are generally more tolerant; if they do not believe in integration, neither do they accept intimidation and brutality. In addition, the minister, himself more highly educated, is more likely to have insisted on some degree of freedom from narrow restrictions on specific issues as a prerequisite to his service. [12]

In addition, the number of years the minister has served the congregation is positively related to his freedom to act contrary to its will. [13] Ministers who have served a congregation for many years have developed strong, close relationships and have provided personal services that represent a form of invested capital on which, theoretically, they may draw when differences of opinion develop. As one prominent and well-loved pastor said, "When you've been with a congregation for a long period of time, there will be many people who have been converted under your ministry. They will have toward you a warm conversion feeling that will support you and do a great deal of good when you are trying to get them to see that something is right and proper from the Christian standpoint."

Related to this is the pastoral image carried by the congregation, that is, whether their definition of the minister's role requires, permits, or prohibits his participation in controversial issues. Theoretically, the congregation that expects a ministerial posture on social issues reacts less negatively when his position differs from their own than the congregation that expects him to abstain from participation. Also relevant is the question of whether the minister has expressed himself over a previous time period on the racial issue. We would expect that a pro-integration posture during crisis would encounter a less vigorous negative reaction if the minister has prepared his congregation to expect this posture by his previous announcements and activities.

A third variable that affects the minister's activity is the rate of turnover in his membership. This is what the minister calls "lettering in" and "lettering out." Generally speaking, the higher the rate of turnover, the greater the freedom of the minister to take unequivocal positions including unpopular ones. One pastor of a large, well-established and stable church told us of overhearing a member say to a visitor after the minister had made some unpopular comments on race: "Now of course, you know the preacher doesn't speak for the people in the church when he says things like that." But in a newer church, or one with rapid turnover owing to a mobile population, the minister in a special sense is the church. He speaks for it. He determines its policies. Lacking a sense of continuity and of tradition, and a mature sense of relationships among themselves, the laymen are poorly situated to challenge the minister's decisions. New arrivals are more likely to turn to the minister than to lay groups for their perspective on the church and its program.

A fourth variable is the type of pronouncement the national headquarters of the church issues on the subject of race policy. The beleaguered liberal minister finds it a source of strength to tell his detractors that he is, after all, only explaining the official position of his church. When artfully executed, this manuever requires the lay critic either to withdraw his criticism or seem to repudiate his church's position; in the latter case he appears as a poor church member. To the extent of his loyalty to his religious faith, he is vulnerable when criticizing a minister whose behavior seeks to implement the policy of the church. His vulnerability strengthens the hand of the minister.

The matter of lay loyalty to a church deserves separate attention and may be considered an additional variable. There are various levels of loyalty, of course, to the church at the national level or to administrative subdivisions, and so on down to a particular church body, located in a specific building on a specific plot of ground and possessing its own characteristic history. In discussing the forces that sustained him through a difficult period in which his congregation rebelled against his racial views, a young minister called to our attention the importance of loyalty to a church. He believes that the loyalty of long-time members to the local congregation, combined with the deep-seated habit of attending services and contributing to the church's program, held his church together although his was an alien voice.

"You have to remember that people will develop a loyalty to a church that is pretty strong in the face of a number of things. The loyalty of a lot of the members of a church can be counted on in spite of almost anything the minister says or does. There are a good number of people in my church who would continue to attend even if I recited 'The Cremation of Sam McGee' from the pulpit every Sunday for a month and said nothing else. Some people have developed an intense loyalty to the Lord that leads them to church every Sunday irrespective of the content of the service. Some people have developed a loyalty to me and most of those who remained loyal to me vigorously disagreed with me in this particular matter. But above all, aside from this loyalty of members to me, to the Lord and to the denomination I preach for, I want to tell you that this factor of loyalty to this particular church, by that I mean this building sitting right here on this spot of land, counted for a great deal in seeing me through."

A final factor remains to be considered: the immediacy of the issue to the congregation. As the issue increases in relevancy, pressures develop on the minister to tread softly if his opinions differ from those of the congregation. All ministers had more freedom in challenging segregation in June 1957 than in October. Ministers to congregations in which few if any members had children attending the integrated school—for example, the Pulaski Heights churches—had more leeway in supporting integration than ministers to churches in which large numbers attended Central High. It was not possible to deal with this variable with any precision in Little Rock since the congregations least affected by integration also were those of higher socio-economic and educational levels. It is, however, a variable significant in its own right.

5. Presumably, the minister who expresses his integrationist convictions will do so for reasons over and beyond a simple desire to "get it off his chest." He states his beliefs because he wants to persuade people, to influence attitudes and actions. He becomes, in other words, a practitioner in the social psychology of attitude change, wherein he faces many of the same problems studied by the social experimenter in the laboratory and tackled by the propagandist in the field. His views are alien to those of many in his audience. He hopes to bring his listeners around to his way of seeing things. How shall he best do this? How shall he maximize impact? Viewed in another way, how shall he minimize the effects of failure? The answers worked out to these questions in Little Rock are many, varied, and sometimes idiosyncratic. The following descriptions do not cover the field. They

are instructive only as examples of the devices used by Little Rock ministers, sometimes deliberately, perhaps more often with lesser degrees of awareness.

The *law-and-order technique* is a simple and widely used device. In fact, it was the most popular device used by integrationist ministers during and before the Little Rock crisis. In the pure or extreme case, the minister does not take a stand on the question of integration or segregation; indeed, he may in effect reinforce segregation sentiments by failing to criticize them. In this pure form, the essence of the technique is: "I am not talking about segregation or integration. On this good Christians may honestly diasagree. But the Christian must uphold law and order."

The moral imperative applied to the case is that of legality rather than of Christian brotherhood. In other instances a statement favoring integration is made, but the principal emphasis is on respect for law and order. It is assumed in either case that actions consistent with a respect for law and order require compliance with federal court rulings on integration, thereby assuring that the desired goal of integration will be obtained. One prominent minister, when asked if he had taken a public stand on the racial issue, said he felt that he had done so when he criticized the governor's action in calling out the National Guard, and that this had been interpreted to mean that he was an integrationist. "The trouble now," he said, "is that you just open your mouth and say most anything and people will put you in one camp or the other. But actually that statement condemned the action of the Governor because the action had been against law and order. The action was not justifiable, and it was the duty as well as the right of ministers in this community to point out to the people that it was against law and order and therefore irreligious. I myself didn't see where this was taking a stand on integration-segregation."

The *messenger of the Lord technique*, when used, poses a troublesome dilemma for the listener. It involves a statement in support of integration as "the will of God," and the speaker is only the messenger. What Christian can quibble with the humble yet unequivocal assertion that "I speak God's Word as God requires I speak it?" Strategically, one might expect this feature to commend the technique to many users. Despite its apparent virtues, however, it was not widely used in Little Rock. The major reason, as we have seen, was that most of the liberal ministers were not convinced that the determination of God's will on segregation as a social issue can be made with great certainty.

We did find, however, one instance in which the technique has been used with conspicious success by a young minister. His case is unique. He is one of a small number of Little Rock ministers who intensified rather than retracted his efforts when the crisis broke and continued them beyond the symbolic termination point of the "peace prayers." Even more significant, he encountered only a slight but manageable resistance from his congregation while doing so.

It would be misleading to attribute his success solely to use of this technique. He uses a southern drawl to good effect, and he possesses a winning personality. It is interesting also that his liberal views on racial matters combine with the conservative, traditional view on sex, sin, and liquor that is indigenous to religion in the southland. For either viewpoint there is a single source of unquestioned authority: the will of God. This is his description of his strategy: "If there were some issue before my congregation and I found out that 20 percent of my congregation was with me on it and the rest were against me, that wouldn't make a bit of difference in the world. I would still have my obligation to express what I see to be the will of God. This is one of the truly unfortunate things about the way my denomination is organized. We have an administrative setup here such that you judge the value of the church, the strength of the church, in terms of whether it keeps growing or not and whether you keep all the members happy or not. This is a very false premise by which to judge a church and whether a minister is doing the work of the Lord. I don't take straw polls. I don't need to take straw polls to find out where I ought to stand; and when I know where I ought to stand I let them know. It is not my responsibility to poll the congregation to find out what they want to be told. It is their responsibility to listen when I tell them what the will of the Lord is."

This unique minister told us that he had had previous "battles" with his growing and vigorous congregation in which he "read the riot act" to them. "I told them," he said, "that I intend to purge my church of undesirable elements and that if some of them continued to believe or act in certain ways I wanted them to simply transfer their membership somewhere else, or at least get out of this church; that I would be glad to give them every assistance in transferring. I also tell them that they can keep right on doing those things if they want to, but if they do they're going to burn in Hell just as sure as you-know-what."

We asked him what some of these "battles" had been about. He replied: "Oh, drinking, gambling, missing church on Sunday, running around with another man's wife and that sort of thing."

The basic essentials for use of the *exaggerated southerner technique* are a good southern drawl and an impeccable southern background. A basic defense of segregationists is that birth, residence, or education outside the region invalidates a man's judgment on racial issues (unless, of course, he happens to believe in segregation). The home-grown integrationist, however, is difficult to oppose. The speaker who uses the technique, a very simple one, reminds his listeners of his background before he expresses his opinions on race. He also may throw in a few flowery phrases about the glory and grandeur of the South. In exaggerated form, the reminder goes like this: "I, suh, of Mississippi planter stock, descendant of slaveholders, born, bred, and educated in our beloved southland, suh, must speak some critical truths, suh." Then he states his position.

One minister who uses the technique to advantage told us: "When my congregation and I get anywhere near the race issue I always remind them in my thickest drawl that I'm more southern than they are. Fact of the matter is, I tell them, suh, that they're out-and-out mid-westerners compared to me."

Like the *law-and-order technique,* the *every-man-a-priest technique* is commonly employed in Little Rock. It also permits the minister to express his own opinions while lessening the moral punch of his remarks. He prefaces his lecture with a statement something like this: "I am going to state my own opinions. We believe in freedom of opinion in our church, and you, also possessing free access to knowledge of God's will, may hold a different opinion, which I assure you I shall respect." Each listener is encouraged to seek his own answer, and the minister does not argue that his anwers are the right ones.

This egalitarian posture doubtlessly is appreciated by many listeners since there is no condemnation of the opposing views which the listener holds. The technique puts the minister on the same level as his audience, removing any special moral force from what he says at the same time that it permits him to express himself "as one of you." Presumably he trusts that the prestige of his position, his protestations notwithstanding, will add special weight to what he has to say.

This procedure was described by one practitioner as follows: "I had no specific purpose in expressing my opinion publicly as far as the congregation was concerned, except, of course, as I lent whatever influence I have to the position I took. After all, in my church we're pretty used to every man being a king and priest before God, and no one speaks for our people as such. So when I take a position, I don't take it as a super-human who is privy to God's innermost secrets, but I take it as an individual among individuals. I've taken my position only on the basis of individual conviction."

Another pastor told us that he worked hard and successfully, he thinks, to cultivate in his congregation a kind of tolerance for the minister, such that the congregation tolerates him when it does not accept him, just as they expect tolerance from him. Practically no one in the congregation was really angered by a liberal sermon he preached on tolerance, he said, and practically no one was willing to "raise a ruckus" about it in any way.

In similar vein, another pastor said that he makes it clear to his congregation and church officers that they are not required, in order to remain in good standing as members of the church, to accept his or the denomination's position on race or on any other matter "that is not basic to the faith." This pastor defined himself as a spiritual counsellor: "I offer spiritual guidance and interpret the church heritage and the Christian heritage relative to particular issues, as best I can, but within broad limits there is a freedom of opinion and a spirit of toleration of differences in my church."

The *deeper issues technique* is also a favorite device employed in Little Rock. The technique emphasizes the "brotherhood of man" with no necessary or explicit translation into the social issue of segregation. The minister intends that the listener make the translation himself. He states the principle, or at most poses the question, but he does not provide the answer. He says in effect, "I want to talk to you about living a Christ-like life, practicing Christianity, humility, loving-kindness, Christian charity." He proclaims these as virtues but is careful not to say that the practice of these virtues requires specified attitudes and actions in relations between whites and Negroes.

One pastor said in discussing the kind of guidance he gives the large number of people who approach him on the subject of race: "The guidance is strictly from the principles of Christianity and the fact that Christianity expects a person to react to another human being in the way he would expect to be treated himself. I have given a number of sermons which, in fact, had direct implication for the segregation-integration issue. I talked on what I considered to be issues deeper than this and these deeper issues concerned brotherhood, justice, the underlying problems of human existence."

As used in Little Rock, the *segregationists are stupid technique* is a counter-measure, quite defensively toned, in which one is less likely to defend the principle of integration than to attack segregationist arguments. The minister may decry the flood of hate propaganda from outside the city or deliver an exposé of race baiters. Or he may declare his disaffection with the Citizens' Council, the Mothers' League, the Klu Klux Klan, and similar organizations. Pastoral letters, church bulletins, or special circulars are sometimes used to answer the argument of segregation ministers that there is Biblical justification for segregation. The generic characteristic of these efforts is an implicit or explicit attitude toward rabid segregationists as being misinformed, stupid, cruel, hate-filled, or vulgar. The listener or reader is left to decide whether he wishes to be thought likewise.

One aspect of the *segregationists are stupid technique* requires separate discussion. Basically, the minister tries to achieve a stated degree of integration (for example, in the schools) by debunking the reality of dreaded consequences suggested by opponents. Specifically, since most measures designed to improve opportunities for Negroes are met with fears that Negroes will "run things" or that intermarriage ("mongrelization of the races") will result, the minister attacks the idea that power for Negroes or amalgamation are likely consequences. Of course, he does not say that power and amalgamation themselves might be acceptable results. More likely, he prefaces his attack with statements such as "I am myself opposed to amalgamation," or, "None of us wants wholesale integration," or, "Some Negro leaders are making themselves obnoxious by taking radical positions."

The *God is watching technique* is perhaps the most equivocal device of all. It is beautiful in its simplicity and commends itself to some for this reason. The speaker does not declare himself on the issues, nor even discusses them. Instead, listeners are reminded that the matter of race does have religious significance and therefore they should "act like Christians" in matters pertaining thereunto. As the city's liveliest exponent of this technique described it:

"I know that you can't get yourself into any trouble with God or with your fellow man if you behave like a Christian. If you act like a Christian, you won't ever do anything you're not supposed to do. You won't beat up colored people, or anybody else for that matter, and you won't go around with hate in your heart. If your people understand this, then you won't have to preach sermons on integration for them; they'll do what they're supposed to do. And I never have.

"My people know that an omnipotent God watches every step they take. Sometimes when people get excited or passionate they may forget this. So last month, when things got hot, I felt I ought to remind them that the Heavenly Bookkeeper keeps pretty strict accounts. I'm satisfied they knew what I meant."

The foregoing list of techniques is not exhaustive, nor are the categories mutually exclusive. The list is representative, we feel, of the major means by which liberal ministers in Little Rock communicated with a body of listeners that they felt would grow apart if they had spoken in the forthright and urgent terms the occasion demanded.

6. There remain to be discussed the questions of frequency and force. Even though the minister believes in integration, has decided to express his convictions publicly, hopes to affect the attitudes and actions of his listeners, and has made a choice of tactics and arguments to be used, he still must determine how much attention to give to the topic and how much wallop to put in his punches. Shall he use the sledge hammer or the velvet glove? These decisions in turn rest on certain beliefs he has on how to achieve effectiveness in his work. Generally speaking, he has to define a target group and evaluate his operations in the light of the more general purposes of his ministry. It appears that the following three propositions are basic conditions in his dilemma:

The milder the tone and the less frequent the discussion, the more likely he is to preserve communication with those most distant from his own position, that is, from the position to which he would like to convert his listeners.

This is especially likely to be true when, as in a crisis situation, issue salience is high and the issue is emotionally charged. In such instances the risk is highest of losing contact completely with certain persons who may be targets of the remarks.

The milder the tone and the less frequent the discussion, the less moral compulsion ("upper tension") is felt by a presently unconvinced but pliable group.

If religious interests and cultural values conflict (that is, if the listener prefers segregation but is responsive to religious teaching), failure to apply the moral imperative with significant strength leaves him more subject to persuasion from opposite (segregationist) forces that are not so restrained.

*The milder the tone and the less frequent the topic, the less rein-
forcement is received by an already convinced group of liberals.*

Lacking significant reinforcement from the titular head of the
congregation, and facing strong pressures from within the church and
from the community at large, the liberal elements tend to become a
confused, ineffectual, and perhaps disillusioned body.

It is obvious that the needs of these several groups are not mutually
complementary. The minister, whatever his intention or desire, is
in the familiar position of the man in the middle, unable to be all
things to all men. Whatever decision he makes, certain risks must
be borne. He may drive away from the church, or otherwise alienate,
those whom he most wants to reach as an "over the long haul" target
group. On the other hand he may fail to influence the undecided
by attempting to maintain contact with the extremely bigoted. Again
he may introduce disillusionment and confusion among liberals who
under more positive, vigorous guidance would become an effective
force for peaceful social change inside and outside the church. Or,
faced with these conflicting choices, he may pursue a passive course
as presenting the least evil. Since the same tactics have different
and sometimes opposite effects on different groups, his choice between the sledge hammer and the velvet glove is a crucial decision.

7. Finally, with special reference to activity during a period of
heavy crisis, the minister who favors integration must face the broader
question of timing in addition to questions of frequency and force.

Let us say that the pastor looks back on a set of purposes and a
coordinated activities program that he has inaugurated for his church,
and that he projects these into the future in the form of an anticipated
series of progressive achievements. Specifically, let us say that there
are certain things in race attitudes and racial cooperation in his church
that he has already achieved and others that he expects to achieve.
Then a crisis of immediate relevance, such as the Little Rock situation,
confronts the community and the church. What effect does this
crisis have on his program, and how shall he relate it to his larger
purposes?

The theoretical range of choices here is broad. There may be
vigorous attention to the issue during the period of crisis on the twin
assumptions that during the period of high salience "right thinkers"
need reinforcement and "wrong thinkers" must be influenced. At
the other extreme, he may completely avoid the topic during the
crisis on the assumption that "minds are closed," tempers run high,

and the risk of alienating "wrong thinkers" from eventual influence is too great.

In this connection, it is instructive to note that advisers and teachers caution the young minister on the need to become fully conversant with a congregation's mood before initiating new programs. This policy when followed may pay off indefinitely in an effective and appreciated ministry. Precisely because it brings such gratifying returns, however, there is a real risk that, with the passage of time, the minister becomes less and less likely to initiate programs that deviate seriously from the congregation's expectations. First, he has developed an effective relationship with his members while not offending their tastes. Second, subtle but effective role-expectations have arisen in the congregation which tend to continue the pastor in the role that met with their approval during earlier efforts. [14]

These observations suggest the basic proposition that any disturbance or crisis that affects the community or individual congregations poses a threat to the continuing institutional program of the church. They suggest also that the minister tends strongly to prefer calm water and to distrust controversy and disturbance. When controversy does appear in the community, he is likely to make the response he believes to be most appropriate to the early dissolution of the issue and the restoration of peace.

SUMMARY. In the South, where race relations have assumed such importance, the Christian minister must decide whether the problem is a religious one, and, if it is, he must determine what type of social system, segregated or otherwise, is required by the Christian ethic. It then becomes his task to communicate his convictions to his membership.

If he decides he cannot in good conscience accept a segregated society, his convictions run counter to those of his southern audience, and his task is not to reinforce but to challenge the attitudes of his listeners—a delicate matter in communications and one that becomes extremely delicate when, as in Little Rock, public events and political decisions create a racial crisis. The minister must preserve a church fellowship while applying a Christian judgment that violates values held by members of the fellowship. He must determine what to say, how and to whom to say it. These difficult decisions involve matters of timing, targets, frequency, force, and goals.

Many Little Rock ministers in the fall of 1957 believed that segrega-

tion is neither consistent nor compatible with the Christian message.
Faced with their greatest challenge, in a community in which organized liberal leadership was sorely needed to restore order while respect-
ing the legal rights of Negro citizens, most of Little Rock's ministers
assumed equivocal, cautious positions. Chaos in liberal sentiments
became one of the tragedies of the fall's events. Why did the liberal
ministry, reinforced by the strong stands of major religious bodies
at national and regional levels, fail to become a rallying center for
integrationists, as a conservative ministry had become a focal point
for segregationists?

The explanation lies in the nature of the ministerial role and the
pressures that influence it. It seems clear that in the absence of negative reactions from their congregations many ministers would have
taken effective action to secure a peaceful and numerically significant
integration of the city's school facilities. Given various negative
reactions, however, the minister became increasingly aware of his
responsibility to preserve the church as a church, that is, to maintain
church unity and with it an institutional program. Our analysis
suggests that certain institutional characteristics cause the responsibility to preserve a frictionless congregation to take precedence over
any desire to effectuate social reform. It further suggests that certain
institutional arrangements, working propositions, communication techniques, and reactions of segregation extremists help the minister to
manage his guilt while maintaining his inaction.

CHAPTER SIX

THE CRISIS CONTINUES: "THINGS LEFT UNDONE"

"Little Rock has been badly scarred—economically, morally, spiritually, historically. But it can serve as an example and a lesson. . . . As this crisis continues, it becomes more apparent that the tragedy that makes men weep is the recollection of things left undone; and the realization that centuries of hatred could be unleashed with so little effort."

A LITTLE ROCK CITIZEN, 1958

Further insight into Little Rock's situation can be gained by reviewing the later behavior of the city's ministry, especially in the fall of 1958 when Governor Faubus closed the high schools in order to prevent continued integration.

Was the cautious equivocation and silent assent of 1957 a harbinger of things to come? Or had accumulated frustrations and a deepening despair led some to determine that there were things they must do and say despite the risks?

Generally, the pulpits of Little Rock remained silent. Laymen expressed in very emphatic terms their preferences in this connection. Ministers had been asked to "lay off the subject." During the winter, spring, and summer of 1958 one could attend virtually any church in the city and not hear the slightest reminder that the nation's most critical racial impasse was continuing. The silence was especially marked in the larger, more influential churches.

However, a few ministers worked quietly behind the scenes to support such organizations as the Arkansas Council on Human Relations. Several have attended unpublicized interracial meetings designed to keep open at least some meager lines of communication between the races. Publicity about these activities has been carefully avoided. There have been reports that "cells" have been organized in some churches to discuss the city's crisis, but investigation has disclosed that the extent, continuity, and effectiveness of these groups has been negligible.

While ministerial silence continued, the forces of defiance and segregation grew stronger, and the forces of "law and order" and desegregation became weaker.

By the beginning of 1959 there had been significant changes

in Little Rock's ministerial personnel. At least nine local clergymen had left their pulpits as a reasonably direct result of the
integration conflict. As the reader might expect, the ranks of the
innovators (Chapter Four) have been especially affected by these
changes. Rarely, of course, was disaffection with the minister's racial
activities the stated reason for his departure. Fellow ministers on the
inside know, however, and the lesson is plain for all to see. If the
techniques employed in the quiet removal of a minister who needs
to "grow in wisdom" are somewhat obscure they are nevertheless
instructive.

At least one denomination has had an unusually large number of
quiet transfers and others are in prospect. The denomination structure is such that the means for change of locale are readily available.
Not a word is said about the minister's stand on the integration question. Usually nothing at all is said or it is simply announced that a
routine change is in order. If more explanation is sought, the minister is told: "You have lost the respect of your members", "You no
longer do effective work in your present location," or, "You need a
chance to increase your wisdom and broaden your experience." Those
clergymen who had remained silent or were not involved in Little
Rock's crisis continue to retain their appointments or are given more
attractive positions. Those who had expressed their Christian convictions forcibly do not fare nearly so well. It is not necessary for
administrative officials to spell out the meaning of their policy: those
ministers who have lost members during the past two years have
clearly suffered the consequences.

The most dramatic case of loss of position, involving the most active
innovator, has occurred in a congregationally organized denomination.
As is typical in such cases, every effort was made to secure his departure without forcing his resignation. He was told at a meeting of his
official church board that, what with attendance and contributions
dwinding, economies were in order, and where better to start than
with the preacher's salary. They would, in fact, be required to trim
his salary by 30%—from $6,000 to $4,200. The minister pled that
his reduced pay would not be sufficient to meet his obligations to his
family. He was then told that other means would be sought for effecting economies. Reassuringly, he was given a vote of approval, affec-
tion, and confidence. From then on, however, his best friends did the
work of securing his transfer; his enemies said not a word to him.
Laymen whom he trusted urged him to seek another post, pointing
to the increasing crisis in the church as instanced by dwindling attend-

ance and financial boycotts certain members had instituted. He was told that members complained because he gave too much time to "community affairs" and that matters had become "embarrassing" to his staunchest supporters. Gradually he was prevailed upon to leave Little Rock for a comparable post in a border-state parish.

In an urbanized community adjacent to Little Rock one congregation has been more blunt in protesting their minister's support of public school desegregation. Their protest was submitted to the chief administrative officer in the area. The minister involved was not told to modify his stand. In fact, not a word was said. His superior officer recommended him to another parish, which in turn approached him with an invitation; whereupon the administrator counselled him to accept. He is now in a northern state. His superior's reason for arranging the transfer was a simple one. It was not because the pastor was considered to be an integrationist, nor because he had expressed himself within the context of the local controversy. Indeed, his superior was himself outstanding among the city's clerics in denouncing those who cite the Bible in support of segregation. But the minister had been unable to state his convictions and at the same time maintain harmony within his parish. Harmony had to be retained.

The innovator's difficulties are in part the responsibility of liberal laymen in the city's larger churches, particularly those who were disturbed by the caution of their ministers. The innovator hoped in vain that the city's liberals would reinforce him in his efforts to maintain a congregation while preaching his convictions. In the past year he has seen disaffected segregationists depart to seek more congenial church homes but this trend has not been counter balanced by a movement of liberal elements into his church. Generally, the effect of member realignments has been to increase the segregationist's congregation and decrease the innovator's; the inactives and the influentials remain relatively unaffected. Transfers and forced resignations, the impact of these changes on those who remained, and the lack of reinforcement from liberal lay persons in the community have deepened the despair of the innovators. No recruits have joined their ranks from among inactives or ministerial newcomers; and only one influential has provided encouragement.

Significant action from the city's influentials could not be expected. They were less active by the fall of 1958 than in the preceding fall. Today they have a firmer rationale for their inaction. They have observed the polarization of public opinion; they have seen the spectre of divided congregations and dismissed pastors. Important lay leaders and official boards have urged them not to "embarrass" church members. Perhaps this was the advice of friends; perhaps it was a suggestion or a warning. Members have come to them and bluntly said: "We've had enough; we simply do not want to hear 'the situation' discussed any more." Participants in vigorous segregation groups have not hesitated to identify specific ministers and announce their intention to "rid the city of them."

In September 1957, when the crisis broke, there was some prospect that a statement of conscience would commit the influentials and other clerics following their lead to a stand on principle and a course of action from which they would not retreat and to which their members simply would have to reconcile themselves. That prospect has dissipated entirely. In 1957 the influential's sense of obligation to fulfill a mission, to express the Christian absolute, was relatively prominent in his thinking; obligations to respect his members' values and to preserve the church in harmony were not so clearly thought out. But after a year of problems, he was acutely conscious of these latter obligations; they had become salient values for him. If the compulsion to state the moral imperative in forceful, challenging terms remained important to him it was only in the more remote recesses of his awareness.

There are a few important exceptions to the pattern of relative inaction among the city's leading ministers. As they came forward in 1957 to defend "law and order" but not desegregation, so in 1958 some defended public education when school closing threatened. In advance of a referendum on September 27, 1958, at which voters expressed a preference for no public schools rather than desegregated schools, several leading ministers appeared on a television program sponsored by the local Women's Emergency Committee to Open Our Schools. The Episcopal Bishop, the Methodist Bishop, the new president of the ministerial association, and another prominent pastor were participants on these panels.

Moreover, some of the Presbyterian ministers aroused the ire of Governor Faubus. On September 16, 1958, the Governor was asked whether he knew that the local Washburn Presbytery planned to ask him to revoke his proclamation blocking the beginning of the school term. He replied: "I would not be surprised at that. I am aware that a large number of ministers in the Presbyterian church have been very effectively brainwashed." The Governor further stated that the brainwashing had been accomplished by "left-wingers and Communists" and let it be known that some of the clergymen were "left-wingers." The Presbyterian ministers demanded an apology they did not receive. The following Sunday, the ministerial association's president, a Southern Baptist, urged his congregation to vote for public schools "even if it means integration."

But to say that pastors and ecclesiastica have done their best to steer clear of the desegregation controversy is not to say that their churches are not involved. When the public high schools were closed two of the city's leading Baptist churches made their educational facilities available to the newly formed, private Baptist High School. The Episcopal Interim Academy was opened at the Episcopal Cathedral and the city's leading Methodist church was used for tutorial sessions. Other churches set up their own educational plans. The ministers of these churches may not have been without misgivings in permitting the use of church property for this purpose. Some knew that they were in the morally untenable position of operating a segregated private school, and that any success they had in operating these schools would to that extent lessen the public pressure to reopen the public schools; therefore they had a part, however small, in foiling federal court orders. But they knew also that educational careers had been disrupted, with job and college entrance opportunities threatened. Both the Baptist High School and the Episcopal Academy announced that their classes would be discontinued when the public schools reopened. It remained to be seen how strong segregationist pressure would be to make the church schools permanent.

In addition to these efforts of individual churches to meet the educational needs of their young people, the new educational building of the Highland Methodist Church is available to the Faubus-spawned Little Rock Private School Corporation, which uses the facilities for its tenth grade courses. The corporation pays only the utility bills of the building in return for its use.

Since segregationist forces have continued to increase their strength in the community, the liberal minister has found himself under tremendous pressure. He feels fortunate to hold his own. Though it is difficult to cover the range of these pressures, the following items, from among many, may suggest the subtlety of the pressure.

1. The Pulaski Heights Methodist Church is proud of its Raney Lectures endowment fund, which each year brings in a nationally prominent religious figure for a public lecture. Dr. T. J. Raney is the president of the Little Rock Private School Corporation, an agency established by the Arkansas governor as a means of preventing desegregated schools in Little Rock. His family endowed the lectures.

In honor of its board president, Little Rock's private school was named Raney High School. Thus Pulaski Heights Methodist Church has its Raney Lectures and the segregationists of Little Rock have their Raney High School.

2. The superintendent of the corporation's private school, which taught over 1,000 students during the 1958-59 school year, is a member of the board of deacons at a prominent local church. Some may see a touch of irony in the fact that he is one of the teachers of the Brooks Hays Bible Class at that church.

3. The president of the Southern Baptist Convention, Brooks Hays, was defeated in 1958's elections. He was up for a ninth term in the United States House of Representatives. The victor was Dr. Dale Alford, an eleventh-hour write-in candidate who charged that Hays was "too staunch a moderate" on the desegregation issue. Dr. Alford is a lay reader and past senior warden in the Episcopal Church. In October 1958, he was one of four Arkansas lay delegates to the triennial convention of the Episcopal Church in the United States.

4. The Methodist Episcopal Church South, the Methodist Protestant Church, and the Methodist Episcopal Church USA united into one body a scant 20 years ago (in 1939). A Council of Methodist Laymen, which spoke threateningly of the need for formation of a new Methodist Church South, was formed in Little Rock in the fall of 1958. Stout segregation sentiments were expressed at the organizational meeting, attended by some 300 persons, including prominent Methodist lay leaders. Sentiments were voiced that their "ministers' minds were befuddled."

5. At a public meeting on the evening of November 14, 1958, Jimmie Karam, crony and clothier to Governor Faubus, announced his candidacy for the Little Rock School Board. An invocation was delivered by the pastor of Little Rock's First Evangelical Methodist Church, who declared his unrestrained support for Karam's program of segregation.[1] The day following, a prominent layman in a leading church told his liberal-but-silent pastor, "would that my preacher stood with the South like that preacher."

6. During the fall of 1958, nationally publicized efforts were made by a few Negroes to attend several white religious services in Little Rock. These Negroes were turned away from churches whose pastors had told us that they had adopted a policy of admitting all comers. In at least one instance, the pastor (an innovator) was not told by his ushers that Negroes had appeared; only later did he learn that the visitors had been turned away without his bring consulted.

Such matters multiply. Together they mount to a crescendo of discomfort for any minister who in any manner whatever has suggested his sympathy for desegregation in the public schools.

Tentative Hypotheses. Since all of the findings of this study have been presented, some tentative hypotheses can now be proposed. First, however, a closer analysis of the Protestant minister's role is necessary to gain the proper perspective for these hypotheses.

In modern mass society there are numerous individuals and organizations whose primary concern is with some portion of the public. They wish to influence, change, even to control. In fact, survival of the individuals as role-persons and of the organizations as institutional entities depends on their success in exercising a continuing influence over public behavior. Of imperative importance for this influence is the ability to establish and maintain satisfactory communication patterns.

One thinks of the cigarette manufacturer who must persuade a smoking public his product is superior to those of competitors; of the college professor whose lectures must be palatable enough to induce students to attend his courses; of the politician who must somehow be able to persuade voters he deserves another term in office; and of the operator of the used-car lot who can stay in business only if he can convince a reasonable number of people that his bargains are better than those offered down the street. There are countless such examples.

All who are dependent on some portion of the public run the risk of offending it. Precautions to avoid offense may sometimes reach extreme proportions. Witness, for example, the care that sponsors of network radio and TV programs exercise against the possibility that program scripts contain offensive or controversial materials.

The situations of the many persons concerned with the response of some part of the public are not all identical, of course. As a first distinction, it is obvious that the reason for "pleasing the public" varies according to the circumstance. For some, a positive public response itself may be viewed as a basic goal of activity since the rewards sought inevitably accompany such response. Thus, the movie star who pleases his public is assured that his movies will sell. He is successful by definition when his public is numerous and happy. For others, however, a positive public response presumably is but a necessary means to another and essentially independent end. The public's response to the person's behavior is not in itself the desired goal. Thus the newspaper editor may want to influence public opinion in order to contribute toward a constructive foreign policy, and a public that buys his papers is necessary to this venture. The lecturer is dedicated to the spread of information which he cannot disseminate if he fails to arouse and hold the interest of his public. In these cases, the public response is desired because there are superordinate goals which can be obtained only with proper public reactions.

Another distinction involves whether the person or organization acts as an agent for its public. The public-office holder acts as the representative of the voters in his district; he is bound by the definition of his role to respect their wishes and act in their interest; he is an agent. This is not true of, say, the cigarette manufacturer. However much he emphasizes his dependence on his public, he acts as an agent for his own interests, and he uses his public, or rather, obliges his public in order to use it.

There is a third distinction. Some agents assume in relations with their public an obligation to guide, direct, and improve either the public itself or some group for which the public is responsible. There is a sense of mission and of service, often involving a moral dimension. This is implicit, for example, in the work of welfare agencies, when the agencies must serve those who want help. And the teacher is concerned with bringing moral as well as material uplift to his students. There are contrasting themes in the occupational ideology of politicians, but many see their responsibility as more than mirroring public opinion. They believe they must creatively lead by opposing currently popular beliefs and practices that seem undesirable.

In one sense the unsettling effects of controversy affecting various segments of the public are viewed with suspicion by all of the persons and agencies mentioned. Controversial issues over which large numbers of people become concerned, divided, and emotionally aroused threaten the security of those who function in the public eye. They pose, in fact, an unavoidable problem. Even though the public figure remains aloof from the issue, he may inadvertently become identified with one side or the other. If he occupies a certain position in the community, he is almost certain to be pressured by opposing factions to declare himself. Yet to do so may damage his ability to function. Because of these considerations, he is often under pressure to avoid becoming personally involved in controversies. He must prevent divisons in the public to or for which he is responsible. The

anch manager is cautioned not to get involved in local fights, and
ore than one physician has avoided declaring himself on the fluorida-
n issue.

Nonetheless decisions are made and issues are resolved. Despite
l of the reasons public figures may have for avoiding offense, despite
l of the dangers that lie in the unequivocal advocacy of solutions
at are unpalatable to segments of a relevant public, policies are
tablished on which leadership has exerted influence.

It is important to understand the means public figures use to in-
ence the dissolution of controversial issues. When does the person
ho sits in the seat of influence work publicly to secure some goal
owever controversial it may be? When does he seek his aims through
ehind-the-scenes manipulation? And when does he run for cover?
nder what circumstances can we expect the main-street business-
an to defend a cause he believes to be just at the risk of offending
ustomers? When will the public-office holder seek a referendum on
question he has the power to decide himself? On what issues, or
nder what circumstances, will an issue be fought out at the front
nes of leadership, with the most prominent citizens involved? And
n what issues is the matter settled by scuffles at minor levels of
ower? These questions are basic to the dynamics of a democratic
ociety.

These general areas of interest led to our study of ministerial
ction in a period of community crisis. Several considerations seemed
o make the minister an especially significant object of study. To
eview certain highly significant features of the occupational role of
ninisters will be useful at this point.

A minister is, in the first place, an employee. His congregation pays
is salary and, in many instances, provides his housing. In return
he minister assumes certain obligations to this congregation. There
re easily verbalized and explicit expectations—he visits the sick, con-
ucts funerals and weddings on request, and delivers sermons on
Sunday mornings. There are other less tangible and less easily ver-
alized expectations—for example, how closely his sermons should
onsist of Biblical exposition, and when he should become involved in
ffairs outside the parish. It is obvious that the public he must please
s his congregation. If he fails, the congregation may request and
secure his release.

The minister is also the advocate of the spiritual and the moral, in
contrast to the material and the expedient. His is one of the few professional roles that by common agreement as well as by self definition

is dedicated to an absolute and timeless ideology, to principle rath
than to the propitious. The nature of his work implies that what
advocates is not yet in fact attained by those to whom he commen
it. Implicitly, then, he deals in criticism. The individuals to who
he speaks, like the society in which they live, are not yet perfect.
commends to them attitudes and behavior from which they dai
depart. He tries, as a part of this effort, to set a standard of justi
and equity for those in other positions of public leadership.

Another significant characteristic of the ministerial role is that th
minister must "go to press" every Sunday. That is to say, similar 1
the newspaper editor and distinct from many others, he must mak
regular appearances before his public. He is, in other words, high
visible. A corollary of his high visibility is his easy accessibilit;
People who wish to see him need only stop at his office or request tha
he call on them. In conference, the area of discourse is not restricte
any topic is open to discussion. Accessibility increases vulnerabilit
In his open exposure to immediate criticism, the minister contrast
sharply to, say, the industrial plant manager, who is protected fror
those under him by the physical arrangement of the plant, by estab
lished patterns of intraplant interaction, and by the fact that he i
the employer rather than the employed.

The minister is intensely involved in the parish and the community
His career advancement depends on the type of immediate interper
sonal response he obtains from local groups. In this sense, circum
stances require that he be a localite rather than a cosmopolite. [2] Un
like the executive of a large corporation, who depends for his caree
advancement on his superiors rather than on local individuals o
institutions, the minister rises or falls with the response of the loca
congregation and community. [3]

These are features that are crucially important to understandin
the behavior of the minister during community crises. To commi
oneself on an issue is to risk defeat; and to be defeated is to lose status
Yet there is a difference between taking a beating on an issue an
taking a beating simply because of one's stand. The latter concerns
the liberal minister in Little Rock. He has a personal protectio
against the former because, like his peers elsewhere, he admits tha
the forces of evil are strong and will win many battles. He is psychologically prepared for defeat on moral issues—liquor, sex, gambling,
immodesty, apathy to religion—for he has tasted defeat on such
matters before and expects to again. He knows that many who
listen reject his premises and his values. To this defeat, too, he is

econciled. But he is neither reconciled nor accustomed to contro-
ersy and rejection simply because he has taken a stand on a morally
elevant issue. Nor is he accustomed to personal abuse for attacking
vil. It appears, then, that it was not the anticipation of failure that
aused him to seem timid in supporting desegregation; rather, it was
he consequences he faced for taking his stand. Perhaps he did antic-
pate rejection, even opposition, from those vigorously and emotion-
lly opposed to his position. What he did not anticipate, however, was
he negative response of those who wish to preserve harmony within
he church, of those who prefer to say that race is not a religious issue,
nd of those whose associates chide them about belonging to his
church. As the Little Rock crisis developed and deepened, the liberal
minister who stated his case found he was approved and supported
only by those who place certain goals in race reform above their personal convenience and above the unity and growth of the church.
This number was not large. Essentially, then, his problem rested in
his communicants' unwillingness to accept the ministerial role and
the Christian message as he wished to define them.

It is difficult to emphasize sufficiently the significance of this lack of
support from his membership. To trace adequately the personal base
of his need for support is beyond our focus. No doubt some readers
will see in it clear evidence of the success motif operating in the
ministry. They will say that the minister seeks fame and glory,
material comfort and worldly prominence, and that he desires a large
church and a massive budget because these are obvious means to
such ends. They will say that he stands ready to compromise whenever the literal service of principle obstructs him in these goals. Or
they will say simply that he does not want to lose his job.

The success motif may be operating. However, that is not a
satisfactory explanation. The answer seems to lie more clearly in
the accumulated weight of years of training and experience in what
may be termed the central ethos of the ministerial profession. The
eyes of the minister are trained to turn constantly outward toward
people, toward numbers. He must help people, guide them, win
them. Their response becomes a measure of his personal worth.
When the plates and the pews are full, and the bricks for the new
wing are stacked outside, the evidence of a job well done is all too
tangible. When old members greet him warmly and newcomers
respond to his invitation to join his flock, he has a sense of well-being.
It is not necessary to posit a worldly success motif nor a calculating,
self-seeking design, to understand this response. It can be viewed

as a logical outgrowth of the types of professional criteria he has accepted as a part of himself. His training teaches him to rest the case for his personal competence on the responses people make to his ministry. He becomes, in this sense, the embodiment of David Riesman's other-directed person.[4] It follows, then, that any persistent defection in the ranks—whether it takes the minor form of tension and surliness, the more threatening form of absenteeism and tight wallets, or the most serious form of an organized resistance movement that aims to oust the minister—is a shattering personal experience. Not necessarily, we repeat, because he sees his personal life-goals becoming more elusive; rather, because according to the institutional norms that he has long accepted, he is incompetent, a failure. Why? Because the message he delivers is no longer attractive to people. Thus he is no longer attractive to people.

There is a significant anomaly here. It would seem that the successful minister is psychologically the most vulnerable of all to discord and dissension in his membership. The aging pastor to whom success has been evasive has had time through the years of rebuke and mediocrity to develop a perspective that protects him from self-condemnation when he does not achieve the public response the successful minister expects routinely. The fresh young seminary graduate may well carry the lamp of world uplift through uncompromised principle so eagerly that he sees in public distaste for his message only a measure of the size of his task. The successful, prominent minister, on the other hand, has been reinforced throughout his professional career by the positive response of members and prospects. These are the terms by which he evaluates himself. To him least of all is the negative response tolerable. Yet he is the best equipped by talent and position to take the strong, unequivocal stand. If he leads, others follow. If he hesitates, others falter. Herein lies the anomaly: those most qualified for effective leadership in crisis are those most vulnerable to its perils. Their vulnerability, we see now, is psychological as well as institutional.

A young minister has this to say: "I talk to the young ministers and I ask them why they aren't saying anything. They say no one will listen to them, they aren't known and their churches are small. But wait, they say, until we get big churches and are widely known. We won't be silent then. Then I turn to the ministers in the big churches and I listen to them trying to explain why they have done so little. Their answer is a simple one; they say they have too much to lose. Only recently, one such man said to a group I was in, 'I've spent seventeen years of my life in building up that church, and I'm not going to see it torn down in a day.' "

Despite the anomalies and the conflicts, despite the explanations for hesitant commitments or cautious inactions, some ministers have taken positions that were unpalatable to many of their constituents. The pattern of ministerial response was not as homogeneous as the preceding paragraphs may suggest. We cannot, then, be content to explain the bases for caution and withdrawal. Our further task is to identify the variables—personal, congregational, institutional—that seem to affect the nature and extent of the minister's response to racial crisis.

This statement of the relationship between variables and behavior can best be made in the form of hypotheses, which may serve as a summary of many of our observations. The reader is cautioned against seeking anything final in them. They are simply a convenient way of presenting the impressions and observations that emerge from this study. The extent to which they apply to ministers in other areas of the South, and to persons in different occupational roles and other types of situations, awaits further research.

The hypotheses rest on two major assumptions.

(a) Most southern ministers in the major denominations are willing to accept gradual public school desegregation; probably most of them believe it to be a Christian imperative. This assumption is supported by the *Pulpit Digest's* poll, based on a 1958 random sample, which indicated that four out of five Protestant denominational clergymen in the South approve of the racial desegregation of schools. [5]

(b) There is a point at which the minister's defense of desegregation becomes costly to his parish. Segregationist members of the congregation will pressure him to be silent on the subject, and, if he is not, depending on the intensity of their attitudes, they will withdraw from or stop giving to the church.

Given Christian ministers who see race as religiously relevant and who personally accept and favor desegregation, our basic interest is to account for variations in behavior that support these convictions. These are our hypotheses:

1. *The support of desegregation is less in times of racial crisis than in times of noncrisis.* Many Little Rock ministers have carefully retreated from exposed positions since September 1957. Before that time they encouraged in church-sponsored affairs a variety of interracial contacts that promoted an increase in racial tolerance. They managed these activities without undue opposition, sometimes with

enthusiastic response. Such efforts were not, however, good predictors of their behavior during the crisis. As the issue increased in salience and the lines hardened in the community at large, the ministry became less supportive of interracial contacts and desegregation efforts. They suffered abuse at the hands of rabid segregationists after September, but by and large the abuse represented a carryover of hostility for previous policies.

2. *The support of desegregation during a crisis period is not a variable directly linked to social class.* The higher the social class level of both the congregation and general membership of the denomination, the more likely the pastor is to favor integration. And if he is pastor of an exclusively lower or working-class church, he is very likely to favor segregation. But the class characteristics of the church do not seem to be good predictors of the minister's action in support of desegregation although they are reasonably good predictors of his private attitude.

3. *The more popular the denomination in the local area, the less likely are its ministers to defend positions not accepted by local public opinion.* Ministers in the numerically dominant denominations are those least likely to censure the great population mass from which their membership is drawn. This is a way of suggesting again the anomaly we have noted — that ministers in the positions of greatest potential influence are the ones least likely to attempt its exercise.

4. *The minister is less likely to support desegregation during a crisis if no ministerial figures of high prestige in his denomination lead the way.* These prestige figures may be ecclesiastical officials in the case of denominations that have this form of church polity. In such cases, pastors expect guidance from their superiors as to their own proper conduct. This guidance in its simplest and most effective form is the public statements and activity of the superior. In addition to the church hierarchy, there are religious leaders whose prestige is not vested with the robes of formal office. Often, these patterns of informal leadership are not restricted by denominational loyalties. Such men receive the respect and adulation of their ministerial peers. When they are silent, their silence influences pastors over whom they have no formal control. When they are vocal and active, others may be expected to support the pace they set.

5. *With an increase in the number of years that the minister has served his congregation, there is a decrease in the probability that he will support desegregation during a crisis.* The explanation seems to lie partly in the network of personal relations the minister develops

over the years. Parishioners form an increasingly rigid image of the pastor and his expected behavior. The pastor reciprocates with an image of himself that in large part reproduces member expectations. The mold becomes harder to break. The pastor feels an ever-increasing obligation to respect the preferences and expectations of his members, to continue an ongoing system of relationships. The new pastor, by contrast, is not so thoroughly entwined in these systems of subtle pressure. While he is governed by general normative systems that define the conduct of pastor and congregation vis-a-vis each other, he is in a position to exploit the more idealistic aspects of these norms.

A part of the explanation lies also in the pastor's increasing identification with his parish as a going concern. Each year means another year of his life that has gone into developing and maintaining it. To risk its decline is to deny the worth of what he has worked to build. Increasingly he hesitates to vary from established patterns, and increasingly he is committed to conserve that which he has.

6. *The minister is less likely to support desegregation during a crisis period if he is over 50 than if he is under 40.* This is a regularity that emerges from our data. But its significance is not altogether clear. It may be due in part to an increasing social consciousness in the training of recent seminary graduates or to more general changes in public opinion. It may be that this hypothesis is to a large extent a corollary of the previous hypothesis. Older ministers hold the more prominent appointments, and therefore risk more by acting. Probably all of these factors play some part.

7. *The minister's support of desegregation is less if his church is engaged in a membership drive, building program, or fund-raising campaign than if it is not so engaged.* We come again to a vital point in the analysis. The minister hopes to maximize the number who are fully participating members of his church. There are certain times when he is acutely aware of the need to secure the maximum response from the maximum number of people. During these crucial times he takes all available steps to soothe hurt feelings, settle old resentments, and avert possible controversy. There are very few places in the South where the minister can secure a more favorable response from a large number for the straightforward defense of desegregation than for silence or cautious platitude. Were such places more frequent, the number of ministers voicing liberal sentiments would be larger.

8. *Given two churches of comparable size and drawing members from the same social class, the one a neighborhood church and the*

*other a community-wide church, the pastor of the latter is the less
likely of the two pastors to support desegregation during a crisis period.*
The pastor of a community church serves as a catalyst to a larger
number of interests in his congregation. His members only infrequently contact each other in their daily rounds. Faced with the need to
reconcile a greater diversity of interests, and finding that members
do not often see each other outside church, the minister finds it more
difficult to control negative responses to his personal activities.
Realizing these difficulties, he is less likely to assume avoidable risks.

9. *The minister whose orientation is primarily to his parish is less
likely to support desegregation than the minister who is oriented to
the community at large.* We greatly oversimplify when we speak
of parish-oriented and community-oriented ministers in any absolute
sense. Clearly there are many shadings and degrees of these differences. Nevertheless, there are those who restrict their obligations
almost exclusively to the affairs of their church and its members, as
there are those who assume an obligation to be active in civic affairs
and to voice the Christian witness in community issues.[°] By its
nature, the issue of public school desegregation involves complex
political and social matters, and the character of secular educational
institutions; it may touch the churches only as a secondary effect.
The parish-oriented minister may take the position that he ought not
be an advocate so long as he sees nothing remiss in the conduct of
his own members. Those who are community-oriented, however,
are more likely to enter the fray as a symbol of the Christian social
conscience.

10. *The more stable the membership of his church, the less likely
is the minister to support desegregation during a crisis period.* When
the membership is continuous, a strong lay leadership develops that
in some sense may be said to challenge the minister's own position
as church leader. A sense of "our church" develops that to some
extent is independent of the minister's own program and preference.
At the very least, he must recognize this leadership and work with
and through it to achieve the goals he sets. When there is rapid turnover, it is less easy for laymen to represent themselves as voicing the
mind of the membership.

11. *The freedom of the minister to defend desegregation is more
restricted if he was born and educated outside the South than if he is
a social and educational product of the region.* This statement probably needs careful qualification. When the emotional fervor accompanying a social movement becomes so intense that all who defect

from the cause are defined in traitorous terms, then the home-grown deviant can be rejected as a quisling and a turncoat.[7] When freedom is absent, patently neither this nor any other variable distinguishes persons by degree of freedom. In less intense periods, however, the segregationist finds the local product more persuasive than the imported leader, for he cannot charge that the former fails to understand the problem. The outsider is acutely aware that he is vulnerable to this charge, as he is aware that the response to him may be, "Yankee, go home." This combination of factors—the outsider's self-imposed hesitancy to speak from limited knowledge, the local person's prerogative to speak "as one of you," and the segregationist's greater difficulty in attacking the locally rooted—seems to provide a rationale for the hypothesis.

12. *The less personally affected are the members of a congregation by the issue, the greater is the freedom of the minister to support desegregation during a crisis period.* In the broader sense, the minister in Butte, Montana, has more freedom to defend desegregation in Little Rock than the local minister. But even within the same urban community, not all citizens, not even all parents of school-age children, are equally affected by the desegregation process. Some schools or classes receive more Negro students than others; or Negro students are admitted to some schools but not to others. In Little Rock, Negroes were admitted to Central High but not to the newer, socially exclusive Hall High. Some parents may send their children to private schools or possess the means to do so if it becomes necessary. These suggest the possible differential salience of the desegregation effort. When the congregation feels less intimately involved in the situation, or when it sees the possibility of escape from the desegregated situation should it become personally intolerable, the minister has a greater freedom to give his support to the desegregation effort.

13. *Success (speaking numerically and financially) in the ministry is negatively related to the probability of strong advocacy of unpopular moral imperatives during crisis periods.* At least in Little Rock, ministers who took the lead in defending the continued presence of Negroes in Central High School tended to be younger men who were not pastors in the prominent churches of the city. Our data suggest that the larger the size and the greater the prominence of the church, the less likely is its pastor to engage in activities that seem to threaten its continued stability and growth. This seems to be related to having a greater investment, a sense of having more to lose.

14. *Ministers in the small, working-class sects will support segre-*

gation, and many of them will be publicly active in its defense. (The assumptions stated earlier for denominational pastors are not relevant to this final hypothesis.) We have commented earlier that should a minister of this type support racial desegregation, he would be so aberrant as to justify the most intensive scientific analysis. The extent of his action in support of his segregation values, however, may be in large part determined by the local situation. In Little Rock, not only did the segregationist minister have the encouragement of the political power of the state, but local moderates permitted him to define the battleground on his own terms. The experience of more peaceful communities, however, seems to indicate that the sect segregationist may not be vocal when moderate elements are in firm control.

These are the hypotheses. Hopefully, the research necessary to their proper test can be carried out. It is hoped as well that other research efforts may investigate their possible adaptation to different types of professional personnel and to other types of community crisis.

CHAPTER SEVEN

THE PROTESTANT DILEMMA:

"THE WAY UP IS THE WAY OUT"

"To advance your career in the ministry today you must succeed in an organizational way. You must get for your church a bigger building, more members, and more money. But to do this you have to dilute the gospel enough to insure its appeal for everybody—even sinners. ..As you advance, then, you must go out of God's favor. ..It looks like the way up is the way out."—A LITTLE ROCK MINISTER, 1958

A basic dilemma is posed for every social movement that attempts to influence society—whether it be a political party or a religious organization. At one extreme, the movement can hold uncompromisingly to its principles even at the cost of alienating most of its potential and needed adherents (the idealistic alternative). Or, at the other extreme, the movement can modify its ideals so sharply that it attracts a wide following but sacrifices its distinctive aims (the organizational alternative). Thus the problem for the movement becomes one of gaining power without surrendering the principles for which the power was originally sought.[1]

On the American political scene, militant third parties generally choose the former extreme; the two dominant parties choose the latter. In the religious realm, sociologist Milton Yinger has shown that the "sect type" religious bodies follow the idealistic approach and the "church type" bodies follow the organizational approach.[2]

The sect tends to have a small and disciplined membership, to combat the secular world defiantly with a firm and literally interpreted doctrine, and to appeal to the lower socioeconomic classes.[3] It often fails to gain influence by not organizing broadly. The church tends to have a large membership, to be adaptive, and to claim universality: "It dominates the world and is therefore dominated by the world."[4] It often loses its influence by sanctifying the status quo. Some balance of these two extremes seems most effective. Yinger in his analysis, *Religion in the Struggle for Power*, concludes that "religion maximizes its power as an agent in social change when the church and sect tendencies are combined by some kind of organizational principle."[5]

But this combination of tendencies is difficult to achieve, and modern Protestantism has not yet found the optimal balance. Many denomi-

nations in America are losing what sectarian elements they have left
and are becoming more completely "church type" in orientation. This
process has meant an ever-increasing base of support but an ever-
decreasing insistence on fundamental doctrine. Thus Protestantism
today is faced with the irony that while its memberhip rolls grow,
secular trends in America continue unabated.

Accompanying this denominational willingness to compromise with
the secular culture is a reluctance to support social reform—even
reform that is proclaimed by the churches themselves as consistent
with Christian principles. Reacting to this situation, Reinhold Niebuhr has urged a more socially aware Protestantism: "A Christian
pessimism . . . becomes a temptation to irresponsibility toward all
social tasks which constantly confront the life of men and nations . . .
The Christian gospel which transcends all particular and contemporary social situations can be preached with power only by a Church
which bears its share of the burdens of immediate situations in which
men are involved." [6]

Hesitancy toward social reform is enhanced by two basic aspects
of Protestantism: the responsibility placed in the individual and
the responsibility placed in the local church. Protestant individual-
ism, Liston Pope maintains, makes it "possible for a churchman to
delude himself into believing that the church is simply what he thinks
it is, and that it is his prerogative to define policies for his local
church." [7] This belief can in specific cases completely undercut a
church effort at reform in a realm of life in which particular members
have strong vested interests. The same can be true for local church
organization. Commenting specifically on the race issue and local
church autonomy, Niebuhr points out that "religiously sanctified racial
parochialism . . . has . . . been the negative by-product of one of
the genuine achievements of the sectarian church in our nation: the
creation of integral communities on the level of local congregations.
. . . . The actual 'chumminess' of the local congregation has invalidated the universal principle at the heart of the gospel. Particular
brotherhood, ethnically based, has invalidated the universal brotherhood implicit in the Christian ethic." [8]

Yet these tendencies can be exaggerated. Modern Protestantism
is not by any means a pure "church type"; a small sectarian cluster
within the denominations prevents a complete compromise with the
secular world so that "there remains an explosive element in Christianity which seems never to be completely bottled up." [9] We have
discussed how this "explosive element" is beginning to operate in

the desegregation controversy in the South, and have noted too that the church could become important in the process through its ability "to plant the seed of moral doubt." But this ability implies at least a modicum of sectarian zeal within the laity as well as the clergy. This brings the social movement dilemma down to its individual dimensions. Many Protestants want their religion to be alive and important in the rapidly changing world, but, at the same time, they would prefer for the church to compromise in those realms of life (like race) in which they have strong emotional involvements counter to religious doctrine.

The Little Rock Ministry and the Dilemma. Just how this dilemma operates in a specific crisis situation has been illustrated in detail in the present survey of the Little Rock ministry. We have seen that most of the community's denominational clergymen view racial integration as morally right and desire to do something about the conflict. But when they seek to exert their influence, the Protestant dilemma becomes sharply conspicuous. In Chapter Five we outlined three foci of the dilemma: the laity, the minister himself, and the institutional structure of Protestantism.

All of our available data indicate that the large majority of the Christian laymen in Little Rock desired that their churches not take a stand on the city's integration issue. Significantly enough, they did not demand that their ministers publicly defend segregation but only that they remain silent. This concession in itself is tribute to the fact that they realize a religious defense of segregation from their clergy would be too much to expect. Their insistence that the ministry remain silent, however, had real teeth in it: decreased contributions, lowered attendance, and even removal of particularly offending clergymen (Chapter Six). Perhaps, the full realization that they cannot expect lay support for their new role as social reformers is the most alarming aspect of the crisis to many of the Little Rock clergy. One Little Rock minister has written: "One of the most disappointing and frightening aspects of this task has been the realization by Little Rock clergymen of the position the Church actually holds in the eyes of so many in the world. . . . [The] staggering fact[is] that the Church is largely without influence in the day of society's trouble. . . . Thus, the ministers of Little Rock have been made to see that for a great many people, religion receives that tip-of-hat respect as for an aged gentleman who has been effective years past but who has nothing to say or to give to the present." [10]

The minister also finds himself unprepared for the new role. He is trained and experienced in the roles of coordinator, evangelist, and administrator. He knows what the specific criteria are for success in these roles. But he has no comparable training, experience, and criteria of success for the social reformer role. "Actually, we've been taught that controversy is un-Christian," pointed out one pastor. "I knew I should be doing something," confided another, "but I'm afraid I simply did not know what to do."

The internal sanction of guilt was allayed by the silent Little Rock ministers in a number of ways. First, since they had no concrete criteria of success as a social reformer, they could easily accept the sect segregationists' evaluation of themselves as firm integrationists. Second, the denominational clergyman usually operated on a number of (not necessarily incorrect) working propositions that protected him from guilt in the crisis situation: the efficacy of slow education rather than rapid conversion; the necessity to maintain close communication with the congregation at all costs; and the intrinsic value of preserved fellowship. Third, the minister frequently attempted to ease out of his dilemma by expressing his true feelings on race in such a manner as not to disturb his communicants. For this purpose he employed such communication devices as "every-man-a-priest," deeper issues, "God is watching," disparagement of segregationists, and exaggerated southerner techniques.

The last and possibly the most basic focus of the Protestant dilemma lies in the institutional structure of the denominations themselves. The role of social reformer is not nearly as institutionalized in Protestant structure as the organizational roles of the ministry. No clear sanctions, positive or negative, apply to this role within the church structure. Indeed, it was considered excellent by church superiors in Little Rock for a pastor to publicly advocate integration and simultaneously build up his church organizationally. But such an achievement is not possible when the great majority of churchgoers oppose such public action and apply negative sanctions against it. Defense of racial integration in Little Rock came to mean lost members, lost financial support, and a lost opportunity to build the proposed north wing. And these results were concrete evidence of a minister not performing his "proper" duties. The organizational aspects of "church type" Protestantism have become so important in comparison to social reform that failure in these administrative regards in Little

Rock frequently meant the removal of the minister. Church superiors, rather than protecting such men, keep a close eye on administrative records and usually act accordingly.

Thus the "church type" solution to the Protestant dilemma translated itself in this case into differential emphases and sanctions placed on the alternative roles available to the minister. Given this denominational structure, it was infinitely easier for the clergyman to continue on as the quiet and coordinating "shepherd of his flock" than to enter the conflict. If he remained silent, he received appreciation from his congregation for not being like the ministers "who dragged their churches into the whole mess," and he did not have to face the unaccustomed abuse from the community. But in taking this path of least resistance he ran the risk of becoming the tool of his parishioners. As one southern theologian has expressed it: "I often think, 'Am I the shepherd of my flock or its pet lamb?' "[11]

One of the "innovating" ministers of Little Rock summed up these structural restraints on clerical action as follows: "To advance your career in the ministry today you must succeed in an organizational way. You must get for your church a bigger building, more members, and more money. But to do this you have to dilute the gospel enough to insure its appeal for everybody—even sinners. As you advance, then, you must go out of God's favor. It looks like the way up is the way out."[12]

The most influential and the least active ministers illustrate the "church type," organizational approach to the Protestant dilemma most clearly (Chapter Four). Two other kinds of ministers in Little Rock, however, evidenced a rather sectarian, idealistic approach: the sect segregationists (Chapter Three) and the denominational innovators (Chapter Four).

Though on opposite sides of the conflict, these two ministerial types have definite similarities. Both believe that their religious principles compel them to voice strongly partisan views. Both feel that the issues involved are of deep moral significance. Both are usually confident that the Bible supports their position on the question. And neither is willing to let organizational demands stand in the way of their public actions.

Apart from these sectarian similarities, there are, of course, important differences between the groups. The segregationists represent churches which are almost prototypes of the "sect type." These small churches, predominantly lower class in membership, emphasize Biblical literalism, and encourage both fervor and congregational participation in their services.[13] The pastors themselves are isolated from and hostile to other religious and political views. They are poorly educated and consequently have no national or international perspective on their city's crisis. [14] Their open advocacy of segregation did not lead to conflict; their congregations, fellow ministers, and gospel interpretations all supported their stand. Indeed, some of them gained considerable acclaim outside their churches, acclaim that as sect leaders they were neither accustomed to nor prepared for.

The innovators constitute the "explosive element" among Little Rock's denominational clergy. Young and not long settled in the community, this ministerial type comes much closer than either the sect segregationists or his denominational colleagues to establishing a balance between the idealistic and organizational extremes of the Protestant dilemma. Perhaps his lack of experience and his smaller parish made it possible for him to disregard administrative concerns more than other denominational leaders. In any event, the failure of his protest movement in Little Rock offers evidence of the nonsectarian nature of modern Protestantism.

Future Desegregation and the Dilemma. Hypotheses concerning specific ministerial behavior in future desegregation crises have been advanced in Chapter Six. But in terms of the Protestant dilemma, a broader question needs to be asked: Will modern Protestantism regain enough sectarian zeal to command an effective part in the complex process of ending racial segregation? We concluded in Chapter One that "an aroused southern ministry . . . could become the next decade's most important agent of social change." But will it?

The major Protestant churches "have come to a remarkable degree of unanimity about the requirements of their faith in regard to racial questions." [15] A solid front of top-level pronouncements favoring racial integration have committed the church unequivocally. Encouraged by these statements, Negro Protestants are demanding aid for their cause from their fellow Christians. The Reverend Martin Luther King, Jr. voices their appeal when he says: "If ever the white ministers of the South decide to declare in a united voice the truth of the gospel on the question of race, the transition from a segregated to an integrated society will be infinitely smoother. . . . Here, then, is the hard challenge and the sublime opportunity: to let the spirit of Christ work toward fashioning a truly great Christian nation. If the church accepts the challenge with devotion and valor, the day will be speeded when men everywhere will recognize that they 'are all one in Jesus Christ.' " [16]

The successful efforts in race relations of the Roman Catholic Church provide further incentive for Protestant action and serve as reminders of what religion can do. [17] And Protestant theologians such as Reinhold Niebuhr furnish constant prods to the church by contending, for instance, that: "For every person who disavows religion because some ancient and unrevised dogma outrages his intelligence, several become irreligious because the social impotence of religion outrages their consciences." [18] Counter these many pressures for action with the forceful opposition of the southern laity, and you begin to appreciate how crucial the race issue has become for Protestantism.

The long-term course that the church follows in this realm will be largely determined by how it continues to meet the idealistic and organizational dilemma. If "church type" characteristics continue to dominate almost exclusively, if attracting more members and more money remain as the most important goals, then obviously Protestantism will not enter the integration conflict in any unified and effective manner. As in Little Rock, it will largely be left to the young clergymen of small parishes to implement in any way they can the lofty pronouncements made at the denominational conferences. Such a course on an issue as crucial as desegregation would signify to society that Protestantism can only proclaim, not act. In the terms of the dilemma, it would mean that the church had chosen to accept the solution of compromising completely with the secular world.

Effective involvement of the church in the race question necessitates a closer balance of sectarian and church qualities. To achieve this balance, the Little Rock findings suggest that changes would have to occur within the laity, within the clergy, and within the institutional structure of the denominations.

Two steps could be taken to win southern churchgoers' acceptance, if not approval, of a publicly active clergy.

First, issue a warning of impending ministerial action before any anticipated development of community tension. Once something is expected and assumed to be inevitable, it is more easily accepted when it comes. [19] The experience of the Little Rock ministry confirms this general principle. The minister who forthrightly tells his congregation how he feels and what he is going to do about racial desegregation before a crisis develops will neither shock nor outrage his laymen when he engages in public action. His communicants may not like it, but they will at least be steeled for it.

Second, work to achieve united clerical action; it is not only more effective but also better accepted by individual congregations. No solid, pro-integration ministerial front —neither all of the clergymen of one denomination nor through the ministerial association—was ever established in Little Rock. (The innovators tried to form this but failed.) As a result, the consequences of individual efforts were more devastating. "Why should our rector make such a public spectacle of himself and draw critical attention to our church when the Reverend Dr. X down the street has been so understanding and has not said anything during the crisis?" Strength in unity is illustrated in Dallas, where 300 white ministers of 13 Protestant denominations announced together that ". . . enforced segregation is morally and spiritually wrong." [20] In the face of this solid clerical block, what can a Protestant segregationist in Dallas say about his particular minister? Each of these clergymen made a public declaration, but no one man is conspicuous by his single statement. Thus the ministry acting early and together can establish lay acceptance of a more sectarian approach to social reform.

Clerical changes are also necessary to achieve idealistic and organizational balance. The minister will have to accept the responsibilities of a social reformer as seriously as he now does his coordinator, evangelist, and administrator roles. He will have to learn to overcome the lack of experience in his social reformer role in spite of unaccustomed abuse and no immediate rewards.

The clergyman has to question the applicability of some of his working propositions in these new situations. And he will have to reevaluate the effectiveness of his techniques for discussing race. Such radical readjustments are not easily made, but several considerations might be helpful. The Protestant minister has been taught to think in terms of individual effort and individual responsibility. But in the role of social reformer he will find that united action is necessary for complete effectiveness. Remembering that his role is partly a critical one by definition, he must move forcefuly enough to define the battle on his own terms.

Our review of the 1958 activities of the Little Rock ministry indicates clearly that silence allows segregationists to assume control of the entire situation. After this happens, all of the liberal clergy, innovators, influentials, and inactives alike, lose ground both in their churches and in the community. In defining the situation in their own terms, the clergy must invoke the moral imperative. In Little Rock, neither of the two major clerical moves—the condemnation of Faubus and the peace prayers—declared segregation morally wrong. Yet moral judgments are the unique source of ministerial influence. Ministerial social action as a reaffirmation of the distinctive features of Christianity requires the full force of moral sanctions. Community action directly supported by the denominations' moral pronouncements is most useful. Hence unified efforts in terms of moral imperatives can assist the clergy in its attempt to balance the demands of the Protestant dilemma.

The Little Rock data indicate that the most important modifications necessary for a shift toward sectarianism must occur within the church itself. It will be difficult to establish the social reformer role as firmly as the deeply institutionalized organizational roles. Yet, at the very least, negative sanctions against this new role could be removed. Criteria in addition to the sheer number of communicants and contributions attracted will have to be used in assessing the work of a clergyman. Administrative records must not be allowed to tell the whole story. Then a man who by invoking the moral imperative on the race issue has refused to become his flock's "pet lamb" would not lose his pulpit because some members were offended. The point is not that social action will have to override all administrative concerns, but merely that something resembling parity will have to be established between them. No consistently forceful support of racial integration can be expected from the church until the social reform aspects of religion become more institutionalized in denominational structures.

But even if these changes within the laity, the clergy, and the structure of the church are achieved, there remain severe intrinsic limitations on the church's influence. Religious values are dominant in the lives of only a minority of men. Regardless of how well Protestant ministers employ their power, they cannot remove the influence of other values and institutions. Thus if the Little Rock ministry had made the most efficient use of its influence it could have modified the scene in that city, but in all probability it could not by itself have prevented "the march of Faubus." Our study has shown, however, that a large part of the limitations on Protestantism are not intrinsic but are imposed by the institution itself. Notwithstanding the real restrictions placed on them in a tragic situation, the fact remains that the Little Rock ministry did not make the most efficient use of their influence. Our problem extends beyond Little Rock; it challenges Protestantism throughout America. The church could eliminate these self-imposed limitations in the future by evolving a closer idealistic and organizational balance. Then, and only then, could Protestantism become both more effective in the race conflict and more influential in society.

STATEMENTS OF THE CHURCHES ON
DESEGREGATION AND RACE RELATIONS

The major religious bodies show a remarkably consistent concern with the problems of race relations in the United States. Their conventions and other policy-setting sessions have insisted repeatedly and urgently that the practice of racial segregation is a blight on the Christian conscience. These bodies have worked over a long period of time to mobilize religious opinion in supporting racial equality. They have been prompt to commend the Supreme Court decisions that attack racial segregation in public facilities. There is no reasonable doubt that the major religious bodies of America believe that the church must condemn race separation.

The following statements of official church policy affirm this conclusion. Let it be noted that they are representative of a larger number of similar statements. In many instances, local and state denominational bodies have issued strong statements to support the positions of their respective churches. Similar stands have been taken by interdenominational and local church councils in many southern states.

BAPTIST BODIES:

In the light of the recent decision handed down by the Supreme Court of our nation declaring segregation of the races to be unconstitutional, and in view of the position of this Convention in adhering to the basic moral principles of our religion as they apply in race relations, we recommend:

1. That we recognize the fact that this Supreme Court decision is in harmony with the constitutional guarantee of equal freedom to all citizens, and with the Christian principles of equal justice and love for all men.

2. That we commend the Supreme Court for deferring the application of the principle both as to time and procedure until the nation

shall have had time to work out methods by which transition from the present practice may be effected.

3. That we urge our people and all Christians to conduct themselves in this period of adjustment in the spirit of Christ; that we pray that God may guide us in our thinking and our attitudes to the end that we may help and not hinder the progress of justice and brotherly love; that we may exercise patience and good will in the discussions that must take place, and give a good testimony to the meaning of Christian faith and discipleship.

4. That we express our belief in the public school system of our nation as one of the greatest factors in American history for the maintenance of democracy and our common culture, and we express the hope that in the working out of necessary adjustments, its place in our educational program shall not be impaired.

5. That we urge Christian statesmen and leaders in our churches to use their leadership in positive thought and planning to the end that this crisis in our national history shall not be made the occasion for new and bitter prejudices, but a movement toward a united nation embodying and proclaiming a democracy that will commend freedom to all peoples. (Resolution of the Southern Baptist Convention, June 2-5, 1954, St. Louis, Missouri.)

*   *   *

We appeal to our Baptist brethren, white and Negro, and to other Christian friends, to give careful consideration to the following statement of principles made by a group of Southern Baptists that set forth, we believe, the truth of the Bible and which are offered in the spirit of good will and Christian love:

(1) God created man in his own image. Therefore, every man possesses infinite worth and should be treated with respect as a person.

(2) Christ died for all men. Therefore, the Christian view of man, every man, must reflect the spirit of the cross.

(3) God is no respecter of persons. Therefore, prejudice against persons or mistreatment of persons on the grounds of race is contrary to the will of God.

(4) Christ said, "Thou shalt love thy neighbor as thyself." Therefore, Christians are obligated to manifest active goodwill toward all people and to help them to achieve their fullest potentialities as persons.

(5) Christian love, as exemplified by Christ, is the supreme law for all human relations. Therefore, Christians have the assurance that such love, conscientiously practiced, will resolve tensions and bring harmony and good will in race relations.

(6) All true Christians are brothers in Christ and children of God. Therefore, they are obligated to cultivate prayerful concern for one another and to show confidence in one another.

(7) Every person is accountable to God. Therefore, the right of individual opinion, tested by the teachings of Christ, and of freedom to express it, always in the spirit of Christian love, should be granted to all and respected by all.

In accordance with these principles of our Christian faith, and as free citizens, this Commission protests the violence in all its ugly forms that is being used against the Negro people in the current segregation issue or at any other time. In recognition of the Negro's rights as a citizen of these United States, we call upon the law enforcement agencies of local, state, and national governments to protect him, irrespective of his position or culture, from lawless attacks on his person or property; and to protect any other individual or group who seeks to live in a chosen community as free citizens engaged in peaceful pursuits according to their own convictions and conscience.

We believe that our nation cannot long endure these lawless attacks made upon the person and property of its citizens in contempt of the law and the courts of justice. We, therefore, call upon these law enforcement officers and agencies to bring to legal justice the perpetrators of these crimes, regardless of their position or influence in the community.

Furthermore, in keeping with our historic Baptist position on the freedom of conscience and of expression in religion under the leadership of the Holy Spirit, we call to the attention of the people in our churches and other citizens of our country the fact that any suppression of these freedoms, whether it be by the laws of state or by economic, civic, social, or church pressures, denies the voluntary principle in religion and imperils both religious and political freedom at its source.

We are witnessing today in some communities and churches the betrayal of these freedoms by vocal minorities who are able to arouse sufficient opposition to force the resignation of pastors and to incite retaliation against peaceful citizens who speak or act according to their convictions on racial justice and interracial goodwill. The people of our region and throughout our land are reminded that both the voice of God and the verdict of history warn us that those who deny these freedoms to others do not long retain them for themselves. (The Southern Baptist Convention, 1957.)

* * *

We recognize that during the past ten years great strides have been made in race relations in America and that it was a logical next step for the Supreme Court to declare two years ago that our public schools must be integrated to assure equality of educational opportunity.

We fully support the Supreme Court decision and deplore the resistance to this decision in certain states where integration of public education has met organized opposition.

Our Convention has spoken out against segregation and has repeatedly urged church leaders to work as unceasingly for a nonsegregated church as for an integrated society.

We rejoice that integration is progressing in the churches of our American Baptist Convention. Recent staff and missionary appointments testify to our intent as a religious fellowship to see that there is no racial "wall of separation" in our common service in the Kingdom. At the same time, we confess the urgency of accelerating this trend, which still is marked by futile effort, insincerity, and unwillingness to change.

Since the probability of developing integrated church congregations is contingent on the spread of open housing, we acknowledge our responsibility to work for conditions in our communities which will assure to persons the right to rent or own a home anywhere in the community solely on the basis of personal preference and financial ability rather than on the basis of race, creed, or color.

Thus, in prayer and in penitence for our own failures, we pledge ourselves to work at all levels for justice, equality, and brotherhood among the races of America. (American Baptist Convention, June 22, 1956.)

* * *

. . . we dedicate ourselves to the following objectives:

1. That membership in each Baptist church shall be open to all people of its community regardless of their race or national origin.

2. That each church shall choose its minister on the basis of character and ability without regard to racial background.

3. That each church shall work to assure equality for all people in education, employment, housing, and political activity.

4. That members of our churches shall base their fellowship with others on individual merit without regard to racial origins.

5. That we shall not align ourselves with any organized group or movement that works to retain segregation whether in country clubs, sororities, fraternities, service clubs, organizations of property owners, the Ku Klux Klan, White Citizens Councils, and all exclusive groups that deny membership to others on the basis of race.

6. That each Baptist organization, school, home, and hospital shall follow practices that are consistent with clear policies of racial non-discrimination. . . . (American Baptist Convention, May 31, 1957.)

*   *   *

Almost any American tourist of Europe and other eastern countries meets with the question of the attitude of America toward the intermingling of the races composing the population of the United States.

Some of these peoples are quite "scathing" in their remarks concerning the American claim of Democracy and Christianity on the one hand and the treatment America permits to be accorded her minority peoples on the other.

For many years Negroes have been puzzled as to the attitude they should adopt regarding the sincerity of the American claim of the policy of "Justice to all and special privilege to none."

When, however, the Supreme Court issued her memorable decision outlawing segregation in the public schools, the race took heart and reorganized her thinking with regards to America being in truth "The Land of the Free and the Home of the Brave."

Negroes love America and entertain no bitterness toward her despite the vicious wrongs some commit against them in certain sections of the country. They have too long agonized in prayer for her security. They have given too freely of their blood to vouchsafe her institutions—not to love her with undying devotion. They believe the Supreme Court on May 17, 1954 justified the faith, the hope and the love they exercise toward this country. (National Baptist Convention, U.S.A., Inc.)

CHURCH OF THE BRETHREN:

We reaffirm our belief that discrimination owing to color is out of keeping both with the teachings of the New Testament and with the stated position of the Church of the Brethren. We realize that, as we attempt to sharpen our efforts to practice genuine brotherhood, we are dealing with an issue that is not sectional in nature, and therefore, we speak firmly and in love to all Brethren who have been less than Christian in this matter, in every area of our land. We commend governmental agencies, our own churches and those of other denominations who have declared their intention to support the Supreme Court decision. We would repeat that our goal must be no less than an integrated church and public school in an integrated community. Such a goal involves housing, equal access to medical care, jobs in industry, the right to vote, and membership and participation in the affairs of the community and of the Christian body. We commend those in areas where racial tension is acute, and in other areas, who are pursuing these goals in a nonviolent way and pledge to them our continuing support. We appeal to all Brethren to give leadership now, with courage, so that we may move toward this goal with calmness, sympathy, and seasoned judgment, realizing that He who made of "one blood all nations of men for to dwell on the face of the earth," shows no partiality among the races. (Annual Conference, June 12-17, 1956.)

In spite of racial tensions that have developed in many areas we are grateful for the steady progress toward integration in many communities and in an increasing number of churches. We believe that the teaching of Scripture is clear. God has no favorite race or nation; in Christ there is neither Jew nor Gentile, bond nor free. We renew our pledges, made in past Conferences, to work for an integrated church in an integrated community. Toward this end we urge every church (1) to develop an education and action program aimed at bringing about interracial understanding, (2) to open its membership to all Christians regardless of their race or national origin, (3) to support orderly and peaceful means of eliminating discrimination in education, employment, housing, medical care, and voting privileges, (4) to oppose every organized effort to deny equal opportunity to any minority group, and (5) to maintain such cordial relations with all groups that the church may display both a reconciling and a redemptive spirit wherever tensions exist. (Annual Conference, June 1957.)

CONGREGATIONAL CHURCHES, GENERAL COUNCIL:

The General Council of the Congregational Christian Churches has repeatedly declared itself strongly for a society without barriers based on race, color or religious affiliation and has pledged itself, and called upon the conferences, conventions, associations, local churches, church-related institutions and individual church members and pastors, to work for a non-segregated church in a non-segregated community.

A primary responsibility of the churches is to transform the minds and hearts of men and women so that fear, prejudice or inertia no longer determines their outlook or behavior. This comes through the grace of God for which the church is called to be a channel.

Recognizing that there are varying viewpoints on relations that should obtain between persons and groups of differing race, we stress the necessity for keeping creative communication open between all Christians, those within each racial group and between those of different racial ancestries.

We are convinced that patterns of residential segregation based on race or religion constitute a major barrier to integrated churches, schools and communities.

We are encouraged by recent decisions of the United States Supreme Court that have consistently followed the doctrine that legally enforced racial segregation in public facilities such as schools, busses, dining cars, parks, and the like, is unconstitutional. Thereby a firmer legal basis for sound and just human relations has been created.

Moreover, these decisions are in harmony with the Christian teaching of the dignity of all men under God and are, in significant part, the result of preaching and teaching by the Christian churches.

The President of the United States, in his capacity as chief executive of the whole nation, has a very critical duty to discharge in this period of transition to non-segregated public facilities and institutions. We commend him for the important steps that he has taken in carrying out his constitutional responsibility for the enforcement of judicial decisions. In these actions we pledge our continuing support.

We note with gratification that the 85th Congress passed the "Civil Rights Act of 1957" setting up a temporary Commission on Civil Rights to study specified problems, particularly those connected with the right of Negro citizens to vote, and to report to the President and Congress its findings and its recommendations for legislative and other action. This act also provides for an additional Assistant Attorney General in charge of a separate Civil Rights Division in the Department of Justice. It further strengthens procedures under which the voting rights of citizens can be protected.

For many years our churches, through their boards and agencies, have supported a far-reaching program in the field of race relations, including schools and colleges in the South, institutes and conferences, research and community surveys, and education in local congregations.

However, in view of the Christian imperative, the numerous denials of the opportunity to share in the privileges of our democratic society and the critical state of world affairs, we confess our shortcomings as a denomination and as a nation.

With renewed dedication, we press towards more rapid achievement of full equality of rights and of recognition of the worth of persons regardless of racial ancestry, religion or national origin. This constraint is particularly pressing upon our consciences in respect to discrimination and segregation within the churches and church-sponsored agencies, institutions, and organizations.

In the light of these Christian commitments and historic developments we reiterate our often expressed conviction that pastors, church officers and members, and boards and administrators of church-related agencies and institutions are bound by their Christian faith to acknowledge and fulfill their obligation to accept persons in every phase of life and work of the Church on the basis of their qualifications. We call upon Congregational Christian agencies, conferences, conventions, associations, local congregations, colleges and schools, social service homes and other institutions to move with steadfast purpose towards the removal of such racial barriers as still remain in our church life. We further urge our members to give careful consideration to the racial policies of church-related and other colleges, universities and institutions to which they make financial contributions.

We commend the Executive Committee of the General Council for having carried through the three consultations on the problem of segregation in our churches, conferences and conventions in the South. We request the Executive Committee to continue this process. We respectfully request that the Board of Home Missions and the Council for Social Action increase the appropriation of finances and make provision for leadership in order to accelerate the process of moving from a racial to a geographical basis in all areas of our fellowship. Further we request that a progress report be made to the General Council in 1961.

We call upon the members of our churches to work for adequate housing and community facilities that shall be available to all persons without regard to race or religion and to refrain from lending their resources to or participating in extending or creating ghettos.

We strongly recommend to our churches that they work with other Christian organizations and civic agencies to prepare communities for new residents of different ethnic background and to insure peaceful neighborly relations when such residents move in. To this end we commend securing and publishing of the names of signers to covenants of open occupancy such as: "We welcome into our neighborhoods any residents of good character, regardless of race, color, religion or national origin."

We further affirm the importance of increasing the supply of new or rehabilitated housing, especially for middle and low income groups, open to all without discrimination. The churches should encourage the use of personnel skilled in intergroup relations especially during transitional periods.

We urge all those engaged in financing, buying, selling, renting and leasing residences or apartments to make their resources and services available to all persons without consideration of race or creed. We also urge those engaged in city and community planning to lend their support and skills to create and maintain racially inclusive neighborhoods.

We respectfully call upon the President of the United States and the Executive Department to give firmer leadership in meeting problems arising from the changing relationships between the races and to use the Chief Executive's constitutional powers to uphold court decisions affecting civil rights.

Likewise we call upon the Congress to declare itself affirmatively on the issue of school desegregation.

We heartily commend the brave Negro children and their parents upon whom falls, in such large measure, responsibility for pioneering the new patterns of integration in our schools. We also recognize with appreciation those teachers, school administrators, members of boards of education and white pupils who have exercised self-restraint and conducted themselves in just and friendly ways, sometimes under conditions of great stress.

We applaud the courage and prophetic Christian witness of scores of pastors and lay members of both races in areas where public authorities are resisting the desegregation decisions of the United States Supreme Court and we pay tribute also to many in the ranks of the United Church Women. We pledge our support to them as we hope and pray for the emergence of more numerous and more articulate lay Christian leadership.

We urge our church members, individually and collectively, to lend their support to officials, governmental bodies and citizen groups that are seeking to obey the law of the land as expressed in judicial decisions in regard to desegregation of public schools and other public facilities. Every effort should be made to revive the active interest of officials and enlightened citizens in all areas of racial tension in the development of effective interracial cooperation in behalf of the removal of barriers to the full enjoyment of the opportunities and rights of American life by all ethnic elements. (General Council of The Congregational Christian Churches, Boston, June 1958.)

DISCIPLES OF CHRIST:

Churches . . . are now faced with the fact that their responsibility is one of moving from principle to practice within their own local situations. The following concrete suggestions as to procedure represent the direction in which our brotherhood should move:

Local churches should make unmistakably clear the witness of their individual congregations as to the inclusive nature of their fellowships.

For some this may mean the employment of a multi-racial staff; for others it may mean an active evangelism program among persons of "other" races; for still others it may mean public announcement from pulpit or in advertising, "We welcome all people," and for still others it may mean long study and painful experimentation as they seek to fulfill the teachings of Christ under the leading of the Holy Spirit. . . .

Local congregations should cooperate with one another in making surveys of their local communities regarding discrimination in housing and the use of public facilities. . . .

Whereas we are witnessing in our time the disintegration of colonialism all over the world and the unprecedented struggle of people and nations for liberty, equality, justice and dignity;

Whereas the denial of any of these unalienable rights of men and nations is a denial of the Christian Gospel in that it strikes at the nature of God, and, thus, the nature of man; . . .

Whereas the declared position of the Christian Church (Disciples of Christ) has been in accord with the position of the World Council of Churches and of the National Council of the Churches of Christ in the United States—which declared a non-segregated Church in a non-segregated Society is the Christian Ideal;

Whereas many of the churches, confronted with a population change in racial or ethnic character in their areas, are following the special pattern of selling out and relocating rather than become an all-inclusive fellowship; . . .

Whereas other churches, confronted with the same challenge, are endeavoring to let the church be the Church—letting it be known that their church is open to any and all people, regardless of race or ethnic origin, who espouse the doctrines of New Testament Christianity as proclaimed by the Christian Church (Disciples of Christ) . . .

BE IT RESOLVED:

First — that we urge and encourage all ministers and churches of our communion to be willing to bear any cross of persecution or reprisal brought upon them by their fearless witness to the rights of all people, regardless of race or ethnic origin, to liberty, equality, justice and human dignity, and to the true nature of the Church and the proclamation of the Gospel of Christ without fear or favor:

Second — that we urge and encourage agencies, congregations and members of our brotherhood to support all Christians who are under persecution for conscience sake.

Third — that because of the emergency nature of many situations where churches are in areas of racial change, we urge that those responsible in our brotherhood organizational life give attention to allocating funds to this critical need.

Fourth — that we discourage our churches in areas of racial change and transition from selling out and relocating where the move has been based on the change in the racial or ethnic character of the population, and encourage our churches to remain on the field and bear fearless witness to the true nature of the church.

Fifth — that we, as a brotherhood, provide a counselling service and, if needed, financial support to churches confronted with a population change in racial or ethnic character, in order to help the church remain in the field and weather the transition period. (International Convention, October 11-16, 1957.)

EVANGELICAL UNITED BRETHREN:

1. *Church Life.* Believing it to be God's will and His way of life, we urge our local Evangelical United Brethren churches to develop a fellowship which is racially and ethnically inclusive. To this end we strongly advise our local churches to meet the opportunities of ministry to their communities regardless of races and/or nationalities.

2. *Employment.* We believe that discrimination in employment based on race is un-Christian. Therefore we urge all Evangelical United Brethren General Departments and Institutions as well as each local church to take immediate steps to end any such discriminatory practices now obtaining and to enlist all concerned to refrain from any

such policies in the future. We urge our laymen in positions of leadership in employment circles to practice nondiscrimination.

3. *Education.* Believing in the democracy and Christian fairness of desegregation in the public school, and recognizing the vital relationship between such democracy and the future welfare of our nation, we urge our Evangelical United Brethren people to participate in and encourage the development of school integration in their communities.

4. *Housing.* Families should be free to choose where they shall live without discrimination because of race. We reject any policy to the contrary and appeal to our members to bring their own practices in line with this idea. We urge our members in the vocation of real estate and home financing to adopt Christian principles of non-discrimination. We furthermore urge our local churches to help counteract panic tactics of community change by encouraging their members to consider carefully every aspect of a contemplated move to a new community. (General Conference, December 8-9, 1955.)

*   *   *

. . . We suggest that we take the following specific actions to better human relationships between the races:

1. Promote a Christian ministry in our communities without regard to race. This means welcoming all races in all phases of Church life.

2. Appoint ministers of other races as well as white ministers in our churches that are multi-racial in character, as has been done in several of our churches.

3. Welcome people of all races when they move into any section of our community. Let us not listen to those who, for the desire of personal gain, encourage panic when Negroes or other minority groups purchase real estate in previously all-white communities.

4. Give active and consistent support to the Supreme Court decisions on desegregation and resist all attempts to circumvent them. We uphold the civil liberties of all American citizens irrespective of color.

5. Withhold permission to use our church buildings as segregated schools in an effort to disobey the mandate of the Supreme Court. We commend the Virginia Conference for the strong position they have taken on this matter. (General Conference, Evangelical United Brethren, October 9-17, 1958.)

EPISCOPAL BODIES:

. . . Whereas, the Supreme Court of these United States has ruled that every citizen shall have open access to the public schools and colleges of the entire nation; therefore be it

Resolved, That the 58th General Convention of the Protestant Episcopal Church in the United States of America now commends to all the clergy and people of this Church that they accept and support this ruling of the Supreme Court, and, that by opening channels of Christian conference and communication between the races concerned in each diocese and community, they anticipate constructively the local implementation of this ruling as the law of the land; and be it further

Resolved, That we make our own the statement of the Anglican Congress that "in the work of the Church we should welcome people of any race at any service conducted by a priest or layman of any ethnic origin, and bring them into the full fellowship of the congregation and its organizations." (Resolution of the General Convention of the Episcopal Church, September, 1955.)

*   *   *

This letter is written against the background of our unforgettable experience at the recent Lambeth Conference. For forty days we had, once again, the privilege of meeting with bishops of the Anglican Communion from many parts of the world. We came from every continent, were members of every race and many nations, and revealed in our fellowship, not only the encouraging growth of our Communion, but also that it is part of the Holy Catholic Church which includes members of every race and nation. We saw anew, against the background of the world's terrible divisions, the oneness of mankind in Christ; we saw that "in Christ there is no East or West"; we saw that only a world body, freed from the passions and enmities that divide men, can bring a healing and reconciling word to our world. The Lambeth Conference was a symbol of that unity toward which the whole world groans and travails . . .

The Sacredness of Law: . . . Since Lambeth Palace is close to the Houses of Parliament, many of us were led to reflect anew on the meaning of law and government. In Christian thought government is a structure appointed by God for the common good. Its function and responsibility is to care for the outer order and framework of our common life. We, all, need to be protected. We need the orderly and impartial administration of justice for the protection of our property, our safety, and our hard-won rights.

St. Paul recognized this when he appealed to Caesar, and when in the Epistle to the Romans he wrote, *the powers that be are ordained by God*. The laws is a minister of God for good. It is God's instrument. It makes civilized life possible, and enables us to live together in peace. It restrains our selfishness and wildness, and, while it cannot change our hearts, it does provide the indispensable outer framework of our unity.

The people of this land do not need to be reminded at this moment of the evils of tyranny, but we do need to be reminded now of the evils of anarchy. Anarchy, the absence of law and order, is a greater evil than tyranny, and leads to tyranny. Anarchy is the absence of order; tyranny is an order of sorts. It is for this reason that Christians are taught to honor government and to pray for *all Christian rulers, that they may truly and impartially administer justice, to the punishment of wickedness and vice*. Without that outer framework of order no unity is possible, and any man who seeks to undermine the rule of impartial justice is inviting disaster for the nation. It is only for the gravest and clearest principle of conscience relating to a serious moral issue that one may contemplate civil disobedience. And, because all order is at stake, such disobedience can only be justified when it is based on a higher ethical principle than the law represents. Never is it right when the disobedience is the expression of a lower ethical standard than the law would enforce. We call upon you, therefore, at this time to honor and obey the laws of this land.

God's Judgment upon our Divisions: . . . We saw vividly at Lambeth the judgment of God upon all our divisions and conflicts. This judgment is a great fact that concerns us all and because of which we all will suffer. The judgment of God; what is it? It is not some extraneous power falling upon us with no relationship to our behavior. It is not the capricious will of an arbitrary tyrant. It is not the opinion of bishops. It is not a quotation from the Bible.

God's judgment is the response of a just God to the offences of mankind against His loving will. It is the inevitable result we bring upon ourselves when we move against the grain of His universe. It is the inevitable result of our inner contradictions. It is God frustrating our purposes when we oppose His will. This judgment is as real as God is, and as powerful, for it is God Himself seeing our sins and acting in history to accomplish His will in spite of our sins. You will find the judgments of God reported in your daily newspaper, in the events of history, in the clash and contradiction of rival ambitions and fears, in the hatred and suspicion we earn when we fail to deal justly with hose with whom we share this narrow world.

We must remember that the majority of mankind belong to the colored races, and that the American racial problem is discussed the world over. Much of the good will which our nation once enjoyed has been lost. If America continues to lose friends as others become convinced that we do not mean what we say about justice and equality, the reason will be obvious. The judgments of the Lord are true and righteous altogether. These judgments are the plain cost we pay in God's universe for not practicing what we preach, and for not being ready to grant to others the opportunity and equality we cherish for ourselves.

Two strong motives, therefore, should drive us to our duty. One is the love for all men which the Holy Spirit pours into our hearts, the Divine Spirit that urges us toward unity. But if our hearts are sometimes dull, let us then do the will of God because the fear of His judgment grips our hearts. *Imprint upon our hearts,* says the Prayer Book, *such a dread of thy judgments, and such a grateful sense of thy goodness to us, as may make us both afraid and ashamed to offend thee.* This is God's world, and He punishes us together as we move against His will. If Africa and Asia should turn finally against us, it could well be because the colored races became convinced they must look elsewhere for justice. It is only when we lift our eyes from our immediate problems to see God's reign, His grace and wrath, that we think and act truly. (From Pastoral Letter of House of Bishops of the Episcopal Church, October, 1958.)

LUTHERAN BODIES:

Segregation and social stratification, both based on essentially external differences, regrettably occur in Christian churches. . . . The presence of segregation and stratification in the churches undermines the power inhering in the Gospel of uniting men through Christ in fellowship with the Father. . . .

Were His Spirit truly to rule in men's hearts and lives, problems of race segregation and social stratification would disappear. The free and voluntary actions of men who love neighbor as self because of God's love for them will exceed in justice and equity the compulsion forced by decree upon the unwilling.

It is incumbent upon Christians, their churches, and their church agencies, so far as it lies within their power, to practice to the full the realistic insights of their faith in dealing with issues of race and class. Pride and smug assumptions of superiority or privileged position draw the Master's censure today as they did for the sons of Zebedee

It is the unique task of the churches, shared by every Christian, to seek to bring the power of the Word of Sacraments to bear upon individuals, thereby changing their hearts and lives. This course alone promises the ultimate corrective for the evils of segregation and stratification. (American Lutheran Church, Biennial Convention, 1954.)

*   *   *

. . . We urge our members to use their influence in the securing of full rights of citizenship for all, and in discouraging any activity in their communities which would seek to circumvent orderly judicial procedure in the implementation of the Supreme Court decisions of segregation. . . .

We recognize that the evils of racial discrimination are not restricted to any one section of the nation, and we encourage our people to oppose all forms of racial discrimination whether they be found in the North or in the South.

We point out to our members, especially those in the northern states, that discrimination in housing, real estate transactions, and employment is just as much a violation of Christian principles as discrimination in places of public assembly, public transportation, or schools. . . .

Where there are members of local churches in which racial integration is taking place, or is likely to take place, who are unwilling to continue their membership in such congregations for this reason, we encourage such members to examine their consciences in the light of Holy Scriptures, and in the doctrines and decisions of the Church, specifically that God has created all men in His image, that Jesus Christ has given His life for the salvation of all men, that the Holy Spirit would call all men into the fellowship of the Church.

We remind congregations of their inescapable responsibility to bear witness in its locality to these truths, as well as the privilege of demonstrating that the Christian fellowship transcends barriers of race and class.

We urge pastors of congregations to which such disaffected members may be seeking letters of transfer to encourage them to remain in their own congregations and to demonstrate Christian acceptance of and love toward those whom they have deemed different from themselves. . . . (Augustana Evangelical Lutheran Church, June 11-17, 1956.)

. . . *Resolved*, That The Lutheran Church—Missouri Synod affirm its adherence to, and application of, the Scriptural principles of fact concerning race relations and church work as adopted by its representatives in conjunction with representatives of the sister synods of the Synodical Conference, and as reported in the Proceedings of the Forty-Second Convention of the Evangelical Lutheran Synodical Conference of North America of August 12 to 15, 1952, . . .

And be it further . . .

Resolved, 1. That all congregations of Synod regard all persons regardless of race or ethnic origin living within the limits of their respective parishes, and not associated with another Christian church, as individuals whom God would reach with the Gospel of His saving grace through the ministry of the local congregation;

2. That congregations operating in changing communities be encouraged to continue operations in those areas rather than relinquish their properties through sale to other denominations, and that the various District Mission Boards be encouraged to subsidize these congregations when this becomes necessary, so that the souls in those communities, regardless of race or ethnic grouping, may be won and served;

3. That synodical institutions, agencies, and offices continue to make no distinction, based upon race or color, in their entrance requirements or employment policies; and be it finally

Resolved, That since Christians are constrained to do justice and love mercy, we acknowledge our responsibility as a church to provide guidance for our members to work in the capacity of Christian citizens for the elimination of discrimination, wherever it may exist, in community, city, state, nation, and world. (Lutheran Church—Missouri Synod, June 20-29, 1956.)

*　　　*　　　*

. . . We believe that Christians have special responsibilities to keep open the channels of communication and understanding among the different groups in this controversy. Our congregations are encouraged to contribute to the solution of the problem by demonstrating in their own corporate lives the possibility of integration.

We furthermore state that due heed ought to be given the following principles by all and especially by those holding civil office, since they hold their power under God and are responsible to him for its exercise:

(1) The public school system so necessary to the maintenance of a democratic free and just way of life, must be upheld and strengthened.

(2) All parties to the present controversy are in duty bound to follow and uphold due process of law, and to maintain public order. (United Lutheran Church in America, Convention, October 17, 1956.)

*   *   *

Whereas, the ULCA is sensitive to the present challenges and opportunities in the realm of human relations and is conscious of its responsibilities to provide leadership in this realm;

Therefore, be it resolved: that the ULCA commend the Board of Social Missions for its creative program directed toward improvement of race relations in harmony with the principles expressed by the 1956 Convention of the Church in the Statement on Desegregation; and

Be it further resolved: that the Church extend to all its pastors and congregations the assurance of its continuing approval, support, and prayers in the Christian implementation of these principles. (United Lutheran Church in America, Convention, October 6, 1958.)

METHODIST BODIES:

The historic decision of the Supreme Court abolishing segregation in the public-school system is in keeping with the attitude of The Methodist Church. In our official pronouncements, including the Social Creed and the Episcopal Address adopted by the 1952 General Conference, our position has been clearly stated.

The Supreme Court recognized that such a ruling brought with it difficulties of enforcement, and therefore, made provision for sufficient time to implement its decision. The declaration of the decision was made in the magnificent home of the Supreme Court in Washington, but the ultimate success of the ruling will be determined in the hearts of the people of the nation. Thus the church is furnished with an unequaled opportunity to provide leadership during this period in support of the principles involved in the action of the court.

We accept this responsibility, for one of the foundation stones of our faith is the belief that all men are brothers, equal in the sight of God. In that faith, we declare our support of the ruling of the Supreme Court. (Statement by the Council of Bishops of the Methodist Church, Chicago, November 18-21, 1954.)

*   *   *

The teaching of our Lord is that all men are brothers. The Master permits no discrimination because of race, color, or national origin.

The position of The Methodist Church, long held and frequently declared, is an amplification of our Lord's teaching. "To discriminate against a person solely upon the basis of his race is both unfair and unchristian. Every child of God is entitled to that place in society which he has won by his industry and his character. To deny him that position of honor because of the accident of his birth is neither honest democracy nor good religion." (The Episcopal Address, 1952 and 1956.)

There must be no place in The Methodist Church for racial discrimination or enforced segregation. Recognizing that we have not attained this goal, yet rejoicing in the progress made, we recommend that discrimination or segregation by any method or practice, whether by conference structure or otherwise, in The Methodist Church be abolished with reasonable speed. The growing spirit of brotherhood throughout the church strengthens our confidence that, under the leadership of the Holy Spirit, we will continue to go forward.

There is a changing racial climate in our world, largely growing out of the teachings of the Christian Church. The conscience of society has become increasingly sensitive regarding racial discrimination and injustice. Methodists unite with peoples of all lands and all faiths in a determined effort to eliminate these unchristian practices. We look to the ultimate establishment of a truly Christian society.

The decisions of the Supreme Court of the United States relative to segregation make necessary far-reaching and often difficult community readjustments throughout the nation. We call upon our people to effect these adjustments in all good faith, with brotherliness and patience. In doing this all racial groups must be willing to admit their imperfections and seek to correct them. Let these things, however, be done in love lest the cause of Christ suffer at our hands.

It is our desire to accomplish the realization of Christian brotherhood and full participation by all in every aspect of the church's life. We join other people of good will around the world in moving toward the day when all races shall share richly without discrimination or segregation in the good things of life. Therefore, we resolutely go forward with the work begun with respect to race relations in the church and in our world. (From *Doctrines and Disciplines of The Methodist Church*, 1956, Section 2026, pages 723-724).

*   *   *

. . . "An integrated church in an integrated society" is the declared policy of American Protestantism. Virutally every major denomination in the United States has hailed the Supreme Court decision on the integration of schools as a milestone in the achievement of human rights. Likewise, the Roman Catholic Church has condemned racial discrimination as "unjust and un-Christian."

In this struggle for universal acceptance of an integrated society, the Negro church plays an increasingly vital role. We have witnessed instance after instance of sacrifice, toil and even bloodshed by ordained ministers of the Gospel determined to make a reality out of the professions of Democracy. . . .

Our people must know that all men are created equal, and that any divergence from this principle is hypocrisy, in fact, immoral. The people must likewise know that the law of the land is second only to the law of God and that to openly flout the dictates of the highest tribunal is flirting with tragedy. . . .

We believe it to be our Christian duty to awaken a social consciousness concerning these vital issues. This represents teaching the Gospel of Christ in a practical sense. Telling our Brethren how they can live and play in peace and harmony is a task of our ministry. . . .

As followers of Christ we are opposed to violence and mob action. This latter must not be confused with mass action, a technique we must learn to employ in certain fields against those who would exploit us. Who would sell their wares to us for profit must not at the same time oppose our march to freedom.

We commend therefore the citizens of Montgomery, Alabama, who in protest against injustice have refused to lend sustenance to their oppressors. The "Spirit of Motgomery" must be applied wherever possible against individuals, corporations, local and national, who fail to stand up and be counted. . . .

May God grant us the strength and courage to fight on, never once turning backwards in our march. May the scourge of race hatred, segregation and unjust discrimination vanish forever from the face of the earth. (African Methodist Episcopal Church, Council of Bishops, February 15-18, 1956.)

NATIONAL COUNCIL OF THE CHURCHES OF CHRIST:

The unanimous decision of the Supreme Court that segregation in the public schools is unconstitutional gives a clear status in law to a fundamental Christian and American principle. The decision will have far-reaching effects in the whole nation and the world.

It offers the promise of further steps for translating into reality Christian and democratic ideals. The decision is a mile-stone in the achievement of human rights, another evidence of the endeavor to respect the dignity and worth of all men.

The complexity of implementing the decision is recognized by the Court which has set the cases for further reargument on the formulation of the decrees. To put the decision into effect will test the good-will and discipline of people in many communities. Adjustments will be more difficult in some localities than others. In the period of transition from one pattern to another (whatever the length of the period to be prescribed by the Court), we know that the churches and individual Christians will continue to exert their influence and leadership to help the authorized agencies in the several communities to bring about a complete compliance with the decision of the Supreme Court. The law of neighborliness is the great guide available to Christians as they deal with this situation in their local communities. "Thou shalt love thy neighbor as thyself." The second part of the Great Commandment contains the potential for lifting men to a new level of social responsibility and for creating new dimensions of human brotherhood. (Statement of the General Board, National Council of the Churches of Christ in the U.S.A., May 19, 1954.)

PRESBYTERIAN BODIES:

THE BIBLE AND HUMAN RELATIONSHIPS

Any study of relationships involving people of different cultural and racial background is essentially a study of human relationships. It is important in such a study to recognize the authority of Scripture. Attention is called to the following basic truths relevant to our study which are taught in Scripture:

1. *The Sovereignty of God.* The first of these truths is that God is one and he is ruler over all creation. His will is right and shall be done in heaven and in earth. This truth is set forth in striking terms by John on the Isle of Patmos when he had a vision of God's judgment upon the evil forces of the world: "And I heard as it were the voice of a great multitude, and as the voice of many waters and as the voice of mighty thunderings, saying, Alleluia: for the Lord God omnipotent reigneth."—Revelation 19:6.

God being sovereign ruler of the universe, "Man's chief end is to glorify God and enjoy him forever."

2. *The Dignity of Man.* A second basic truth found in Scripture relevant to our study is that every person is of infinite value and has infinite possibilities. This truth is set forth principally in the doctrine of creation; in the doctrine of the incarnation; and in the doctrine of redemption. Scripture teaches that man was created *in the image of God.* It is believed that this has reference to man's capacity to think, to feel, to will—a spiritual being who can know God, love him and communicate with him.

The dignity of man is further set forth in the incarnation of Jesus Christ. Said the writer of the Fourth Gospel: "And the Word was made flesh, and dwelt among us, and we beheld his glory, the glory as of the only begotten of the Father, full of grace and truth." — John 1:14.

In Jesus we behold the perfect man, "the image of the invisible God." In him we see God's ideal for man.

The infinite value of every person is finally and completely demonstrated in the sacrificial death of Jesus Christ.

"For God so loved the world, that he gave his only begotten Son, that whosoever believeth in him should not perish, but have everlasting life."—John 3:16.

3. *The Oneness of Mankind.* A third basic truth is the oneness of mankind. This truth is supported in Scripture by five facts. The first of these is the fact of creation. The story of creation as given in the Book of Genesis shows the common origin of man.

The second fact in support of man's oneness is the Providence of God. The Hebrew people were chosen by God not because they were better than other peoples, but that he might use them in revealing himself to the world. His blessings are poured out upon all people. It is significant that in Scripture the usual division between peoples has to do with the two groups, Jews and Gentiles, or believers and non-believers.

The third fact is that God's plan of redemption applies to all people alike. The circumstances of one's birth do not affect God's will to redeem that individual. It is God's will that all should come to a knowledge of the truth. Said the Apostle Peter: "Of a truth I perceive that God is no respecter of persons: but in every nation he that feareth him, and worketh righteousness, is accepted with him." — Acts 10:34, 35.

The fourth fact is that God's law for human relationships, the law of love, applies to all people alike. Jesus in the Parable of the Good Samaritan indicates that one's cultural and racial background is not to be determinative in the application of this law. The Christian law of love transcends the barrier of race.

The fifth fact supporting the oneness of mankind is that God's judgment upon people is impartial. His judgment is based upon moral principles and not upon externalities. In the Parable of the Judgment, Jesus warned that all nations would be gathered before the Son of Man to be judged. The basis of the judgment would be their relationship to him manifested in their behavior toward their fellowmen.

CONCLUSIONS

Five conclusions concerning human relationships are reached from a careful study of the Bible:

1. God is the sovereign ruler over all creation. Man's chief end, therefore, is to glorify him.

2. God in his concern for, and in his dealing with man, is no respecter of persons. The people of Israel were chosen for his instrument in the salvation of all people which points up this truth. Since Christ died for all, Christians are constrained to look upon all people as those for whom Christ died, even as the Apostle Paul said: "Henceforth know we no man after the flesh."—II Corinthians 5:16a.

3. Every person is of infinite value, and therefore of equal value in the sight of God. In his sight there is no "superior race." Rather, all people have been created in his image and are to be treated as such.

4. People, while differing in outward appearance, are essentially one. They have fundamentally the same needs, aspirations, hopes and fears. God in Christ is the goal of their life and their souls are restless till they repose in him.

5. It is God's will that the law of Christian love be operative in all human relationships. Guided by this law Christians recognize and meet need apart from the circumstances of one's birth and culture.

People are to be looked upon and treated as people. Whatever injures or prevents the growth of human personality is contrary to the law of love. The Christian's conduct toward others must be guided by the law of neighborliness which seeks the welfare and happiness of all people. . . .

THE POSITION OF THE CHURCH

Since segregation of the white and Negro people continues to diminish it is time to determine the church's relationship to this trend. This state of flux is due to two dynamic forces at work, the Federal Constitution and the Christian conscience, the one legal and the other spiritual; the one finding expression in statutes and court decisions, and the other in personal conduct, in the voice and policies of the church. If it be judged that segregation is not merely the separation of two peoples, but the subordination of one people to another, we can, on good evidence, observe that the courts have shown more sympathy toward the Negro than has the church. The church would then find itself in the embarrassing position of having to adjust its sense of morality to measure up to the morals of the state. This would belie its pristine nature. Our Christ was and still is ahead of the times; the customs, traditions, and laws of it. The church must strive to keep apace of its Master or become bereft of his spirit.

Our religious convictions form the dynamic for the making, amending and repealing of laws.

We recognize three levels of relationship, the legal, the ethical, and the spiritual. A law is the least common denominator of human behavior. It is a restraint so generally acceptable that it can be enforced without curtailing freedom. Behind every set of laws is a code of ethics which contains the unwritten laws of corporate life.

Unwritten laws, as they become generally taught and observed, are subsequently codified. Behind every code of ethics is a concept of God so that ultimately every human relationship, whether it be voluntary or prescribed by statute, is determined by what a man believes about God. It will be a sad day for the church if these three levels of relationship should be inverted, that is, if our belief in a personal God should permit us to foster a relationship inferior to that which impersonal law demands. If this should happen, the church would lose its status as the conscience of society, its intangible, controlling and quickening force.

With special reference to the resolution placed in the hands of the Council of Christian Relations by the 93rd General Assembly for study and recommendations the Council recognizes that in Presbyterian procedure the General Assembly does not *direct* that certain changes in educational and cultural patterns be apoted. On the other hand, the Council understands that the General Assembly may properly *urge* the adoption of such changes in the practices of the Church.

In keeping with this procedure, therefore, the following recommendations are offered:

1. That the General Assembly affirm that enforced segregation of the races is discrimination which is out of harmony with Christian theology and ethics and that the church, in its relationship to cultural

patterns, should lead rather than follow.

2. That the General Assembly, therefore, submit this report for careful study throughout the church, and that it especially urge:

(1) That the trustees of institutions of higher education belonging to the General Assembly adopt a policy of opening the doors of these institutions to all races.

(2) That the synods consider earnestly the adoption of a similar recommendation to trustees of institutions under their control.

(3) That the governing bodies of the various conferences held throughout the church consider the adoption of a similar policy.

(4) That the sessions of local churches admit persons to membership and fellowship in the local church on the scriptural basis of faith in the Lord Jesus Christ without reference to race.

(5) That in this time of crisis and concern, we commend to all individuals in our communion and especially to all leaders of our churches the earnest cultivation and practice of the Christian graces of forbearance, patience, humility and persistent goodwill. (Report of the Council on Christian Relations, adopted by the General Assembly of the Presbyterian Church in the United States [Southern], May 27-June 1, 1954.)

* * *

. . . As the Christian people of the South face [the] problems of race which now present us with an unparalleled obligation and opportunity, the General Assembly proposes for careful consideration the following principles which in its judgment should guide them:

All people have been created in the image of God and are to be treated as such. Therefore, we should confront problems of race against the background of a world perspective. . . .

To do unto others as we would have them do unto us, we must seek sympathetically and imaginatively to understand their point of view, their needs, aspirations, and fears; this is a rule for individuals, groups, and nations.

The Christian conscience cannot rest content with any legal or compulsive arrangement that brands any people as inferior; which denies them the full right of citizenship on the ground of race, color, or social status; or which prevents them from developing to the fullest possible extent the potentialities with which they, as individuals, have been endowed by the Creator.

The recent decision of the Supreme Court regarding segregation in

the Public Schools must be recognized as the law of the land, and
obeyed as such unless it is changed by legal and constitutional
methods.

The public school system must be preserved and strengthened. To
withhold the benefits of a public school education from any child, to
prevent any community by punitive means from carrying out its educational responsibility is an unwise and dangerous expedient.

Violence, and furious or unrestrained language which may incite
thereto, must be avoided; all organizations, hooded or otherwise, which
seek to take the law in their own hand, and all movements which would
prevent citizens from resorting to law in their own defense must be
opposed.

The right to vote must be made secure for citizens without restrictions based on race or color, without preventive stratagems which
make a mockery of democratic processes.

Communication between responsible leaders of the two races in the
South must be developed, strengthened, and maintained. It is essential that individual church members seek to be led by the Spirit of
Christ in their daily contacts with those of other races, and so preserve
the fellowship of believers in Him as Lord and Savior.

To the Christian people of the South there is now given an opportunity to demonstrate the effectiveness of the Gospel in solving a
difficult problem in human relations whose far-reaching effects are in-
calculable. God grant that we may not fail our nation or our Lord in
this period of crisis. (General Assembly, The Presbyterian Church
in the United States [Southern], 1958.)

*   *   *

As Christians we hold that all forms of racial discrimination and
segregation are denials of human worth and are contrary to the will
of God.

We call for the launching of "operation desegregation" in our
churches and church-related institutions and in the communities in
which our churches work and serve:

I. The action of the Supreme Court of the United States with
reference to racial segregation in public schools points up the failure of
the church to achieve true fellowship within its own life. The church
must act now to abolish from its practices all forms of segregation.
We note progress already achieved on this front, but we must continue
to work earnestly for desegregation with respect to

—local churches, presbyteries, synods;
—boards and agencies of the church, at all levels, professional as well as clerical staff, and in the distribution of funds;
local church organizations and activities, sessions, church boards, employed staff, and volunteer leadership;
—church-controlled and church-related hospitals, homes for the aged, children's homes, and other institutions, both as to occupants and staff;
—all missionary enterprises;
—church-related schools, colleges, and seminaries, as to student bodies, faculties, and boards of trustees.

II. We call upon the members of our churches
—to work for desegregation in the businesses, professions, and unions to which they belong, and to urge the passage of fair employment practice laws with enforcement provisions in states in which legislation of this type is not already in effect;
—to work for desegregation in housing in their communities, private as well as public housing, and to refrain from entering into arrangements or covenants that tend to encourage segregation;
—to encourage and support all measures for facilitating the desegregation of public schools, both as to students and faculties;
—to seek the election or appointment of qualified representatives of Negro and other minority groups to public positions. (The Presbyterian Church in the U.S.A. [Northern], 1955 General Convention.)

REFORMED CHURCH IN AMERICA:

We believe that the problem of race is a problem of human relations. We believe that the Scriptures of the Old and New Testaments provide the final authority for all matters of human relations. We believe that all problems of human existence are resolved in the love for God above all, and for our neighbor as ourselves. We further believe that such love has been fully revealed to us in the life and work of Jesus Christ, our Lord and Savior; and that the grace to participate in that love is readily available through the Holy Spirit by faith. We believe that the primary function of the Church of Jesus Christ is to witness to that love to all people in every walk of life.

We believe that in the light of the Biblical revelation, we have fallen short in the demonstration of that love. We hereby make an act of confession and repentance. . . .

We believe that sincere repentance manifests itself in acts of obedient love. We therefore believe that our sincerity will be demonstrated through concrete local acts, such as:

. . . conscientious efforts to open the doors of all churches to all people.

the support of those laws and agencies designed to uphold and guarantee the rights and health of all. . . .

the education of our youth in the privileges and responsibilities of life in a free, mixed society.

We believe that Christian love represents the highest criterion for all human relations. . . . We believe also, that in a responsible society, the immediate goals of such love will be structured into laws. We believe that the Church exercises its prophetic role when it inspires its constituent society to construct such laws, and when it subjects such laws to the scrutiny of Divine revelation. In that spirit, we believe that the recent Supreme Court decision on the ordered, gradual desegregation of the public schools of our land, represents an effective legal expression of Christian attitudes and convictions at the present time. We believe that we should support and implement the intent of that decision. . . .

We believe that marriage is a Divinely appointed institution to perpetuate the human race, to preserve the order of society, and to realize the fullness of human personality. We believe therefore that when two people are so joined, regardless of race differences, society and church must respect that marriage.

We further believe that the Church recognizes the sanctity of marriage, and bestows God's blessings on those who marry "in the Lord". We believe that being "in Christ" transcends all ethnic and cultural barriers. We believe that the Church misconceives its function when it actively hinders, forestalls, or denies, the marriage of any two people who, loving Christ, love each other. We also believe on the other hand, that the Church has received no Divine mandate to actively foster interracial marriage. We believe that when two people present themselves before God and the Church for marriage within the Scriptural context, the Church unites them with the blessing and under the aegis of God, and welcomes them as a family into the full Christian fellowship. We further strongly believe that when children born into this creative relationship receive the stings and outrages of a sub-Christian society, the Christian fellowship as the Body of Christ acting in compassion and mercy, binds up the wounds and heals the hurts of its injured members. We also believe that, at the same time the Church must bring the righteousness of Christ to bear on a society wayward in its offenses of "these little ones". We believe that by so bearing one another's burdens, the burdens of offended and offender, we fulfill the law of Christ. . . .

We believe that the racially inclusive and culturally integrated church represents the highest demonstration of the transforming fellowship of reconciliation which characterizes the Christian fellowship at its best. We believe that where opportunities for such churches exist, conscientious efforts be made to realize this ideal. We further believe that those who are ministering in these frontier areas of Christian faith and life be actively encouraged and warmly supported.

We believe that racially restricted housing covenants, real or implied, are inconsistent with Christian integrity. We believe that according to Scripture, the rights of property are subservient to the needs of people. We believe that there is nothing inherent in race differences to necessitate the decline in property values. We believe that restrictive pressures and flight-in-panic on the part of dominant groups lead to unnecessary real estate declines and contribute to the establishment and perpetuation of ghetto-existence. . . .

We believe that each generation inherits from the past problems for which it cannot be held directly accountable, but for whose solutions it is held responsible. We believe that the Cross of Christ, seen as vicarious atonement, points the way to the Christian resolution of this dilemma. We believe that we are called to bear the wounds (or crosses) of vicarious suffering, so that the least of Christ's brethren may find their rightful places in the society of men and the Kingdom of God. (Credo on Race Relations, The Reformed Church in America, June 7, 1957.)

ROMAN CATHOLIC BISHOPS:

. . . We have preferred the path of action to that of exhortation. Unfortunately, however, it appears that in recent years the issues have become confused and the march toward justice and equality has been slowed if not halted in some areas. The transcendent moral issues involved have become obscured, and possibly forgotten.

Our nation now stands divided by the problem of compulsory segregation of the races and the opposing demand for racial justice. No region of our land is immune from strife and division resulting from this problem. In one area, the key issue may concern the schools. In another it may be conflicts over housing. Job discrimination may be the focal point in still other sectors. But all these issues have one point in common. They reflect the determination of our Negro people, and we hope the overwhelming majority of our white citizens, to see that our colored citizens obtain their full rights as given to them by God, the Creator of all, and guaranteed by the democratic traditions of our nation.

. . . The time has come, in our considered and prayerful judgment, to cut through the maze of secondary or less essential issues and to come to the heart of the problem. The heart of the race question is moral and religious. It concerns the rights of man and our attitude toward our fellow man. If our attitude is governed by the great Christian law of love of neighbor and respect for his rights, then we can work out harmoniously the techniques for making legal, educational, economic, and social adjustments. But if our hearts are poisoned by hatred, or even by indifference toward the welfare and rights of our fellow men, then our nation faces a grave internal crisis.

. . . Among all races and national groups, class distinctions are inevitably made on the basis of like-mindedness or a community of interests. Such distinctions are normal and constitute a universal social phenomenon. They are accidental, however, and are subject to change as conditions change. It is unreasonable and injurious to the rights of others that a factor such as race, by and of itself, should be made a cause of discrimination and a basis for unequal treatment in our mutual relations.

The question then arises: Can enforced segregation be reconciled with the Christian view of our fellow man? In our judgment it cannot, and this for two fundamental reasons.

(1) Legal segregation, or any form of compulsory segregation, in itself and by its very nature imposes a stigma of inferiority upon the segregated people. Even if the now obsolete Court doctrine of "separate but equal" had been carried out to the fullest extent, so that all public and semipublic facilities were in fact equal, there is nonetheless the judgment that an entire race, by the sole fact of race and regardless of individual qualities, is not fit to associate on equal terms with members of another race. We cannot reconcile such a judgment with the Christian view of man's nature and rights. Here again it is appropriate to cite the language of Pope Pius XII: "God did not create a human family made up of segregated, dissociated, mutually

independent members. No; he would have them all united by the bond of total love of Him and consequent self-dedication to assisting each other to maintain that bond intact."

(2) It is a matter of historical fact that segregation in our country has led to oppressive conditions and the denial of basic human rights for the Negro. This is evident in the fundamental fields of education, job opportunity, and housing. Flowing from these areas of neglect and discrimination are problems of health and the sordid train of evils so often associated with the consequent slum conditions. Surely Pope Pius XII must have had these conditions in mind when he said just two months ago: "It is only too well known, alas, to what excesses pride of race and racial hate can lead. The Church has always been energetically opposed to attempts of genocide or practices arising from what is called the color bar."

One of the tragedies of racial oppression is that the evils we have cited are being used as excuses to continue the very conditions that so strongly fostered such evils. Today we are told that Negroes, Indians, and also some Spanish-speaking Americans differ too much in culture and achievements to be assimilated in our schools, factories, and neighborhoods. Some decades back the same charge was made against the immigrant, Irish, Jewish, Italian, Polish, Hungarian, German, Russian. In both instances differences were used by some as a basis for discrimination and even for bigoted ill-treatment. The immigrant, fortunately, has achieved his rightful status in the American community. Economic opportunity was wide open and educational equality was not denied to him.

Negro citizens seeks these same opportunities. They wish an education that does not carry with it any stigma of inferiority. They wish economic advancement based on merit and skill. They wish their civil rights as American citizens. They wish acceptance based upon proved ability and achievement. No one who truly loves God's children will deny them this opportunity. (Statement of the Roman Catholic Bishops of the United States, November 13, 1958.)

SOCIETY OF FRIENDS:

We the 120 Friends gathered here at Wilmington from 16 Yearly Meetings, as well as other Friends groups, greet you all in Christian love.

Coming from North, South, East, and West, we have been made

tender in the deeper realization that "all of us have sinned and some short of the glory of God" in our relations with our brothers. We have stood in the light of Christ "which lighteth every man that cometh into the world," and which makes all men equal in God's sight.

We have been led to face our failure to met the urgent challenge of the worldwide revolution in human relations. We recognize our confusion and our lack of faithfulness to our principles. In all parts of the nation we have failed. Through ignorance or complacency or fear we have neglected our moral obligation. We have not treated all men as brothers.

Group statements sometimes mean very little, but this we know: that right relations with God must lead to right relations with all men. Instead of passing judgment on one another, our task lies in helping one another to move forward in a practical application of this truth. Here, at this Conference, Friends, pastoral and nonpastoral, urban and rural, Negro and white, have prayed together and spoken to one another honestly in a spirit of love. We have gained insight into one another's problems and have seen barriers fall. We urge Friends to create opportunities for similar experiences.

We see a service for Friends in the quiet, experimental action taken by the individual Meeting and the individual Friend in their home communities. We earnestly pray that we can move under a sense of the urgency of world events from where we are to where God would have us be in race relations. More important than where we are is the direction in which we are going.

In the midst of tension and conflict at home and abroad, we see the immediacy of this problem. . . . (Philadelphia Yearly Meeting of Friends, August 31-September 3, 1956.)

SYNAGOGUE COUNCIL OF AMERICA:

The Synagogue Council of America greets with deep satisfaction the historic decision of the Supreme Court of the United States ending segregation in the public schools of America.

This decision is another expression of the Prophetic insistence that in the eyes of God all men are His children and therefore equal, regardless of their religion or race.

The sincere believer in the Fatherhood of God must believe in the brotherhood of man and consequently that what is basic in our neighbor is the color of his conduct, not his skin.

This epic pronouncement illumines again this great soul of America; it is conclusive repudiation of the Communist challenge to the genuineness of America's democratic avowals. (Statement of the Synagogue Council of America, 1954.)

UNITARIANS (AMERICAN UNITARIAN ASSOCIATION):

Therefore be it Resolved, That the American Unitarian Association at its 130th Annual Meeting urge our churches and fellowships to cooperate in their communities with all efforts to facilitate the transition to non-segregation, and we assert our opposition to all efforts, including the weakening of the public schools, to evade the Supreme Court decision. (May 24, 1955.)

*   *   *

Therefore be it resolved,

1. That we the delegates to the 131st Annual Meeting of the American Unitarian Association favor every attempt to meet and search for areas of agreement and mutual understanding among men of all races and persuasions and will ourselves foster and join with all such attempts;

2. That we respectfully urge the President of the United States, the governors of the separate states, and all persons in civil authority to call and persistently support, within their respective jurisdictions, conferences of good citizens of all races in order that a groundwork of healthy communication may be established and just solutions to these problems may be found;

3. That we urge upon all governmental officials and agencies their duty to accord the full protection of the law to all citizens in the exercise of their rights, including the right to vote, and the other rights guaranteed by the Constitution of the United States; and

4. Finally, that we call upon the Congress of the United States to enact such legislation as may be necessary to accord this protection wherever it is not provided by the local community. (May 22, 1956.)

Therefore be it Resolved,

That the American Unitarian Association urge all people of good will to work unremittingly in all phases of local, state, and national life towards:

1. Abolishing all official sanctions and practices which would require racial segregation in public schools, public transportation, public

housing, and other publicly supported facilities;

2. Eliminating racial restrictions on membership in churches, professional organizations, labor unions, and similar semi-public bodies;

3. Eliminating racial discrimination in employment and housing;

4. Promoting mutual understanding between members of different races by all available means, including working together in organizations having members of different races;

5. Encouraging the spread of information about successful action to end or lessen racial discrimination and promote racial understanding. (May 28, 1957; a similar resolution was approved on May 27, 1958)

REFERENCE NOTES

CHAPTER ONE

1. Weldon James, "The South's Own Civil War." In Don Shoemaker (ed.), *With All Deliberate Speed*. New York: Harper, 1957; p. 23.

2. From a spring 1957 address to a Unitarian Church conference held in Nashville, Tennessee. *Ibid.*, p. 34. The statement can be supported by such facts as the University of Mississippi losing a third of its associate and full professors from 1955 to 1957. *New South*, 12 (July-August 1957), pp. 10-11.

3. Public opinion polls have consistently shown that white, college-educated southerners—those who can be expected to be typically the most influential—are far more willing to accept integrated facilities than other white southerners. Thus in 1956 the National Opinion Research Center found that 42 percent of their white, college southerners approved integrated transportation and 28 percent favored school integration while the corresponding percentages for the grammar school educated were only 13 and 5. H. H. Hyman and P. B. Sheatsley, "Attitudes Toward Desegregation," *Scientific American*, 195 (December 1956), pp. 35-39.

4. James, *op. cit.*, p. 23. This contention is documented by the results of a 1958 mail survey by *Pulpit Digest* of a cross section of Protestant ministers in the South. Four out of every five respondents favored compliance with the Supreme Court's order for public school integration. "Southern Ministers Speak Their Minds," *Pulpit Digest*, 39 (December 1958), pp. 13-17.

5. A more complete review of recent pronouncements concerning race from the leading religious groups in America is provided at the end of the present work.

6. James, *op. cit.*, p. 24.

7. Robert Penn Warren, *Segregation*. New York: Random House, 1956; p. 100. This is a general phenomenon, applying to many if not all denominations on a wide variety of issues. A widely held rule of thumb is that the farther away the ministers are from their home churches, the more liberal they are on all issues.

8. "Protestantism Speaks on Justice and Integration," *Christian Century*, 75 (February 5, 1958), pp. 164-166.

9. James, *op. cit.*, p. 27.

10. *Southern School News*, 4 (May 1958), p. 16.

11. Bonita Valien, *The St. Louis Story: a Study of Desegregation*. New York: Freedom Pamphlet of the Anti-Defamation League of B'nai B'rith, 1956; p. 63.

12. James, *op. cit.*, p. 27.

13. Wallace Westfeldt, "Communities in Strife." In Don Shoemaker, *op. cit.*, pp. 49-50.

14. *Ibid.*, p. 47.

15. *Ibid.*, p. 51.

16. *Southern Schools News*, 3 (January 1957), p. 15.

17. *New South*, 12 (July-August 1957), p. 11.

18. Other frontier regions also tend to develop religious forms with a strong, unyielding, but protective God. Consider, for example, the extremely fundamentalist aspects of

172

the Dutch Reform Church that Afrikaner frontiersmen evolved in the Union of South Africa.

19. W. J. Cash, *The Mind of the South*. New York: Knopf, 1941.

20. *Ibid.*, p. 335; and Gunnar Myrdal, *An American Dilemma*, New York: Harper, 1944; p. 563.

21. F. S. Loescher, "The Protestant Church and the Negro: Recent Pronouncements," *Social Forces*, 26 (December 1947), pp. 197-201.

22. Myrdal, *op. cit.*, p. 563.

23. Samuel Stouffer, *Communism, Conformity, and Civil Liberties*. New York: Doubleday, 1955; p. 141.

24. T. F. Pettigrew, "Regional Differences in Anti-Negro Prejudice." Unpublished Ph.D. Dissertation, Harvard University Library, 1956. Poll studies which do not show a regional difference are combining northern Protestants with northern Catholics, the latter group usually the most frequent attenders of all. The present regional discrepancy under discussion is just Protestant attendance. Leo Rosten (*A Guide to the Religions of America*, New York: Simon and Schuster, 1955) cites studies showing regional breakdowns without breakdowns by religion.

25. B. T. Prothro and J. A. Jensen, "Interrelations of Religious and Ethnic Attitudes in Selected Southern Populations," *Journal of Social Psychology*, 32 (August 1950), pp. 45-49; and "Comparison of Some Ethnic and Religious Attitudes of Negro and White College Students in the Deep South," *Social Forces*, 30 (May 1952), pp. 426-428.

26. S. W. Gray, "A Note on the Values of Southern College Women: White and Negro," *Journal of Social Psychology*, 25 (May 1947), pp. 239-241; and G. W. Allport, Phillip E. Vernon, and Gardner Lindzey, *Study of Values: Manual of Directions*. Boston: Houghton Mifflin, 1951.

27. 1950 census data illustrate a related point of importance. The South has the smallest percentage of professional and technical people in its labor force of any region but still has more ministers. Thus only five percent of Arkansas' employed male labor force is professional compared with New York and California's ten percent though Arkansas has almost twice the proportionate number of ministers. In rural areas particularly this means that southern ministers are unusually influential simply because of the lack of competition from other professional people.

28. These data are from the 1947 North-Hatt occupational prestige study. See National Opinion Research Center, "Jobs and Occupations: a Popular Evaluation." In R. Bendix and S. M. Lipset (eds.), *Class, Status and Power*. Glencoe, Ill.: Free Press, 1953; pp. 411-426. These previously unpublished results were kindly furnished by Dr. Albert J. Reiss, Jr., of Vanderbilt University.

29. John Gillin, "National and Regional Cultural Values in the United States," *Social Forces*, 34 (December 1955), pp. 107-113; and John Gillin and Emmett J. Murphy, "Note on Southern Culture Patterns," *Social Forces*, 29 (May 1951), pp. 422-432.

30. Floyd Hunter, *Community Power Structure*. Chapel Hill: University of North Carolina Press, 1953; pp. 82-83.

31. *Southern School News*, 3 (January 1957), p. 15.

32. From an address by Dr. George at Dartmouth College, October 12, 1956. Church lay leaders in the South have sometimes made similar statements. Witness the announcement of L. Randolph Thompson, senior warden of St. Peter's Episcopal Church of Altavista, Virginia, as reported in a June 6, 1958, Associated Press release: "What disturbs me is to see so many conservative, consecrated and experienced

ministers leave the diocese and to see them replaced by a group of young and immature men, who are disposed, evidently with the bishop's blessing, to conduct themselves with the zeal of a John Brown or a Harriet Beecher Stowe. Their selection seems to be in line with a definite plan of reorganization. . . . It seems to me that the clergy of the diocese of Southwestern Virginia are inclined to go far beyond the limits set by the average Southerner with regard to race relations and they seem to be full of the zeal of crusaders in their unswerving determination to sweep aside the customs and traditions of the Church of Virginia and reshape our social ways to their concept of political expediency and Christian doctrine."

33. Myrdal, op. cit.

34. In this connection, it is significant that segregationists never once question the Constitution, but attempt to argue instead that others—the Supreme Court, the President, etc.—are not abiding by the Constitution. Indeed, this tendency of the southerner to cloak himself with the Constitution can be demonstrated even back in the pre-Civil War debates when the South, rightly or wrongly, claimed that the North was departing from the Constitution.

35. Myrdal, op. cit., p. 9.

36. Helen V. McLean, "Psychodynamic Factors in Race Relations," The Annals of the American Academy of Political and Social Science, 244 (March 1946), pp. 159-166; and Lillian Smith, Killers of the Dream. New York: Norton, 1949.

37. R. P. Warren, op. cit., p. 93.

38. T. F. Pettigrew, "Personality and Socio-Cultural Factors in Intergroup Attitudes: a Cross-National Comparison," Journal of Conflict Resolution, 2 (March 1958), pp. 29-42.

39. S. E. Asch, "Effects of Group Pressure Upon the Modification and Distortion of Judgments." In G. E. Swanson, T. M. Newcomb, and E. L. Hartley (eds.), Readings in Social Psychology (2nd edition). New York: Holt, 1952; pp. 2-11.

40. C. Y. Glock and B. B. Ringer, "Church Policy and the Attitudes of Ministers and Parishioners on Social Issues," American Sociological Review, 21 (April 1956), pp. 148-156; and Ringer and Glock, "The Political Role of the Church as Defined by its Parishioners," Public Opinion Quarterly, 18 (winter, 1954-1955), pp. 337-347.

41. Our previous polling experiences in the South led to this decision. The change in identification has little effect on the analysis of the results, in any event, since no direct comparisons between the sect and church ministers are made.

42. One or both of us returned to Little Rock in December 1957 and in August and November 1958. Many of our 42 clerical respondents were interviewed on several different occasions before the 15-month study ended.

CHAPTER TWO

1. Published as an open letter to "Methodists of Arkansas and Louisiana" in the *Arkansas Methodist*, October 10, 1957.

2. We have depended on certain daily news media—in particular, the *New York Times*, the *Christian Science Monitor*, and Little Rock's two dailies, the morning *Arkansas Gazette* and the evening *Arkansas Democrat*. Such sources may be incomplete; page one treatment in newspapers one day may receive scant or no mention the next day, depending on the news value of concurrent events. Likewise, internal affairs of the individual church—sermons, group sessions, pastoral letters, etc.—may not have been released to the press. There was an inevitable selectivity in whose sermons the reporter attended and in what telephones he rang to obtain statements.

Fortunately for our purposes, however, there was considerable lack of overlap between the two local newspapers in reporting news of racial relevance. Relatively at least, the *Democrat* gave prominent space to those who defended segregation while the *Gazette* gave space to the critics of Governor Faubus and to those who gave tacit acceptance to token integration. This condition corrects to some extent the restrictions imposed by use of newspaper sources.

These published reports have been supplemented and checked against what the minister himself told us of his activities and efforts at both the congregational and community levels, and of his views about what was happening. We tried particularly hard in our interviews to discover the kind of quiet work with congregations or small groups within the congregation that by its nature would not receive wide publicity. We believe that we have assembled, if not a complete, certainly a representative picture of ministerial involvement in Little Rock's racial crisis. However, the reader should know that what we have written is based on what the press published and on what the minister himself told us of what he had said, done, and tried to do.

3. This sermon is reprinted in full in *New South*, 12 (July-August 1957), pp. 4-9 (published by Southern Regional Council, Atlanta, Georgia), and in the *Arkansas Gazette* just before the schools opened in September 1957.

4. This sermon was printed and circulated by the Southern Baptist Christian Life Commission. Copies may be obtained upon request to that source.

5. The entire statement read as follows: "We, the undersigned ministers of Little Rock, strongly protest the action of Governor Orval E. Faubus in calling out the armed forces of the state to surround Central High School, thereby preventing integration in compliance with the Supreme Court's decision of May 1954 and the order of the Federal Court of August 1957.

"We deplore: (1) the overriding of the authority of the local school administration; (2) the disregard of national law; (3) the abuse of the autonomy of the local school districts; (4) the policing of the great majority of law abiding youth of the city; (5) the exciting of racial tensions; (6) the reflections cast upon our local law enforcement officers; (7) the destruction of the respect of our citizens, young and old, for proper constitutional authority.

"We appeal to every citizen to unite with us in earnest prayer to God that justice will be brought about and a right example set for every child in the community."

6. The number of local ministers who since the first of September of 1957 have said publicly and unequivocally, in unison or individually, that segregation is a moral wrong is extremely small.

7. These two associations are organized as the American Baptist Association (ABA) and the North American Baptist Association (NABA). They do not differ in doctrine from each other; the latter split from the former in 1950 over matters of policy. We will refer to them both as Missionary Baptists, which corresponds to Little Rock usage within both bodies.

The ABA was formed in 1905 as the Baptist General Association and adopted its present name in 1924. Its members deny that those Baptists organized in convention (for example, the Southern Baptist Convention) are faithful to Bible precedent. Their strength is chiefly in the South and Southwest. They believe that salvation is solely by grace through faith and not by law or work. Their theology is generally conservative. The ABA reported 287,000 members and 2,105 churches in 1951; by 1957 these figures had increased to 630,000 and 3,025 respectively.

The NABA was organized in 1950 in Little Rock, which remains the center of its strength. It reported nearly 2,000 churches and 160,000 members in 1951; by 1957 there were 1778 churches with 261,000 members.

Clearly, these two organizations are not small sects in any numerical sense, loosely federated as the individual churches may be. They are relatively small in comparison to the Southern Baptist Convention, which in 1957 reported almost 9,000,000 members, or the Methodist Church, which claimed 9,500,000 in the same year. Our use of the description "small" is derived from the fact that each relatively independent church is small. Thus, when in 1957, there were 287 Southern Baptists and 242 Methodists per congregation, the ABA had only 165 and the NABA only 147 members for each church. Even so, these latter organizations showed a marked average increase over 1951, when the ABA had 136 members per church and the NABA only 83.

For further data on these and other bodies, see Benson Y. Landis, *Yearbook of American Churches for 1959*. New York: National Council of Churches of Christ in the U.S.A., 1958; and Frank S. Mead, *Handbook of Denominations in the United States* (revised and enlarged edition). New York: Abingdon Press, 1956.

8. For example, a year later (September 26, 1958) the signers formed the nucleus of a group of 80 ministers of "Greater Little Rock" which took nearly a full-page advertisement in the *Arkansas Democrat* to declare that "integration is contrary to the will of God."

9. Those who wish to understand the life of Arkansas must begin by a simple division of the state between the flat delta land of eastern and southern Arkansas and the rolling hill country to the west and north. Segregationist sentiment is concentrated in the former. It is relevant to observe that Clarksville is in northwestern Arkansas, approximately 55 miles from the Oklahoma border and 75 miles from Missouri. Little Rock sits astride the boundary between the two parts of the state.

For documentation of the political significance of this distinction, see V. O. Key, Jr., *Southern Politics*. New York: Knopf, 1949; ch. 9.

10. By contrast, the effort of one liberal minister simply to reprint the racial pronouncements of his national church and circulate them to members and to news sources met with defeat when he could not secure support for his venture from either his fellow pastors or members of his church hierarchy.

11. Southern Baptists and Roman Catholics are not represented in the United Church Women. Neither are the small sects.

12. We found the use of sermons that have an inferential but not a direct relevance to the issue of race relations to be a common procedure for ministers with liberal racial views. To choose from several available cases, one pastor had scheduled sermons on the "Toleration of Differences," "Daring Not to Conform," and the "Human Need for Kindness" for the weeks after our interview with him in late October.

13. On October 8, a local segregationist minister became treasurer of a newly formed Freedom Fund Inc., of Nashville, Tennessee, established solely to raise money for the legal defense of persons arrested in connection with the Little Rock school integration disputes. Although the charter did not so specify, we are safe to assume that the fund was for the defense of whites only.

14. The complete statement follows: "In the very beginnings of my remarks, let me say that I am an American first, last, and always, and that I believe in the Constitution of the United States. In no sense of the word am I opposing the Constitution. But the Constitutional rights of the citizens of Little Rock, Ark. have been violated and trampled into the ground by the invasion of Federal troops into a sovereign state and a local school matter.

"There was no violence in Little Rock when Gov. Faubus called out the National Guard as there was in other cities. He called out the National Guard to preserve peace and order. All of the violence that has erupted in Little Rock came as the result of the President's sending Federal troops into this city.

"I protest with every ounce of energy at my command, the violation of State's Rights and personal rights. At the close of World War I, as a member of the 89th Division, I was with the troops that went into Germany forming the Army of Occupation. We were instructed that there was to be no violence offered to German civilians. We did not behave in Germany as the 101st Airborne behaved here in Little Rock. I have many members of my church who served during World War II and in Korea and they tell me that they received instructions to lay no hands on civilians. They are unanimous in their opinion that Federal troops should never have been sent to Little Rock. The Constitutional Rights of all the citizens of Arkansas have been violated.

"I saw the troops move into Little Rock and their attitude was that of conquerors. I have the feeling that many Germans must have felt under Hitler and that Hungarians now feel under Russia. We have no right to criticize the Russians for moving into Hungary under the pretext of preserving law and order when our own President has done the same thing and on the same pretext.

"The commanding General in Little Rock, General Walker, in speaking to the high school assembly said in substance that when the Supreme Court ruled concerning the Constitution, that ruling became the law of the land and could not be changed until an amendment to the Constitution of the United States had been adopted; that only by such democratic means could the law be changed. The General was 100% right. But he was confused in his thinking for this reason. The Supreme Court had already ruled many years ago that segregation in the public schools was legal, provided that the facilities were equal. Little Rock has met every requirement of that decision of the Supreme Court. In addition to the original decision, there have been many more decisions confirming the original decision of "separate but equal" facilities. Therefore, the Supreme Court itself violated the Constitution since no amendment to the Constitution has been adopted.

"Little Rock has completely complied with that decision. The negro schools of Little Rock are superior to the white schools. The negroes now have a modern, first class, high school that provides facilities better than those at Central High School. Central High is 30 years old and obsolete in many respects.

"However, the big issue in this whole thing is not a matter of segregation, but centralized power dictatorship government. If Federal troops can be sent in on a local school situation, they can be sent in on any pretext the President so desires.

"How long are Federal troops to pace the corridors and patrol the grounds of Central High School? One officer of the 101st Airborne Division when asked that question answered, 'We were in Germany for 15 years.' Before God, are we a conquered people? Are we a satalite [sic] state? Have we no rights? Is every decision now to be made in Washington? Is there no local self-government? Where are we headed? What is the answer?

"Violence is not the answer either on the part of the Federal Government or the local citizens. Therefore, I plead with the members of my congregation to avoid all violence; that though the provocations may be great, that we as Christians, must not yield to them."

15. The italicized questions are given for clearer exposition of content. They did not appear as such in the original advertisement. Only the sections within quotations marks appeared in the advertisement itself.

16. The qualifying phrase, "at the community level," is used because the noncommittal prayer services may well have helped mend some fences at the level of individual congregations. Many ministers who earlier in the crisis had expressed liberal positions were faced by this time with increasing signs of disaffection and unrest among their congregations.

17. No doubt one reason for the plan's failure to receive uniform support lay with the pubicly expressed dissatisfaction of some supporters with its moral neutrality. In the planning stages, for example, one leading religious figure unsuccessfully proposed "some action such as a moral pronouncement which would reaffirm the dignity of the individual and proclaim aloud justice for all peoples, all races." His proposal was not well received.

18. It probably is not coincidental that these three church bodies have an ecclesiastical form of church polity.

19. Vagueness and ambiguity such as this were frequent, indeed typical, characteristics of Little Rock ministers who were known on the basis of other evidence to prefer public school desegregation. In this case, the "situation" can be the violent efforts to keep nine Negro students out of Central High School or it can mean the efforts to get them in the school. And it appears from the statement that the Communists' use of the situation for propaganda purposes, less than its intrinsic qualities, made it deplorable. In a similar vein, it is difficult to establish clearly any explicit challenge, standard, or guide to conduct in the quotation at the beginning of this chapter.

20. As in the previous instance (note 15), the separate statements are summaries given for the sake of emphasis. Only the statements in quotations were made by participants in the service.

21. The president of the Mothers' League was one of the choir members of the church served by the president of the Capital Citizens' Council.

CHAPTER THREE

1. Their insularity expressed a fundamentalistic theology and a hostility toward both religious and secular out-groups. Neither the minister nor his constituents hold positions of high status in the community. The ministers are convinced that their faith is the true one and that other religious bodies, especially those serving middle and upper classes, practice a type of religious quackery. In the words of one: "Paganism covered over with a thin, thin veneer of religion is the dominant religious force in this country, and in Little Rock."

2. This figure (30) is the total number of times any name was mentioned, not the number of different names given. The number of persons named is, naturally, much smaller.

3. Conversely, not a single Missionary Baptist or other sect pastor was named by any of the "peace prayer" pastors in their lists of co-workers or of influentials in the ministerial body.

4. Frequently ministers who at one point in the interview had told us of their sermons or lectures in defense of segregation, at another point would tell us that they kept "politics and such subjects" out of their sermons. Probably the most striking case was that of a man who had devoted virtually his entire service to the subject of racial separation the Sunday preceding our session with him. His opening response to our request for an interview was: "I can tell you in a very few words about this integration business. We do not preach the social gospel. We preach the Gospel of Our Lord Jesus Christ and we do not discuss integration with our congregation. It simply does not come up and is not a part of our church work."

5. For an interesting demonstration that religious beliefs are related to socioeconomic status, even within particular denominations, see Russell R. Dynes, "Church-Sect Typology and Socio-Economic Status," *American Sociological Review,* 20 (October 1955), pp. 555-560.

6. It remains a real fascination to us that almost 300 newsmen descended on a city of 125,000 to cover its school tensions during the fall of 1957, yet only a few reported the existence, not to mention the significance, of Hall High School. Even Pulitzer prize-winning Harry Ashmore, editor of the *Arkansas Gazette,* who got the news out fast in September and who also has written compellingly of the deficiencies in news coverage of that city's crisis, seemingly did not consider Hall High important enough to inform his national audience about it.

Yet there it sits. Brand new in the fall of 1957, it looked out on a pine forest and a still unpaved road. Sewer pipes still were unlaid. Located on land outside the corporate limits of the city when the Supreme Court handed down its historic decision of May 17, 1954, Hall High, built to serve 1,000 students, had much space to spare in the 1957-58 school session. It stands on the western tip of the city, in the path of residential movement. Virtually no Negroes are in its district, and there are informal but workable arrangements to see to it that this situation does not change. Hall High School was built to serve a major portion of Little Rock's middle and upper class groups—and whites only.

Whatever else it means, Hall High School stands as a monument to everything

179

that ought not to be done when a community wants to desegregate its schools peacefully. Granting the real and honestly given reasons for building the school—that Little Rock needed another school, that its population was moving westward, that the possibility of admitting Negroes to Hall could be considered after the pattern had been established at Central—the fact remains that its existence drained off a large portion of responsible student leadership and parental interests from Central High when that school desperately needed good citizenship. Nor can it be denied that the elements in the city most prone to violence, who because of their inferior power positions had not participated in the decision to establish and locate Hall High, viewed the entire matter as a contrived means of forcing school integration on the lower classes while establishing a segregated system for upper-class groups.

One anomaly of the desegregation process is that the students who by their demeanor show the least interest in their own education, and the parents who never attend school functions and whom the principal cannot corral for conferences, are the ones whose efforts to "protect" their school from Negroes are the most vigorous, even violent. Their love for alma mater was never so great. The proportion of these types in the student and parent bodies at Central High School automatically increased when Hall High came into being. The use of violence and of gross, brutal physical injustice simply are not part of the pattern of life for the students who attend Hall High, whatever their preference in the matter of attending school with Negroes. And so it is with their parents. Civic leadership in Little Rock is residentially concentrated in the area served by Hall. These men were genuinely shocked and disturbed when violence erupted. They were chagrined that external restraints in the form of federal troops had to come to restore order. Yet any effort they made to restore local autonomy by restraining the violent was both compromised and accompanied by a discomfort akin to guilt. Lines of communication between the classes were cut; lines of authority were challenged. To any effort to restore reason, there was the inevitable response: "You can't tell us what to do. Your kids go to Hall. We're not in the same boat."

Whether the Little Rock police force conducted itself with maximum efficiency at Central High School in September 1957 is an open question. Nonetheless, its mere presence around the school identified it as the enemy of those intent on keeping Negroes out whatever the cost, and its officers were seen as the tools of those who wanted to integrate the school. It was in this light that a petition circulated by the Capital Citizens' Council for the removal from office of Police Chief Marvin Potts is of particular significance. It read in part: "He lives in the Central High attendance area, at 7th and Martin, but has side-stepped the Blossom law that all other Central High parents must obey, and has placed his daughter in Hall High . . . This privilege of transfer Mr. Virgil T. Blossom (school superintendent) has stoutly denied all other parents of the Central High area."

7. We do not know how much duplicity was involved in the plans for Hall High School. It was described to us by former Superintendent Blossom as part of an overall plan to provide three high schools for the city: one all-white, one all-colored, and one mixed. We do know, however, from our interviews with civic leaders that there was strong sentiment for keeping Negroes out of Hall High. When we asked one prominent citizen why the city did not admit Negroes into this new and middle-upper class school in preference to admitting them into the older and middle-lower class Central High, he spread his arms wide and exclaimed: "Why, our kids had a new location, new school, new teachers, an entirely new setup. You couldn't expect

them to have new Negroes, too." Also, the segregationist was right when he claimed that it was the vote in the Hall High area (he refers to it as the silk stocking area) combined with the Negro vote which elected school board members who favored the Central High integration plan in the spring of 1957.

It is interesting to recall that Governor Jeff Davis, the last man before Faubus to be elected governor of Arkansas three consecutive times (1900, 1902, and 1904), liked to refer to the upper class of Little Rock 60 years ago as "the high-collared roosters and the silk-stocking crowd." See V. O. Key, Jr., *Southern Politics*. New York: Knopf, 1949; p. 189.

8. One correspondent wrote as follows to the editor of the *Arkansas Democrat* (December 2, 1957): "I am turning integrationist for one reason and that is to see Hall High School integrated with all deliberate speed. If they don't integrate Hall then they have no right whatsoever to do so at Central High. The federal government is always talking about discrimination against the Negroes, but now hundreds of white children at Central High are being discriminated against."

We do not in the least mean to imply that ministers in the Hall High district were in any manner involved in the plans to initiate and maintain its all-white status. To the contrary, some of them felt keenly that whatever voice they might have was muted because they and members of their congregations were not so intimately involved in the issue at hand. Under a plan by which seniors in Hall High area might attend Central High if they so chose, the several Heights ministers who were thus affected as parents, all sent their children to Central.

9. There is a vast and expansive religious literature developing from many sources in the South in defense of segregation. The revival of this type of literature during the past several years is a significant social phenomenon in its own right. As one of many possible citations, see the *Missionary Baptist Searchlight*, Little Rock, Arkansas, September 25 and October 10, 1957.

10. We learned from interviews with other ministers that in a few instances members had been attracted to the churches of vocal segregationists even though the minister in their former church did nothing more than remain discreetly silent on the matter of segregation. In these cases, it seems obvious that "pull" rather than "push" factors operated. One would suspect that such transfers as these were distinctly related to social class variables, in that some lower-class members of a generally sophisticated, cosmopolitan church might seize the segregation issue as an excuse for a break they had long desired to make. One "uptown" pastor told us that several disaffected members of his church had affiliated with the congregation of a prominent sect segregationist. His only comment: "Good riddance, I say!"

11. The forthright manner and sure-footedness of these men stands in startling contrast to the holding actions and evasive manuevers of many among the more liberal ministers. A pastor of a substantial middle-class suburban church which is relatively detached from the issue because its children do not attend school in the city related this incident to us: "At the last meeting of my official board there was a movement within the board to declare our church in favor of segregation of the races. I believe in integration. At this meeting, I didn't state my own beliefs, but I took the position that if the church declared itself in favor of segregation, some members, a third or maybe even close to half, wouldn't like it, and if it declared itself in favor of integration, more than half the people wouldn't like it. Therefore, I recommended that the church should simply not declare itself on the matter, and they accepted what I said. That was the way I avoided a hot issue coming up. There's

no doubt in my mind that if this matter should come before the congregation at this time, the decision wuld be in favor of segregation by a good majority."

12. Of the many anomalies that have followed in the wake of the Supreme Court's historic desegregation decision, perhaps none is more striking than the use of public referendums to decide whether or not public schools should remain open. Not so many years ago compulsory school attendance laws were passed to require children to attend school. Now, the people for whom such laws were necessary are permitted to cast their votes in favor of impeding the educational plans of those for whom the law was never needed.

13. Actually, most of the integrationist ministers also were opposed to the proposed visit but for different reasons. They saw it as a matter of poor timing, on the grounds that Graham might open incipient schisms within the various congregations, and that at any rate he would not be able to reach the groups whom it was most crucial to deter from violence. They also feared that racial incidents might mar the services if Graham insisted on unsegregated seating. Therefore, it would be better if the date for a "crusade" be postponed. Plans have since been formulated to hold a Graham crusade in Little Rock in late 1959. As United States Congressman Brooks Hays reportedly wired Billy Graham, "The patient is recovering from shock and while the chaplain is always welcome, he might not be as effective unless the patient is ready to listen."

14. Here is an interesting exception to our observation that conscience conflict seems absent among these segregationists. (Since we have commented on the group's insularity, it is important to consider that the exception is less isolated from the general community than is typical.) The pastor of an extremely small church in an outlying area of the city has been forced to seek a supplementary income. His second job is a clerical post in a downtown business establishment, where both business associates and clients contrast sharply in class and economic characteristics to his religious associates; in fact, his work brings him into contact with quite important and influential members of the community.

The pastor's ambivalence was apparent in several areas: in his attitudes on the high school issue, in his comments on the segregationist prayer services, and in the appraisal he gave us of his local seminary training. Though he defined himself as a segregationist, he said he really couldn't see anything basically wrong with admitting Negroes to Central High School provided the public went along with the idea. He defended his support of the Friday night service because he felt something had to be done to show that not all of the city's pastors were integrationists, but he expressed a strong concern that this type of action tends to encourage the lawless elements in the community. In speaking of his own background, he said that his work brings him in contact with many highly educated and interesting people with whom he would like to talk, yet he finds they do not speak the same language. But he fears that modern education is leading the people away from the kinds of values and religious beliefs he favors. He said that students at the local seminary receive a doctoral degree when they graduate, yet he wonders whether a graduate really ought to refer to himself as "doctor."

15. Gunnar Myrdal, An American Dilemma. New York: Harper, 1944; especially chapters 1, 2, and 45.

16. Just as the segregationist sought the sanctity of the Constitution in defense of his position, so he also tried to find inconsistency in the arguments of the opposition. The following quotation from a sect minister illustrates this technique: "Now these

integrationists do a lot of talking about 'equality.' Well, just look at the President himself. He made some statements that there were no second-class citizens in this country. Now you know that's foolish, him with all that military rank of his— general and everything—don't tell me he wouldn't pull his rank on a buck private."

17. There are some interesting comparisons between these points and the arguments advanced in support of the Dixiecrat political movement in 1948. See Sarah McCulloh Lemmon, "The Ideology of the 'Dixiecrat' Movement," *Social Forces*, 30 (December 1951), pp. 162-171.

18. The meanings of the terms "sect" and "denomination" as we use them are given in Chapter Seven.

CHAPTER FOUR

1. To term the efforts of these eight men "a social movement" is not to imply that there was a unified coordination of action or a single strategy on their part. Indeed, the eight were divided into three small, informal groups of their own. They form a movement only in the sense that they were all trying to accomplish the same thing at the same time: concerted, public defense of integration by the entire Little Rock clergy.

2. The two authors and a third person, studying the ministerial actions during the crisis, independently divided the 29 denominational ministers into eight innovators, seven influentials, and 14 inactives. We were in close agreement on our judgments. The seven influentials, though less than one-quarter of the sample, received more than 80 percent of the ministers' nominations as the most influential among Little Rock's clergy. Further evidence that these ratings make sense in terms of other variables is demonstrated in the next section of this chapter.

3. Though not officially linked, this organization works closely with the Southern Regional Council in Atlanta. This local council was quite often the instigator of specific actions by the clergy in Little Rock and offered an opportunity to ministers to work for integration behind the scenes. One influential remarked: "I can do things quietly as a member of the Arkansas Council on Human Relations that I cannot do through my church." Yet such action by ministers is not clerical action; it could just as well, if not better, be performed by businessmen. Our interest, however, is in ministerial action as church action, not secular activities, effective as these may sometimes be.

4. This offer, as well as similar offers, was summarily refused by the school officials. With the debatable logic that "too many cooks spoil the broth," the education authorities preferred to go it alone. For critical statements concerning this policy by a Little Rock clergyman, see Colbert S. Cartwright, "Lesson From Little Rock," *Christian Century,* 74 (October 9, 1957), pp. 1193-1194; and "Failure in Little Rock," *The Progressive,* 22 (June 1958), pp. 12-15. A more general review of the mistakes of Little Rock in the school desegregation process by another Little Rock clergyman can be found in Chapter 3 (appropriately titled "Hindsight") of Robert R. Brown, *Bigger Than Little Rock.* Greenwich, Conn.: Seabury Press, 1958.

5. The presidency of the association rotates each year among the various denominations represented in the group. As in many types of such organizations, the influential members either were officers some years ago or have never held office. Rather, young, innovator types are frequently chosen as president.

6. Details of this condemnation, which took the form of an announcement released to the newspapers, television, and radio stations, are provided in Chapter Two.

7. This was not the day of the rioting (September 23, 1957), which did not occur until after Governor Faubus removed his National Guard soldiers. The event under discussion occurred when the Negro children were first turned away from the school by the guard on orders of the Governor. Accompanied by Negro leaders and a small band of white men, seven of the Negro children safely made their way through a menacing crowd of segregationists. The remaining two Negro children came up to the school individually.

8. This man's interest in race relations had been shown in a widely quoted sermon delivered several months before the crisis. Slowed by poor health, he still participated in some quiet, organizational work for integration.

9. This is not to say that the prayers for peace effort was a total failure. But from the point of view of the innovators' protest movement it was the death blow. For a very different interpretation of these services, see Robert R. Brown, "Little Rock and the Churches," *Union Seminary Quarterly Review*, 13 (January 1958), pp. 19-27; and *Bigger Than Little Rock, op. cit.*, pp. 66-109.

10. The term "reconciliation" (from *II. Corinthians*, 5:18-19) led to difficulties in interpretation. Some observers took it to mean "conciliation," others took it to mean "passive resignation." One organizer of the services has written: "In view of such misunderstanding perhaps the use of the phrase was ill-advised." (R. Brown, *Bigger Than Little Rock, op. cit.*, p. 101). The use of such descriptions as "neutral" and "compromising" for the peace prayers in the text is not based on such a misconception of the Christian concept, reconciliation, but, rather, is determined by the actual aims and arrangements of the services.

11. One leader of the services, at least, feels that the results were "valuable." He has written: "Although it is impossible to assess [the results] with complete certainty, there was an immediate lessening of tension and, interestingly, a large segment of troops was withdrawn shortly thereafter. In addition, more people appeared to come out in the open to witness their belief in law and order. Clergy and laity alike were made to feel that there were 'seven thousand men who had not bowed the knee to the image of Baal.'" R. Brown, "Little Rock and the Churches," *op. cit.*, p. 25. We found little evidence that the prayers could be considered the cause of any "lessening of tension." At any rate, if there were any effects of the services, their lack of permanence is attested to by later events in Little Rock.

12. Not all eight of the innovators sensed this, perhaps, but all of them in one way or another attempted to strengthen the tone of the services in a pro-integration direction.

13. *Esther*, 4:14.

14. Another innovator, feeling that it was too late to change the nature of the prayers themselves, moved that the five-man initiating committee continue to meet after the services in order to give leadership and guidance to both the clergy and laity of the city. The motion was passed. The group never met again, however.

15. Most of the denominational leaders interviewed did not so much as know the sect leaders' names, let alone know them personally.

16. One of these efforts was a Little Rock attempt to draft a "statesmanlike" pronouncement on the whole civic problem. Two delegates from each denomination made up the committee that was to formulate the statement. Though several meetings were held, further discussion was suddenly ended. The second of these efforts came from the floor of the annual December meeting in 1957 of the Arkansas State Council of Churches. This attempt to have the Council present a strong statement failed also.

17. From the best evidence we could assemble, these discussion groups were established largely in Episcopal churches. The effectiveness of this communication attempt is difficult to ascertain, but we could find little positive gain from them as late as the fall of 1958. For a fuller discussion of this effort, see R. Brown, *Bigger Than Little Rock, op. cit.*, pp. 107-109.

18. The first of these pamphlets is a National Council of Churches report on the

National Association for the Advancement of Colored People. The second pamphlet, which was both printed and distributed by the Council, is titled *What Saith the Scripture.* It is a detailed presentation of the scriptural defense of integration by the Reverend Richard C. Jahn, pastor of First Lutheran Church of Little Rock and the second vice president of the western district of the Luthern Church, Missouri Synod.

19. "Peace, peace; when there is no peace" is taken from *Jeremiah,* 6:14.

20. S. I. Goldstein has pointed out that the rabbi actually must play many more roles than the Christian minister. He must be teacher, scholar, educator, preacher, prayer leader, pastor, organizer, administrator, and—most important for our present purposes—ambassador of good will to the non-Jewish world. The two rabbis in this sample bear out Goldstein's contentions. S. I. Goldstein, "The Roles of an American Rabbi," *Sociology and Social Research,* 38 (September-October 1953), pp. 32-37.

21. Three innovators were born in Arkansas, others in such states as Mississippi, South Carolina, and Kansas.

22. The pastors of the remaining three large churches are all members of this sample and were judged as inactives in the crisis.

23. A southern-born social scientist has expressed the point to us cogently: "When a Baptist preacher dares defy his flock, he's liable to be out of job; but when an Episcopalian rector opposes his parishioners, he's liable to be promoted by his bishop." It is unfortunate that there are no data in this study from the Roman Catholic churches of Little Roc.k. Though Roman Catholic leaders in Arkansas did not take an active role in the crisis, their Church has in other areas distinguished itself for its support of integration (for example, St. Louis and New Orleans, as discussed in Chapter One.) Reinhold Niebuhr has discussed the difference between the Roman Catholic and Protestant churches in this regard: "Catholicism has been much more rigorous and successful than the Protestant churches on the racial issue. Partly this success is due to the hierarchical structure of the Church, and the consequent ability of bishops and priests to set standards even in defiance of lay opinion. . . .If one compares the record of this 'undemocratic' church with the 'democratic' Protestant churches that have the most dismal history of sanctified racial prejudice, one must come to the conclusion that absolute democracy is not necessarily a resource of justice. . . .Perhaps this is just another proof that we must approach this vexing problem from above and from below . . ." Reinhold Niebuhr, "A Theologian's Comments on the Negro in America," *The Reporter,* 15 (November 29, 1956), pp. 24-25. For a further discussion of this factor see note 7 of Chapter Five.

24. Details of the rating procedure are enumerated in Chapter One.

25. A third possibility can be offered: that the relationship is an artifact of the rating procedures, both of the variables having been judged from the same protocols. Actually, the variables were judged from totally different parts of the protocols. The three types of ministers were categorized solely on the basis of the interviewees' actions (see note 2), while the involvement rating was based solely on a personality judgment from his detailed remarks, apart from either actions or influence.

26. Only a minority of the influentials and the inactives actually thought that the achievements of the church in race relations had been satisfactory, but none of the innovators thought so.

27. The largest group in our sample of denominational ministers, the inactives, reveal less homogeneity than the other two types. A few inactives, for example, are only in their thirties. But particular explanatory factors could be found in such

exceptional cases; for example, admonishments from church superiors together with a dangerous lack of rapport with the congregation extending back prior to the racial conflict.

28. The following discussion of the Montgomery bus protest movement is drawn largely from two sources: Martin Luther King, Jr., *Stride Toward Freedom*. New York: Harpers, 1958; and Preston Valien, *et al.*, "The Role of Public Opinion in the Desegregation Controversy," *Public Opinion Quarterly*, 21 (Fall 1957), PP. 406-409.

29. R. D. Hooper, "The Revolutionary Process: a Frame of Reference for the Study of Revolutionary Movements," *Social Forces*, 28 (March 1950), pp. 270-279. Also reprinted in part in R. H. Turner and L. M. Killian (eds.), *Collective Behavior*. Englewood Cliffs, New Jersey: Prentice-Hall, 1957; pp. 310-319.

30. Max Weber, *The Theory of Social and Economic Organization* (translated by A. M. Henderson and Talcott Parsons). New York: Oxford, 1947; p. 71.

31. Mrs. Rosa Parks, the Negro involved, was the secretary of the local branch of the National Association for the Advancement of Colored People. Her explanation for her decision to ignore the bus driver's order to give up her seat was simply that she suddenly felt "fed up" with the whole business. Being "fed up" strongly suggests that this trigger incident was in fact the result of a long period of ambiguity, tension, and unrest in the situation. See J. A. Morsell, "Comment on Frank F. Lee's 'Changing Structure of Negro Leadership,'" *The Crisis*, 65 (May 1958), pp. 261-265.

32. In Mansfield, Texas, state rangers, called out by Governor Shivers after some violence, successfully prevented court-ordered school integration by refusing to let the Negroes enter. Not waiting for the violence first, Faubus apparently had this technique in mind, but he met with a sterner Federal District Judge than did Shivers in Mansfield. See J. H. Griffin and T. Freedman, *Mansfield, Texas*. New York: Freedom Pamphlet of the Anti-Defamation League of B'nai Brith, 1957.

33. For a firsthand discussion of the difficulties involved in integrating a formerly all-white Protestant church in Los Angeles, see Kring Allen, "Integration by the Cross," *Christian Century*, 75 (August 20, 1958), pp. 943-945.

34. The movement's emphasis on passive resistance aroused considerable enthusiasm among the world's intellectuals, especially in India. The bus boycott idea spread not only to Tallahassee, Florida, but even to the Union of South Africa, 8,000 miles away. In both Port Elizabeth and Johannesburg, dramatic boycotts were carried on, and in the latter metropolis, with 50,000 Africans participating for three months, it actually met with limited success (the Johannesburg Chamber of Commerce arranged to subsidize a one-cent bus fare increase that was the focus of the protest). Yet, interestingly enough, the focus and actions of this movement did not (or could not) become more expansive. Students of the South African scene could point to three reasons for this apparent exception to our general pattern: (1) even in Johannesburg, where militancy and organization among the nonwhites are greater than in any other part of the Union, the Africans' communication channels and efficiency of organization do not begin to compare with those of Montgomery; (2) the protesters live in far-distant locations with no possible means of setting up as efficient a car-pool as Montgomery had; (3) 14,000 members of the protest were arrested in what amounted to violent police interference with the movement. The wonder is not that the boycott did not become more broadly tuned but rather that it ever got started in the first place. Brute suppression can effectively halt a movement—at least for a time—even after it has secured some small gains. *Africa Special Report*, 2 (April 29, 1957), p. 6.

35. Pitirim A. Sorokin, *Man and Society in Calamity*. New York: Dutton, 1942; pp. 158-164, 241-242.

36. Gordon W. Allport, J. S. Bruner, and E. M. Jandorf, "Personality Under Social Catastrophe: Ninety Life-Histories of the Nazi Revolution," *Character and Personality*, 10 (September 1941), pp. 1-22. Also reprinted in part in: Clyde Kluckhohn, Henry A. Murray, and David M. Schneider (eds.), *Personality in Nature, Society, and Culture* (2nd edition). New York: Knopf, 1953; pp. 436-455.

37. James S. Coleman, *Community Conflict*. Glencoe, Illinois: Free Press, 1957.

38. R. Brown, *Bigger Than Little Rock*, *op. cit.*, p. 32.

39. See for instance: Samuel A. Stouffer, *Communism, Conformity, and Civil Liberties*. New York: Doubleday, 1955.

40. Max Weber, *op. cit.*, pp. 363-373.

41. F. V. Cantwell, "Public Opinion and the Legislative Process," *American Political Science Review*, 55 (October 1946), pp. 924-935. Also reprinted in: Bernard Berelson and M. Janowitz, (eds.), *Reader in Public Opinion and Communication* (2nd edition). Glencoe, Illinois: Free Press, 1953; pp. 121-131.

42. "The Role of Public Opinion in the Desegregation Controversy," *op. cit.*, p. 409.

43. R. H. Turner and L. M. Killian, *op. cit.*, pp. 501-502.

CHAPTER FIVE

1. Sections of this chapter have appeared in modified form as: E. Q. Campbell and T. F. Pettigrew, "Racial Crisis and Moral Dilemma: a Role Analysis of Little Rock Ministers," *American Journal of Sociology*, 65 (March 1959).

2. A limited number of interviews with members of congregations in eight Little Rock churches tended strongly to bear out the ministers' estimates of predominately pro-segregation sentiment in their congregations. The results of this sampling are such that we feel safe in agreeing with ministerial estimates that show no dominantly integrationist congregation in the city.

3. There are extremely small Unitarian and Quaker fellowships in the city. No one connected with these groups was asked to participate in our study. It is quite possible that pro-integration sentiment is strong in these two bodies.

4. This may be considered a general scheme for occupational role and decision-making analysis whenever the actor is responsible to some public.

5. The reader may be impressed, as we are, by the practical difficulty of ferreting out this variable whenever the nature of external expectations and sanctions is such that the actor cannot realistically ignore them in making his decisions. It is difficult operationally to distinguish the actor as self-judge from the actor as judged by others.

As we will later show, relevant groups not only make demands and impose sanctions, they also affect significantly the actor's self-expectations and self-sanctions. Nevertheless, we feel it important to treat the self reference system as an independent variable important in its own right in role conflict analysis. This reference system would seem to be especially significant in understanding the case in which action is contrary to the pressure of known and significant groups, and in this area to provide yet another bridge between sociology and social psychology.

6. Of course, the local church hierarchy is an agent of the national church. It has a high degree of autonomy in the implementation of social policy, however, and requires separate analysis.

7. We were somewhat surprised to find the circumstances that are described in the preceding paragraphs. We rather anticipated that ministers in ecclesiastically organized denominations would have greater freedom to defend integration than would those congregationally organized. We expected this greater freedom to be expressed in action that would distinguish between ministers according to forms of church polity. We predicted that the church hierarchy at its various levels would both encourage the pastors to assume liberal postures and reinforce them when they did so. This support would reflect the hierarchy's strong identification with the church at the national level, which would involve accepting the unequivocal opposition to segregation stated by the national church body. If the pastor's liberality brought him into trouble with his members, officials in the hierarchy could use the high prestige of their offices to defend the pastor and rebuke his critics. On the other hand, it appeared that ministers to denominations in which full authority is vested in the local congregation would be at the mercy of church members when critical issues arose. Realizing this, they would go only as far as their congregations would permit them. On the segregation issue this would not be far. There would be no superior to whom to appeal for moral or other support and no superior to urge the pastor to express his convictions, come what may. His congregation could vote to relieve him of his pastorate, and he would have no channels for appeal.

Satisfactory comparisons are not possible since congregational and ecclesiastical churches are not necessarily "matched" on socioeconomic or other variables. It is clear, however, that in Little Rock the indisputable locus of determining influence in all denominations, regardless of church polity, lay with the membership and its representatives. Their sentiments on segregation gave little encouragement to the minister to state the moral imperatives and impose demands on Christian citizens. Perhaps in obeisance to this, perhaps in encouragement of it, the church hierarchy functioned to discourage pastors from taking bold stands.

Also, the public activity of members of church hierarchies served as guides to individual pastors under their jurisdictions regarding what constituted proper conduct. If high officials avoided the issue, spoke in platitudes and generalities, defended Christians against the charge of failure, or in other ways were less than enthusiastic about the threatened changes, these were indirect but effective clues to pastors that a similar course of action was appropriate.

We continue to believe that the ecclesiastical form by its nature offers a potential for effective ministerial leadership in unpopular causes and crisis situations which the congregational form does not offer. However, it is not inconceivable that reality more frequently than not may be the opposite of this potential. That is to say, it seems very possible that a church hierarchy will function to reduce rather than increase the likelihood that a ministry will take stands counter to those preferred by their congregations.

In this respect. it may be noted that a congregationally organized denomination contributed a disproportionate share of ministerial liberalism during Little Rock's crisis, and that one ecclesiastically organized body was notorious in liberal circles for its extreme caution. See Table 2 and note 23 of Chapter Four.

8. It is significant that Blizzard does not include a "community reformer" or "social critic" role in his delineation of major practitioner roles within the work of the ministry. See Samuel W. Blizzard, "The Minister's Dilemma," *Christian Century*, 73 (April 25, 1956), pp. 508-510.

9. An interesting contrast may be drawn here between the minister and the public-office holder. Generally, the politician is "successful" if he gets a bare majority of the votes. An opposition of no more than five or ten percent of a congregation, on the other hand, may be intolerably excessive for the minister. The Little Rock pastor who experienced the greatest difficulty with his congregation believes that the significant opposition constituted no more than 20 percent of his membership. If, as Ringer and Glock's findings suggest, parishioner conservatism varies directly with degree of active commitment to the church, it would seem that the first to take offense are the last persons one wants to offend. See B. B. Ringer and C. Y. Glock, "The Political Role of the Church as Defined by Its Parishioners," *Public Opinion Quarterly*, 18 (Winter, 1954-55), pp. 337-347.

10. Getzels and Guba have shown that in the military situation at the Air Command and Staff School of Air University there is a role conflict between two highly organized roles, those of officer and teacher. These roles are not compatible, and the military actor must make a choice between them. In commenting on this choice, Getzels and Guba say: "There seems to be a *major role* to which one must commit himself in order to determine his action at choice points, despite contrary expectations attaching to other roles he may simultaneously occupy." They indicate that this choice typically is that of officer rather than of teacher.

There is a close parallel between the ministerial office and the military situation described here. Just as "None of the Air University officer-instructors, whatever his personal predilection, may with impunity overlook the fact that he is a part of a military organization", so does the local minister find it impossible to ignore the fact that he has assumed strong obligations to manage and maintain a religious enterprise.

See J. W. Getzels and E. G. Guba, "Role, Role Conflict, and Effectiveness: An Empirical Study," *American Sociological Review*, 19 (April 1954), pp. 164-175.

11. This we think to be a crucial point in understanding the activity of several Little Rock ministers. Let us assume that the minister has expressed his convictions to his congregation such that he feels they understand not only his personal position but his concept of the Christian layman's obligation. Assume further that during a period of crisis, members of his church do not themselves inflame public passions or engage in acts of violence or intimidation. Assume finally that his conception of his ministerial role is that it is bounded by the walls of his parish and does not extend further into the life of the community. His responsibility, therefore, is to his own flock. So long as they do not behave unseemly, and inasmuch as they have knowledge of his own convictions, he feels little motivation for further activity. He can say, as many did: "I am proud of what my people have done."

Of course, this position is open to criticism as being both narrow and negative. In time of crisis the expectations he imposes on his flock are principally negative: "Don't mistreat Negroes; don't engage in violent acts; don't do things you'd be sorry for." They are not corrective; no one is encouraged to ask what responsibility he has to improve the situation. Further, this position involves no effort by the minister to rally either the congregation or the community as a strong moral force to take effective action to correct a crisis evil. It is as if a parent expects of a child only that he stay out of trouble.

12. It is important here, however, to distinguish the freedom to act from the action itself. Many Little Rock ministers who by these criteria of personal and congregational levels of education were most free to act, were in fact among the least active. As is shown in a later section, it appears that this discrepancy is caused by an increased sense of obligation to preserve the church as a church, which comes with high ministerial attainment and, possibly, with age.

13. Again, we must be careful to distinguish freedom to act from the amount and force of the action itself.

14. It seemed at the beginning of this study that the concept of "accumulated capital" would predict the minister's activity in the racial crisis. That is, it appeared reasonable to expect that those ministers with long tenure, growing and prospering churches, wide prominence, large memberships,—in short, successful ministers—would have a larger amount of "capital" which they could "spend" in defense of an unpopular cause without fear of (to complete the analogy) "bankruptcy," without fear of heavy recriminations from their congregations. They, it seemed, would contrast to the less prominent, more recently arrived pastor who would still be in the process of "earning" his "capital" and hence most hesitant to run the dangerous risk of losing out by taking an unpopular stand.

Our results, however, suggest the contrary. It appears that the characteristics and abilities that make the minister successful are precisely those that progressively reduce the probability that he will take decisive and persistent actions that violate the value preferences of his constituents. What he accumulates, in other words, is not risk capital. See Table 5 in Chapter Four.

CHAPTER SIX

1. The Evangelical Methodist Church was organized in Memphis, Tennessee, in 1946. It withdrew from the Methodist Church, protesting against autocratic government on the one hand and a tendency toward modernism on the other. It is congregationally organized. Its approximately 100 churches claim less than 10,000 total members. See Benson Y. Landis, *Yearbook of American Churches for 1959*. New York: National Council of the Churches of Christ in the U.S.A., 1958.

2. For the distinction between localites and cosmopolites, see Robert K. Merton, "Patterns of Influence: A Study of Interpersonal Influence and of Communications Behavior in a Local Community," in Paul F. Lazarsfeld and Frank N. Stanton (eds.), *Communications Research, 1948-1949*. New York: Harper, 1949-49; pp. 180-219.

3. See, for example, R. J. Pellegrin and C. H. Coates, "Absentee-Owned Corporations and Community Power Structures," *American Journal of Sociology*, 61 (March 1956), pp. 413-419.

4. David Riesman makes the distinction between inner-directed and outer-directed persons. See David Riesman, Nathan Glazer, and Reuel Denney, *The Lonely Crowd: A Study of The Changing American Character*. New Haven: Yale University Press, 1950.

5. "Southern Ministers Speak Their Minds," *Pulpit Digest*, 39 (December 1958), pp. 13-17.

6. We are well aware that the minister's inclination to become involved in community issues is probably less a general response pattern than it is a function of the particular issue. There is probably a very low correlation, for example, between willingness to be an advocate in desegregation issues and willingness to be an advocate in local liquor referendums.

7. Little Rock is immersed in a stage of fear and intimidation at the time of this writing (December 1958). Local wags say that the calling card of even the staunchest liberal is the prefatory statement, "Now, I'm a segregationist, but . . ."

CHAPTER SEVEN

1. See J. Milton Yinger, *Religion in the Struggle for Power*. Durham, North Carolina: Duke University Press, 1946; pp. 25-28.

2. *Ibid.*, pp. 16-25. Yinger is employing the well known Weber-Troeltsch typology introduced in: Max Weber, *The Protestant Ethic and the Spirit of Capitalism* (translated by Talcott Parsons). London: Allen and Unwin, 1930; and Ernst Troeltsch, *The Social Teachings of the Christian Churches* (translated by Olive Wyon). New York: Macmillan, 1932. Neither Yinger nor the present discussion assumes that these are two discontinuous types but rather that they are extremes on a series of related continua.

3. For a detailed description of the southern United States' sect, see Liston Pope, *Millhands and Preachers*. New Haven, Conn.: Yale University Press, 1942.

4. From Troeltsch, quoted by J. M. Yinger, *op. cit.*, p. 19.

5. *Ibid.*, p. 221.

6. Reinhold Niebuhr, *Christianity and Power Politics*. New York: Scribner, 1948; p. 216.

7. Liston Pope, *The Kingdom Beyond Caste*. New York: Friendship Press, 1957; p. 144. Related to this point is the concern for individual perfection but little or no concern for social perfection and social responsibility. For the Protestant view of this problem, see Reinhold Niebuhr, *Moral Man and Immoral Society, A Study in Ethics and Politics*. New York: Scribner, 1932. Interestingly enough, this same problem is a pressing one for Roman Catholics, too. The Reverend William Ferree has noted the emphasis of Thomistic doctrine on individual responsibility and individual justice was not fully extended to the social realm until 1930 with the Encyclical *Quadragesimo Anno* of Pope Pius XI. Ferree concludes: "It cannot be denied that at the present time the idea is widespread, that obligations of individual or commutative justice *must* always be met, but that obligations of Social Justice are not so rigid. This is totally false. The truth is that the obligations of Social Justice are *just as rigid* and *much more weighty* than the obligations of individual justice." William Ferree, *Introduction to Social Justice*. New York: The Paulist Press, 1948; p. 25.

8. Reinhold Niebuhr, "A Theologian's Comments on the Negro in America," *The Reporter*, 15 (November 29, 1956), pp. 24-25.

9. J. M. Yinger, *op. cit.*, p. 226.

10. Robert R. Brown, "Little Rock and the Churches," *Union Seminary Quarterly Review*, 13 (January 1958), pp. 21-22.

11. From a speech of the Reverend Monroe Swilley, pastor of Second Ponce de Leon Baptist Church in Atlanta, to the annual meeting of the Southern Baptists of Virginia as reported by the *Richmond Times-Dispatch*, November 14, 1958, p. 4.

12. This comment is from an August 1958 interview.

13. These characteristics are extremely similar to those described by Pope for similar groups: Liston Pope, *Millhands and Preachers, op. cit.* Pope's criteria have been used by Russell R. Dynes to construct an objectively scored "Church-Sect"

attitude scale. Using this scale on a random sample of Columbia, Ohio, residents, Dynes found that pro-sectarian attitudes are associated with low social status not only among sect memberships but also within major denominations— for example, Presbyterian and Methodist. R. R. Dynes, "Church-Sect Typology and Socio-Economic Status," *American Sociological Review*, 20 (October 1955), pp. 555-560; and "The Consequences of Sectarianism for Social Participation," *Social Forces*, 35 (May 1957), pp. 331-334. Peter L. Berger offers evidence from a study of Protestant parishes in southwestern Germany that sectarian characteristics of a "core" membership can develop within a relatively "church type" denomination. P. L. Berger, "Sectarianism and Religious Sociation," *American Journal of Sociology*, 64 (July 1958), pp. 41-44. For a point of view concerning denominational sectarianism that is quite different from the present, widely accepted view under discussion, see Benton Johnson, "A Critical Appraisal of the Church-Sect Typology," *American Sociological Review*, 22 (February 1957), pp. 88-92.

14. Very relevant here is the fact that a large majority of both the pastors and members of these churches were born and raised in rural Arkansas and are now attempting to adjust to the rigors of metropolitan life. J. M. Yinger has written of these sects: "The lower-class sect movement, then, is in this situation an attempt to grapple with the problems faced by the migrant . . ." J. M. Yinger, *Religion, Society and the Individual.* New York: Macmillian, 1957, p. 167.

15. Liston Pope, *The Kingdom Beyond Caste, op. cit.,* p. 144.

16. Martin L. King, Jr., *Stride Toward Freedom.* New York: Harper, 1958; pp. 205-211. This section is reprinted in full as: "The Church and the Race Crisis," *Christian Century*, 75 (October 8, 1958), pp. 1140-1141.

17. Reinhold Niebuhr, "A Theologian's Comments on the Negro in America," *op. cit.*

18. Reinhold Niebuhr, *Does Civilization Need Religion?* New York: Macmillian, 1941; p. 12.

19. This principle is a particularly important one for the whole desegregation process. Southerners who feel that racial desegregation of the public schools is inevitable are much more tolerant of the Negro and feel that opposing the process is not worthwhile. See, for instance: T. F. Pettigrew, "Desegregation and Its Chances For Success: Northern and Southern Views," *Social Forces*, 35 (May 1957), pp. 339-344.

20. *Southern School News,* 4 (May 1958), p. 16.

INDEX

#60
8